TAOIST SECRETS OF LOVE

CULTIVATING MALE
SEXUAL ENERGY

Mantak Chia
Written with Michael Winn

AURORA PRESS

P.O. Box 573   Santa Fe, N.M. 87504

ISBN: 0-943358-19-1
LC #84-71453

A publication of
Aurora Press
P O Box 573
Santa Fe, NM 87504
USA

Also by Mantak Chia

Awaken Healing Energy Through the Tao
The Taoist Secret of Circulating Internal Power

Printed in the United States of America

XCII

ACKNOWLEDGEMENTS

This book has been over a decade in the making. I thank foremost those Taoist Masters who were kind enough to share their knowledge with me, but never imagined it would be taught to westerners. Such is the Tao.

I acknowledge a special debt to H. Reid Shaw for his encouragement after I had just arrived in America and for his hard work on an initial manuscript.

I thank the many contributors essential to its final form: the artist, Susan MacKay, Gunther Weil, Rylin Malone, and all my students for their feedback, Master T.K. Shih, Kim Wang, and Juan Li for their fine artwork; Jeffrey Antin, and Marcia Kerwit for their additions; my assistant Jo Ann Cutreria for typing the manuscript into the computer and endless help; Daniel Bobek for his long hours at the computer, and Barbara Somerfield for her patience as my publisher.

A special heartfelt thanks to Michael Winn for his selfless labors, and for saying so eloquently and insightfully in English what my Chinese does not permit.

Without my wife Maneewan the book would have been academic. For her gifts, my gratitude and love.

A WORD OF CAUTION

Any man suffering from venereal disease or any local illness of his sexual organs or prostate gland should consult a medical doctor and a qualified instructor of Taoist Esoteric Yoga before practicing the methods taught here.

Mantak Chia,Universal Tao World Headquarters
274/1 Moo 7, Luang Nua, Doi Saket
Chiang Mai, 50220, Thailand

Tel: 66 53 495 596 Fax: 66 53 495 852
Email: universaltao@universal-tao.com
Website: www.universal-tao.com for information
on courses, orders of videos, books, cassettes, posters.
U.S.A. Toll Free 888 444-7426
USA Instructors: HealingTaoUSA.com/instructors

TABLE OF CONTENTS

ABOUT THE AUTHOR — Mantak Chia

The author of this book, Mantak Chia, was born in Thailand on April 4, 1944. When he was six or seven years of age he learned to "sit and still the mind" from Buddhist monks while on a summer vacation. This is not to say that he was passive and quiet as a child. In fact, he excelled in track and field events during his grammar school days in Hong Kong. It was during that time that he learned the traditional Thai Boxing and met Master Lu, who taught him Tai Chi Chuan. Shortly thereafter, Master Lu introduced him to Aikido, Yoga and more Tai Chi. His knowledge of esoteric practice did not begin, however, until he was eighteen and he had returned to Thailand. It was at that time that a senior classmate, Cheng Sue Sue, a student of Yi-Eng, taught him the level of Tao Esoteric practice up to the Reunion of Man and Heaven.

When he was in his twenties, Master Chia studied with Master Meugi in Singapore, who taught him Kundalini Yoga and the Buddhist Palm. With the Buddhist Palm, he was soon able to eliminate blockages of flow of life-force in his internal organs and to drive cold, wet or sick energy out of patients who came to see his Master, thereby restoring them to health. The young Mantak Chia felt, however, that Kundalini Yoga produced too much heat and could be dangerous and so he later combined it with elements of Taoist practice, which had cooling effects.

Later, in his twenties, he met and studied with Master Pan Yu, who had created a synthesis out of Taoist, Buddhist and Ch'an teaching, and Master Cheng Yao-Lung, who had also created a new system by combining Thai Boxing and Kung Fu. From Master Cheng Yao-Lung, he learned the Shao-Lin secret method of internal power as well as the Iron Shirt method called "Cleansing the Marrow and Renewal of the Tendon". From Master Pan Yu, he learned a variation of Kundalini and the "steel body", a technique that is said to keep the body from decay. Master Pan Yu still lives and practices in Hong Kong, where he treats patients by transmitting his life-force to them. To better understand the mechanism behind the healing energy, Chia also studied Western medical science and anatomy for two years.

Yet, with all of these achievements, Master Chia was the manager of the Gestetner Company in Thailand, was in charge of sales of offset machines and was well acquainted with the working of the company's copying and printing machines. He may well be the only Taoist master in the world with a computer in his living room. He is also married and has a son. His wife Maneewan works as a medical technician. He is, in short, living proof that his practice is very much down-to-earth, striving to enhance everyday life and not requiring retreat from society to a hermit's life.

The main thrust of Chia's intention is to strip away the mysticism, the mumbo-jumbo, the powers vested in the Guru, the reliance on things-other-worldly or magical. He seeks to present, instead, a fully predictable working model that might be considered as a scientific means of dealing with energy systems. In time, he hopes this will lead to technological developments that might serve to simplify or speed the means whereby such progress might be made. It is with such hopes that he beckons members of the medical community to investigate what he has to offer. There are already physicians and lawyers and computer programmers, who have experienced, first hand, the benefits that Master Chia's methods provide. It is up to them and others in the scientific community to join Master Chia in his lifetime task of bridging the gap between reason and spirit, mind and body, science and religion.

INTRODUCTION

Taoist "Dual Cultivation" and the Quest for Sexual Love
by Michael Winn

"What a pity! A mountain peak as tiny as one square inch has been the source of great inspiration and misery for centuries."

—*Anonymous Chinese Poet on man's obsession with woman's sex.*

Thousands of books have been written attempting to help men and women resolve the problems arising from the endless search for sexually fulfilling love. What could possibly be written that is new?

Taoist Secrets of Love is not just another flowery philosophical treatise on the ecstasies of oriental love. Rather it is a pragmatic handbook that distills the secret teachings on sex of four different living Taoist masters sought out by Mantak Chia during fifteen years of travel and study in the Far East. As he put it, "I read a ton of books telling me how great esoteric love-making was, but none of them explained precisely how it was done. So I decided to write it myself."

Most books on Taoist sex fail to instruct on how to transform sperm energy once it is held in, where to store sex energy in the body, how to best exchange it with a woman, and give cursory treatment to the retention of semen. Chia synthesized the ancient Taoist practices into simple but powerful methods that can be easily learned by western men. This first volume is directed primarily at men, simply because most men are sexually weaker than women and lose more energy through sex than women. A later volume will describe the esoteric Taoist sexual practices for women, which includes voluntary arrest of the menstrual flow.

The sexual imbalance between men and women is obvious. A woman can sexually receive her man for as long as she pleases, and thus the Taoists say her yin essence is nearly inexhaustible. A man's love making is limited to the amount of energy he has to keep his erection. His yang essence is more easily tired. A woman is sexually stronger than a man because biologically she needs to

1

be. Her reproductive organs must bear the strain of physically producing children and nurturing them. The effects on men of this primal biological inequality are profound, setting off a chain reaction that can permeate male thinking and feeling on all levels, from marriage to work to cultural roles we choose to play and to the spiritual models we choose for our inner growth.

At heart most men are as terrified of women's infinite sexual capacity as they are fascinated by it. The general effect on men is to make them feel sexually insecure and causes them to attempt to compensate with some other strength. Sexual insecurity may be the primary reason men have sought physical, political, financial, intellectual, and religious advantage over woman. Correcting this sexual imbalance could have significant side benefits in establishing a more harmonious society, although the primary goal of the Taoist teaching on cultivation of sexual energy was personal health and spiritual fulfillment.

The quest for sexually fulfilled love has taken on the dimensions of a religion amongst those who are too liberal or too scientific to believe in any traditional version of God. The power behind this belief in romantic love, in an ultimate commitment to one person, is the power of sexual experience. If offers something tangible to be shared, a sacrament that is personal and present.

The decline of religion in the west may have begun when the experience of sex became more powerful than the spiritual experience offered by religion in prayer or in fellowship. The current revival of religion in the west ironically may be due in part, to a sexual exhaustion following on the heels of the sexual revolution. Sex became a drug, an opiate for the discontent. Total sexual freedom did not supply the stability people needed most. Today, people are turning back to either marriage or religion to seek their sense of an absolute.

The Taoists offer neither religion nor marriage as the solution to stability, unless it be the marriage of subtle energies they identify as yin and yang. They simply encourage each individual to cultivate his natural inner life-force, or chi. It is in this context the ancient Chinese developed highly refined methods of increasing sexual vitality for the single and the married man. There are two main ways that these energy cultivation methods can be used and this book will accordingly attract two distinct kinds of students.

The first student seeks worldly happiness in the form of physical, emotional, and mental satisfaction. This includes any layman interested in strengthening his personal love relationship, in alleviating sexual frustration, in relieving boredom with sex, in curing impotency, wet dreams and premature ejaculation and in general increasing his longevity and good health. If he is disciplined and does the practices taught in this book, he can attain all of these benefits.

The other student considers himself on a spiritual path and wants to somehow integrate his sexual desires with his meditative practice or spiritual beliefs. The students already drawn to study the Taoists secrets of cultivating sexual energy with Master Chia have come from an amazingly broad range of spiritual disciplines, including every type of yoga: Kundalini, Hatha, Kriya, Tantric, Siddha and martial artists as well as T.M., Zen, Buddhist, Sufi, Hindu, and Christian adherents. The suggestion is that many Americans, however satisfied they are with their basic spiritual beliefs, feel the need to better integrate their sexuality with their spiritual growth.

The Taoist practice of chi cultivation focuses on integrating the divine or subtle energies into the human body, with the goal of achieving a dynamic balance of opposing energies called yin and yang. The Tao is the indescribable sum and absolute source of these energies, which manifest in ever changing form. The Taoists, being practical, proposed that a man can begin with the most accessible energy at hand, namely the sexual attraction between men and women, and use that as a springboard to more subtle realms.

Taoist Esoteric Yoga is neither a religion, nor a path to salvation. Its vision reaches very far, teaching that enlightenment and physical immortality are only stages in a process of coming to wholeness as a human. It also remains very near and practical. The raw materials required for this evolution can be found at any given moment within the life of an ordinary human being.

The Taoist teaching of physical immortality doesn't suggest men no longer die. It means that before they die they have the opportunity to cultivate a "solid" or substantial spiritual body, also known as the Immortal Body, the Solar Body, the Crystal Body, and other names. In the west the closest parallel to a Taoist Immortal is probably an angel. This is different from schools that teach how to become a holy man by dissolving the individual ego into the bliss of cosmic oneness. The Taoists insist each adept preserve his individual nature within a body (physical or spiritual) so he can oversee the growth of his soul until final union with "wu chi," the nothingness from which the oneness of the Tao emerges. This "staying in your own body" precludes the adept from totally surrendering to any guru or divine being or religious authority. No one else can do your spiritual work for you.

Chia sees his role as simply that of a teacher who helps his students empower themselves through cultivation of their chi energy. He passes chi (or "shakti") to his students only so they will have a better sense of what to cultivate and refuses any dependent emotional relationships. He describes himself as the lead driver in a caravan of cars. "I can give each student a road map, a set of tools and instructions on how to fix his car. We start out together, and help and love each other as much as possible along the way. But ultimately everyone has to make it on his own. Some will break down, get lost, or choose a different route. Some may find a better road than the one I plotted. As a teacher, there's no kindness I can offer beyond the map and tools and precise instructions for driving safely."

The Taoist premise is that few men ever penetrate the secret of fully tapping the sexual power that is sleeping deep within their own body. It is revolutionary for the average man to think he can enjoy a deep and radiant pleasure in sex that penetrates permanently to the core of his being, an experience far superior to ordinary genital orgasm. The kind of prolonged "total body and soul orgasm" cultivated by Taoists is normally thought to be the exceptional gift of passionate and sensitive women. It has even become the greatest myth of western culture—the woman as passionate object of romantic love, the one who brings love to its real tenderness. The Taoists taught that men can participate equally in love through a truly exquisite balancing of sexual energies that is as tangible as any physical sensation of genital orgasms.

How is it possible for a man to so radically transform his sexual experience and through it his whole experience of life? Paradoxically, this "higher orgasm" can be discovered only when the "normal" or genital orgasm which so preoccupies America's sexologists is de-emphasized. The beginning three basic stages of Taoist "dual cultivation" of sexual energy for couples are:

1) The male learns to hold the penis erect for as long as desired and does not ejaculate any sperm.

2) Man and woman re-direct sexual energy through specific bodily channels into higher regions of the heart, brain and glands.

3) Man exchanges his super charged energy with the complementary energy of woman.

For the man, it is opening his feelings and subtle energy channels to the woman's essence and absorbing it during sex that is the key.

If you are without a lover, the Taoists offer a modification of this practice known as "single cultivation." This teaches a single man how to put his sex energy to work creatively in daily life or simply to enjoy life in good health without the plague of sexual frustration. The goal of the Taoist masters was not to create a new myth of a super macho orgasm which everyone would struggle to achieve and thus create competition. Rather it was to teach men and women practical ways of using natural energies to go more deeply into life's greatest gift, the freedom to love.

So what does all this cultivation of sexual energy have to do with love, of either the personal romantic type or the compassionate religious variety? The Taoists teach it is the responsibility of man and woman to balance the powers of Heaven and Earth harmoniously within themselves and that harmony in other spheres of life will follow thereafter. On the esoteric level, all acts of human love are the spontaneous transformation of our seed essence. Our seed essence, the seed of our very soul, is physically stored in the body as sperm or ovarian energy. When we love someone, we not only help them, but we also transform some of our own essence to a higher level of energy. Thus the Taoists see sexuality as a primary source of power behind love on the human level. Anyone following "the path of the heart"—the spontaneous and continuous loving of all that one meets—will find their way much strengthened by the Taoist insights into using the power of sexuality to that end.

At the same time it is the larger unseen cosmic harmony of the Tao that is always present that allows the experience of personal love to occur. Thus the Taoist term "harmony" is probably the closest equivalent for the western concept of "love" or compassion, on both the personal and universal levels. The Taoist goal is not to fulfill the human ego with its insatiable desires. It is to quiet the ego and calm the mind so that the subtle energies in the body can be first observed and then cultivated to a high level of awareness. Then the mind can see its true role in the larger order of things and work harmoniously to keep the forces in balance. Personal love relationships can be one valuable stage in this process, a microcosm of the larger subtle energy fields of the universe.

Western sexologists will undoubtedly dismiss these methods as having no statistical or verifiable scientific basis and accuse them of using vague terms such as "energy." It may be shunned by Western religions who are against sexual pleasure as well as by Eastern ascetic schools who believe spiritual enlightenment can be

v

found only by austerities that include sexual abstinence. The fact is that the early Taoists were scientists who based their practices on precise observation of human biology and psychology. They were neither hedonists nor ascetics, but sought a middle path to create the highest spiritual harmony possible between man and woman in accordance with natural laws of the universe. The deeply philosophical poetry of the Taoists, from the I Ching to Lao-Tse's "Tao Te Ching" to the "Secret of the Golden Flower," all testify to the sublime heights of their vision.

The fact these Taoist practices have survived by secret oral transmission for several thousand years is the strongest testimony that they work. The interviews I have conducted with dozens of modern western couples using these Taoist sexual practices, confirmed they still work for an ordinary cross section of urban men, young, old, white, black, Chinese, married and unmarried. Students of yoga, martial arts, and meditation have found it especially easy to learn the technique of seminal retention. Many people were already aware of the importance of sexual energy in their spiritual path, but simply lacked the method of expressing it directly in love making.

The Taoist methods may appear to be similar to the tantric sexual techniques becoming popularized in the west. The principle of balancing male and female and using the body as the crucible for transformation are essentially the same. As Nik Doulgas and Penny Slinger suggest in their authoritative "Sexual Secrets" (Inner Traditions N.Y. 1980) Indian tantra may have originated with ancient Taoists in China and then re-entered China hundreds of years later with the effect of re-vitalizing Taoist sexual practices.

For westerners today the foremost practical difference is that esoteric Taoism never assumed the cloak of secret rituals and invocation of religious deities that can make tantra seem strange and ill-fitting when transplanted to this culture. Sex was used more openly in China as a medicinal form of healing and natural path to spiritual balance without the same religious overtones. I strongly recommend that you obtain Sexual Secrets as a companion volume to this book, as it contains fresh translations of the classical Taoist treatises on sex and has dozens of superb illustrations of Taoist love-making positions not offered in this book.

It must be stressed that Master Chia does not teach his Taoist methods of transforming sexual energy as separate from his practice of meditation, Tai Chi Chuan, Iron Shirt Chi Kung and other Taoist arts. Sexual balance is a very important foundation for building a healthy physical and emotional life, but the Taoist goal is ultimately to gather the primal energies driving all our desires, emotions, and thoughts and cultivate them back into their original state of pure spirit.

The Taoist Masters of ancient China were no fools. They knew love between man and woman is a mystery which cannot be taught. Sex may be only the hand maiden of higher love, but our sexual limitations often confront us with the feeling that our relationships with our lovers or that our life in general is incomplete. The techniques taught in this book are not mechanical substitutes for love. The Taoist secrets of love are meant to be mastered and then discarded when the transformation of sexual energy is experienced as a natural creative power of man, as easy as walking, talking or thinking. Then the pleasure of sex can be ecstatic beyond orgasm and love tender beyond belief.

Michael Winn
June 1984

Michael Winn is general editor of the Taoist Esoteric Yoga Encyclopedia and an instructor at the Healing Tao Center in New York. Born in San Francisco in 1951 and educated at Dartmouth College, he has travelled to over sixty countries as a journalist, photographer, expedition guide and observer of global culture. He has practiced various kinds of meditation, Kundalini yoga, Chi Kung and Tai Chi forms over the last fifteen years. He tested the methods taught in this book during an extended period of celibacy and later with a lover. Only after finding the methods effective, in both situations did Winn agree to this collaboration. The principle ideas belong solely to Mantak Chia as transmitted to him by his Taoist teachers.

CHINESE SEXUAL KUNG-FU:
Will It Work in the West?
by Gunther Weil, Ph.D.

America's fascination with sex in the 1980's is matched only by its massive confusion of attitudes towards it. We need the pleasure of sex but can't decide how to deal with the emotional pain and complexity that often accompanies it. We have all felt guilty, conflicted or alienated by our sexual involvements and commitments at one time or another. From where does sex draw such enormous power to influence our lives?

No doubt, there is a biological imperative at work—the species' need to reproduce and continue itself. Less clear but equally powerful is the way sexual feelings become ensnared in the complex web of our culture. Eventually the culture-wide sex habits become a powerful set of unconscious influences. Most of us have been carrying the excess baggage of the sexual mores of our age for so long that we've forgotten how heavy the load is.

The cultural legacies of the Judeo-Christian ethic were the axis around which the sexual experiments of the 1960's revolved. The neurotic and barren life-styles of this ethic in previous generations were among the major causes of the sexual revolution of the 1960's. Alienated by sexual hypocrisy and the obvious destructive effects of sexual repression, people began searching for new and more honest ways of expressing their desires. Over the last twenty years we have seen the sexual revolution come full circle. What was previously illicit and forbidden became commonplace and banal. Some seek a solution to this current dilemma by returning to the old morality. Some seek refuge in celibacy. And some of us are still searching....

The far reaching implications of the sexual revolution of the 1960's, including the various liberation movements that have accompanied it, are now being re-examined in the wake of widespread conflict and unhappiness between men and women. The recent quest for a "new frontier" for the sexuality of the 1980's, a trend that is beginning to appear in the popular media, is essentially a reaction to the unhappy results of the new morality experiments of the last two decades. We thought we knew what we wanted, but when we got it we realized something else was missing. Individually and culturally we are again examining the meaning of our sexuality and the deeper purposes served by our loving relationships.

Many new ideas are now emerging from the New Age consciousness movement which address this need. Witness, for example, the concept of "High Monogamy" which emphasizes the challenge and excitement of conscious, through-time, relationships that transcend romantic egotism. The much publicized revival of popular interest in Indian and Tibetan sexual tantra is another example. Others are re-examining the merits of celibacy. The sexual paradigm is shifting again, part of the polar shift of the American morality play. As this play continues we are further mystified by the Moral Majority seeking to revive the old repressions and neurotic patterns which drove us to seek relief in the first place.

Many of us are struggling to understand the meaning of the conflict between the old and new sexual morality. Can we avoid the pitfalls of both repressive and "liberated" sexual morality which are by now all too familiar? Where do we turn for guidance in seeking our own truly individual answers?

Unfortunately, our views about human sexuality are constantly shaped by the fads and fashions of science and popular culture. We are influenced as much by these trends—from Dr. Spock to the Herpes scare—as we are by the actual biochemical processes of our bodies and minds. We often "know" more about who and what we are from what we read or see on television than from a deeply lived experience of ourselves. It is obvious that we lack a clear and impartial vision of our own social conditioning. Our self-knowledge is usually derived from the world of well known experts, books, films, TV, magazines, rather than from a patient understanding of our deepest gut feelings or intuitions.

The power of these cultural influences can be understood by carefully noting the cyclical and often contradictory scientific and psychological theories about sexuality found in the popular media. We can easily conclude that consistent valid and practical guidelines for the physical, psychological, and spiritual health of men women are few and far between. This conclusion applies to most of our difficult social and interpersonal problems, but is especially true in the sexual arena. The fact is that we really don't know much from our scientific or popular media sources about the function of sex beyond the obvious reproductive and "pleasure principle" arguments that have influenced all of our thinkers from Freud up to the more recent sociobiologists.

Unfortunately, our lives are powerfully affected by this loss of personal sexual self-knowledge. As a society we have chosen to ignore what the great spiritual traditions once understood about sexual energy and its role in personal transformation and spiritual evolution. What knowledge we once had has been fragmented or distorted by the institutionalized Judeo-Christian religions and re-made to serve the lesser gods of social, political and personal control. Our Western institutional religious tradition has essentially repressed and distorted the sexual instinct and thereby created a variety of personal and social pathologies. In so doing, it has also effectively removed sexuality from its spiritual foundations.

In this respect, Western psychoanalysis correctly perceived the role of repressed sexuality in individual neurosis. Whatever limitations the psychoanalytic view may have as a full representation of human potential, this much can be granted to Freud's insights. Wilhelm Reich and Carl Jung understood quite well the enormous power of liberated sex energy and its connection to a larger universe of spiritual meaning. Jung rightly protested Freud's emphasis on disease as a model for health as well as the narrowness of his understanding of the range and purpose of the unconscious. He correctly emphasized instead the creative and transcendental function of sexual energy within a spiritually attuned and evolving individual.

But all of these psychologists and their legacies have missed the point in one way or another. It is true that the sexual instinct can both liberate and enslave, but in order to be truly liberating, the sexual instinct must be channeled in the direction of another purpose. Only in conjunction with the drive for spiritual transformation can sex become truly liberating.

Because of his lack of knowledge of the great spiritual traditions, Freud was completely unable to see this point. Wilhelm Reich, whose work has influenced so much of the Human Potential Movement's body centered therapies, was bold enough to bring Freud's insights to their logical conclusion. Reich clearly recognized that the ultimate result of repression was individual dis-ease and political fascism.

But in his zeal to emphasize the destructive effects of sexual repression, he also ignored the spiritually transforming functions of sex energy. Carl Jung had just the opposite problem. He clearly emphasized a spiritual and transcendental perspective on the sexual instinct, but he left out the central role of the physical body in this development. This omission made it next to impossible to apply Jung's elaborate intellectual models to daily problems of sexuality.

So we search in vain within Western psychology to find the practical disciplines and principles we need in order to reconcile the conflicts which face us in the sexual realm. This is a simple and ordinary dilemma. But when we want to harmonize our sexual and love relationships with our spiritual goals, our situation seems especially poignant. Time and time again the sexual function proves to be a disruptive influence, generating conflict and division in our lives. It should not be too surprising therefore that celibacy has become an appealing alternative to so many who wish to follow a spiritual path while remaining worldly men and women.

These facts become even more obvious when we observe the behavior of the gurus, swamis and other teachers in "New Age" spiritual circles. The numerous examples of apparently celibate spiritual teachers born and raised in the puritanical context of traditional oriental cultures and suddenly set loose in the American "new morality" is simultaneously sad and funny. We frequently hear of this guru or that master who has fallen into the temptation of sexual relations which their disciples. Scandals have now become almost commonplace in the ashram and dojo. One does not need to become cynical about this in order to recognize that the sexual instinct is bound to find its expression in rather prosaic and predictable ways no matter what the official spiritual dogma may condone or prohibit. This has been true one way or another throughout the history of the institutionalized Judeo-Christian churches, as well as in the New Age spiritual scene, embracing as it does so much of the Buddhist and Hindu life-styles. In regard to sex, institutional religion, old or new, has little to offer us.

Turning to examples of the teachers of sexual tantra, the gap between theory and practical knowledge becomes rather obvious. We hear of the marvelous and ecstatic rewards of tantric inspired relationships. Our New Age spiritual bookshelves and periodicals lend themselves increasingly to the interest and fascination with esoteric sexual practices.

But what is the real purpose of esoteric sexuality and where can one find real knowledge and practical instruction in these publications? How is it possible for someone to actually apply these rituals in a form that is applicable to ordinary life and relationships? And how much do we really understand of the actual esoteric teachings when they are removed from the larger religious and ritualistic context of the Hindu and Buddhist traditions?

In order to answer these questions we need to accurately understand esoteric sexuality as the study and control of sex energy within ourselves having little or no connection with outer rituals of culture. Beyond this, we need practical methods that can be understood by the Western mind and applied in contemporary life.

One way to discover these methods is to identify the essential, life-affirming aspects of sexuality found in mankind's cultural and spiritual traditions and determine which work today. We must carefully separate what we need to guide ourselves in the sexual realm without getting bogged down in outmoded ways of thinking and living.

The tradition of Taoism, the core of Chinese culture, presents an interesting and practical perspective on this question. The ancient Chinese masters observed that the sexual function is closely related to physical and mental health and is also the basis for the cultivation of higher spiritual faculties. The position that effective conservation of the life force energy and its gradual transformation into a kind of spiritual/material substance is both the birthright and responsibility of mankind. When practiced within the monastic tradition of religious Taoism, the conservation and cultivation of sex energy was largely a matter of celibacy.

But in its wisdom the Taoist tradition also provided another or practical way: The path of Sexual Kung Fu (sometimes called "Seminal and Ovarian Kung Fu"). This practice indicated a way by which a married monk or ordinary man and women could cultivate the Tao ("The Way") while remaining in worldly life. Because of its eminently practical orientation in matters of health and living, the Taoist tradition addressed sexual relationships in a straightforward and realistic manner.

The Taoist Sexual Kung Fu was and is today a method of increasing longevity and health, harmonizing the relationship between the sexes, and a means of spiritual transformation.

Aside from some historical distortions in which the basic egalitarian nature of the practice were subverted by emperors and aristocrats in the direction of a kind of male exploitation of the female, the basic premise of the method of Sexual Kung Fu is that of spiritual development and the harmony of the male and female energies.

Accustomed as we are in our Western traditions to consider the field of sexology from within the limits of our religious, scientific and cultural conditioning, it is difficult for us to grasp the essential meaning of the metaphor of Sexual Kung Fu. We have a vague understanding of some kind of relationship to the martial arts, but beyond this, the concept of a sexual kung-fu seems comical if not downright ridiculous.

In fact, the literal meaning of "Kung-Fu" is method, practice or discipline. The concept of sexual Kung-Fu implies a specific method or practical discipline of having sex without ejaculation. At the same time the Taoist tradition recognizes a certain form of conflict between the sexes: a form that is universally represented by the lawful opposition and dynamic interplay of the forces of Yin and Yang. This lawful opposition plays itself out on the "battle-field" of sexual relations and is expressed as the playful conflict between sexual adversaries. A conflict, by the way, in which man is weaker than his "strong enemy," and where the Kung-Fu of ejaculation control is developed as a way of remedying this imbalance of sexual force.

In the western world we also have a related notion of a battle between the sexes. But we easily make a major error by assuming that this expression connotes the same meaning as the Taoist metaphor in anything other than the most superficial sense of conflict. Our Western concept of the battle between the sexes conveys the morbidity and frustration of the ponderously serious sexual dramas which dominate so much of our current thinking about relationships. It has little to do with the playful and transformative aspects of sex as they are understood in the Taoist tradition.

Only when we move our thinking to the level of "sexual energy" is it possible for us to begin to see how the sexual function can be properly understood and correctly employed in the service of sexual harmony and health. According to the Taoist view, man is constitutionally inferior to woman with respect to his sexual capacities.

His energies are easily spent and with the advancement of years his energetic capacity becomes severely diminished. It is this factor that is a major cause of conflict between men and women and it is this factor that is the basic underlying issue of so much of the current sexual counseling and sex therapy.

From our contemporary perspective the idea of a sexual Kung-Fu seems odd and maybe even a little revolutionary. But with the growing interactions of oriental and Western culture and medicine, and the resultant impact on Western sexology, the principles and methods of Seminal and Ovarian Kung-Fu could gradually become accepted.

Considering the fact that Western sexological research is quite young, we might anticipate the kind of confusion that one finds in a teenager exploring his/her sexuality. By contrast, the Taoist tradition is over eight thousand years old and has reached a full maturity in both theory and method. In fact, both traditions are dealing with the control of the same powerful impulse. Whether or not the Taoist Sexual King-Fu can work in Western society will be determined in part by its translation of it into Western forms of scientific understanding and psychology. Its acceptance may hinge equally on the willingness of Westerners to adapt themselves to the wisdom of the Taoist masters.

The ancient Taoist masters would enjoy this play of opposing forces as the inevitable working of the Tao. A young Taoist master has taken the bold step of revealing the secret methodology to the west; it is up to the reader to test its truth.

H-S-S-S
The Sound
of the
LUNGS

HO-O-O-O
The Sound
of the
HEART

SH-H-H-H
The Sound
of the
LIVER

WHO-O-O-O
The Sound
of the
STOMACH &
SPLEEN

HE-E-E-E
The Sound
of the
TORSO

WH-H-H-H
The Sound
of the
KIDNEYS

The Six Healing Sounds
as taught by
Master Mantak Chia

Healing Tao Center
of
Taoist Esoteric Yoga

2 Creskill Place, Huntington
New York 11743 516-549 9452
Poster and Design by Juan Li.
© Mantak Chia & Maneewan Chia

SUMMARY OF THE PRINCIPLES OF
TAOIST CULTIVATION
OF SEXUAL ENERGY

1. The universe is filled with different kinds of dynamic energy, or "chi." The Tao, or "way," for each man is to creatively transform his energy over a course of a lifetime back to its original state of harmonious balance. Sexual essence, or "ching," is a powerful, vital energy that is generated continuously within the human body. Sexual drive propels the course of man's evolution biologically by transmitting the genetic lineage. Emotionally it harmonizes the love between man and woman, and spiritually provides a tangible link between the "ordinary" creative powers of man and the eternal creative process of the cosmos. Refining one's awareness of sexual energy—with or without a partner—is one of the simplist ways of humans to return to pure consciousness and experience the deepest rhythms of life. (Chapters 1 and 2.)

2. Sperm is the storehouse of male sexual energy. A single ejaculation has 200 to 500 million sperm cells, each a potential human being. There are enough spermotozoa lost in a single orgasm to populate the entire United States if each cell was to fertilize an egg. The manufacture of a sperm fluid capable of such psychic super potency consumes up to a third of a man's daily energy output and is especially taxing on the male glandular/immunological system. (Chapters 3 and 4).

3. Conservation of sexual energy is the first principle of cultivation. Ejaculation of the male seed for purposes other than having children is a wasteful loss of an extremely precious treasure. The energy loss over long periods of time weakens the physical health of the male, can lead to unconscious emotional anger towards women and gradually robs the male higher mind/spirit of it's power to rejuvenate itself. For this reason many traditional spiritual orders in the world require male celibacy. Taoists accept sexual love as natural and healthy, but know the momentary pleasure of genital orgasm with ejaculation is superficial compared to the profound ecstasy possible when love is enjoyed without the loss of the powerful male seed. It's every man's birthright to have full control over his bodily functions and prevent this loss. The secret Taoist methods of sealing the penis in order to conserve "ching" are given in Chapters 5 thru 8.

4. Transformation of sex energy is the second principle of cultivation. During sexual arousal, the "ching" or sexual essence stored in the testicles expands rapidly and causes some energy to naturally rise to higher centers in the heart, brain, glands, and nervous system. This upward movement is cut short by ejaculation outward, so most men never become aware of the full power of their sexuality. The Taoist method perfects this upward transformation of sex energy by opening subtle channels from the genitals up the spine to the head and back down the spine to the navel. The expanding sexual energy is chanelled into this "microcosmic orbit" so it flows past all the major vital organs and harmonizes the etheric energy complexes in the body, called "Tan Tiens" by the Taoists (or "chakras" by the Hindus). (Chapters 7 and 8)

5. Balancing the polarity of female-male (yin-yang) forces is the third principle of Taoist cultivation. Once the sex energy has been conserved and transformed up, a single man can use meditation to balance the male and female poles which exist inside every male body. In the practice of "dual" cultivation, a couple balances this field of energy between them by sharing and circulating their subtle energies. The relationship becomes a springboard to transform the sexual attraction into personal love and then into spiritual awareness and service. The power struggle between the sexes gradually diminishes and balancing their differences over work, family, love, and the purpose of existence leads them into deeper harmony. Balancing this core sexual polarity in a couple is true depth psychology, as it nourishes man and woman at their innermost root. Chapter 9 details the "valley orgasm" method of exchanging the yin and yang energy during intercourse. A higher level of this practice involves exchanging energy without sex, or having orgasm within oneself, and must be learned from a master. (Chapter 18)

6. Don't over-emphasize physical sex in your daily practice, as it is easy to get stuck on pleasure without experiencing higher subtle energies. Proper sexual refinement is only one small part of the vast and all-encompassing Tao. If the mixture of your chi (general vital energy), ching (sex essence) and shien (spirit) is imbalanced, it will be difficult to unite yourself and feel whole and peaceful. Cultivating sex energy is important in nourishing your spirit, but without proper diet, exercise, meditation, virtuous moral behavior and love, true cultivation is impossible. Likewise, don't ignore sex and focus excessively on the higher spiritual centers; the roof will easily fall without a strong foundation below. Tao is the wholeness of Heaven and Earth, true harmony for man is the middle way between them, found in the balanced integration of their subtle energies.

7. Avoid sex without love. It creates imbalances in your physical, mental and spiritual bodies and will slow your real growth. The Taoist techniques are meant to be practical, not mechanical. A woman seeks tenderness of feeling in her lovers and will resent a man who is overly compulsive or preoccupied with his mechanical mastery of esoteric love methods. Dual cultivation is impossible without the full participation of the woman, who must transform up her yin essence stored in her ovaries. Regard the woman you love as more than a powerful generator of yin energy; she is foremost a human being worthy of your full love and respect.

8. You do not need a wife or girlfriend to cultivate your sexual energy. In the beginning it is easier to practice controlling your ejaculation alone, without the distracting excitement and heat of a woman. At any stage it is essential to tell your lover exactly what you're doing and ask her cooperation. The same principles of Taoist cultivation apply to women, with sexual essence drawn from the ovaries and this "ching" transformed upward into higher mind and heart. Many women already have an intuitive feel for the process. The receptive nature of women allows them to quickly learn the Tao of love, especially if the man has mastered the process in his own body.

9. Any male in reasonably good health can master the Taoist methods of cultivating sexual energy taught in this book. If you feel impotent or ejaculate prematurely, the rejuvenation exercises in Chapter 15 should be studied before attempting the Big Draw method taught in Chapter 7. The principles of cultivation are simple, but require steady attention. Its like cultivating a garden—hoe a little everyday, and nature will do the rest. One day you will have luscious blossoms and fruits. An impatient mind kills progress. Do not feel guilty or angry when you spill your seed; it may take years to fully master the Tao of love. The key is to relax, enjoy yourself and keep practicing.

PART I

THE FUNDAMENTAL PREMISE:
Sex Energy Can Be Transformed into Spirit

CHAPTER I

MALE SEX ENERGY IS STORED IN ITS SEED

"There is no medicine, or food, and no spiritual salvation that can prolong a man's life if he fails to understand or practice the harmony of sexual energy."
—*P'eng Tsu, physician to the Emperor*

For more than 8,000 years of Chinese history, the "Sexual Kung Fu Method" of retaining the seminal fluid during the act of love remained a deep secret. At first it was practiced exclusively by the Emperor and his innermost circle, who learned it from the Taoist sages that advised the court. These wise men claimed in earlier times it was a natural gift of all mankind. The Emperor needed the method to prevent impotence and illness; improperly educated monarchs were exhausted at an early age by the sexual demands of their wives and concubines. In aristocratic families it passed from father to chosen son alone, excluding wives, daughters and other family members.

Sexual Kung Fu is an internal practice that permits men to retain certain bodily secretions which are a source of incomparable energy when stored and recirculated to higher vital centers. One prevents loss of this biochemical energy by not ejaculating. Stopping ejaculation is not to be confused with stopping orgasm. The

Sexual Kung Fu Method provides an altogether unique and superior type of orgasm repeated over lengthy periods of love making. Its secret is simply, there is no loss of seminal fluid during orgasm.

By practicing control of certain muscles, tendons, and fascia of the lower trunk and by allowing the genital pressure to spread over the entire body, the seminal fluid is withheld. At the same time one thrills to pleasures of infinite variety. Indeed, the joys of this kind of love must be considered quite different from ordinary physical pleasure; the intensity is so great that it often leads to a spiritual awakening.

A man who masters this method will find his sexuality so enhanced that he will feel a revolution has occurred in his life. The pair of lovers becomes a dynamo, generating great quantities of electromagnetic energy. With this method one can make love more often than before, with tremendous benefits to one's health. Sexual Kung Fu stimulates production of precious hormonal secretions instead of depleting them, as is ordinarily the case with ejaculation.

Every vital function is invigorated because one no longer discharges life energy through the genitals. Real sexual fulfillment lies not in feeling the life going out of you, but in increasing awareness of the vital current that flows through the loins. The body is further replenished by a method of "steaming" the vital energy up from the sexual centers to the brain and higher organs such as the heart and crown of head. The life-enhancing energy process is completed by exchanging energy with one's lover during a relaxed meditation following the creation of this supercharged sexual energy.

This powerful release and sharing of life's vital force is the fundamental bond in human love. To awaken this dynamic energy is also to experience the force behind man's biological and spiritual evolution, also known as the Rising Kundalini.

EXTRAORDINARY POWER OF
THE SEXUAL ELIXIR

Wise men of the Orient have from time immemorial sought means of preventing discharge of the seminal fluid. Without exception they have realized the tremendous implications of the sexual act: when performed with love and discipline, it may awaken dormant powers in the mind and body. The nervous and endocrine systems are particularly open to improvement. The act of love has long been recognized as healing, but the Taoist masters sought to go beyond this and find the principles of physical immortality within it. Many schools arose proposing various ways of tapping the secret elixir of sexuality.

Those who fully understand conventional ejaculatory sex, know it grossly exploits every gland and organ. With ejaculation, the internal pressure of life is expelled from the body, leaving behind in some sex-obsessed men only enough life force to fold the newspaper, squeeze food through the bowels and make for the psychiatrists's couch.

The sages considered one drop of semen equal in vital power to one hundred drops of blood. The Hindu holy men refer repeatedly to Amrita, the elixir of life, a rejuvenation substance that may be produced during prolonged sexual activity without ejaculation. The production of this elixir, which westerners might call a higher hormonal secretion, requires a sexual technique that prevents ejaculation and thereby allows the body to enter higher and higher states of energy.

Extraordinary powers, including healing and clairvoyant perception, may evolve when one retains the semen and drives its power back up into the body. Many gifted minds have held that if one could retain these fluids for one's entire life, the body would not decay after death. The Saints—Christian, Buddhist, Moslem, or Taoist—all used the power dwelling in the vital seed to perform "miracles."

DIAGRAM 1

THE SECRET OF SECRETS

Many esoteric sects have urged the eating of the seminal fluid to increase sexual ability and bodily fitness. This practice is at least as rational as buying vitamins. Scientific analysis has found it to contain a treasure house of vitamins, minerals, trace elements, hormones, proteins, ions, enzymes, and other vital nutritional substances.

But there is an additional property in the sperm seed which present-day science cannot analyze and is far more important than any vitamin. This may be called the Life-Force. Though it registers on no scientific instruments, it is far from imaginary since it separates the living from the dead. Ginseng root is an example of another natural substance which shows no special properties under chemical analysis, yet its life restoring powers are now widely acknowledged. Love making is a powerful healing tonic because it involves sharing the human life force, which is far more potent than any herb or medicine.

Chinese aristocrats and adepts seeking the deepest level of fulfillment have long had the capacity to return the energy of the seminal fluid to the brain and vital bodily centers. But ordinary people in our society have, until now, had no technique for recycling this great life power to the body. Most men have found the sexual lure irresistibly attractive and have happily lost their seed when succumbing to it, unaware of the consequences to their health or that there was even an alternative available to them.

With frequent ejaculation of sperm vitality ultimately plummets. The big spender loses stamina, his vision begins to weaken, hair tumbles from his skull: he grows old before his time. At first he will not feel drained, but after years of abuse his capacities will begin to drop alarmingly. When the hormonal secretions of the sexual glands are regularly leached out, the body is sapped at its root. Within a period of time that will range from months to decades depending on the endowment of the individual, creative and sexual abilities are halved, and the ability to withstand disease and the frailties of old age is diminished.

To regain failing powers, the desperate big spender of vital seed sometimes tries to borrow well-being from hormone injections, "uppers," "downers," intoxicants, megavitamins, hallucinogens, and aphrodisiacs. These substances frantically stuffed into the body may appear to help temporarily. He may seek to regain his dwindling sexual powers with personal power purchased with money or political influence. If he is on a spiritual path, or is surrounded by a loving community of family and friends, this feeling of a failing life power will be slowed. But so long as the prodigious energy waste continues, decline is inevitable. The organs of digestion will be unable to assimilate sufficient nutritional energies to replace those irrecoverable life energies lost by ejaculation.

The Taoist method of cultivating sexual energy recirculates to the body the hormones, proteins, vitamins, enzymes, minerals and electrical energies of the semen. When they are conserved and transformed, one enjoys a marvelous sexual life, improved health, deep inner balance, and rising spiritual consciousness.

The Taoist method of love actually stimulates the production of hormonal substances of unusually high quality. One can learn to focus energy on the endocrine glands during the act of love. When the glands are bathed in energy, the quantity of their secretions increases; more importantly, their quality improves. At higher stages in the practice the hormones develop extraordinary properties.

The Sexual Kung Fu method allows one to generate and conserve more nervous and hormonal energy than are necessary for ordinary functioning. This excess vitality may be channeled to strengthen the body and to raise mental and spiritual abilities. When lovers are in close embrace subtle Yin and Yang energies are concentrated into vortexes from the sexual region to the head and eventually remain in the head at all times.

WHY HAS THE SPIRITUAL POWER OF SEX BEEN KEPT A SECRET?

Our race has finally grown aware of the need to conserve natural resources, lest we consume ourselves to total ruin. Fresh water, soil, forests, and fuels must be spared, food produced more efficiently, building and transportation accomplished with less waste. We have already exhausted a major portion of the readily recoverable riches of the planet. The cost of basic commodities skyrockets because, with the few resources left, we continue to over produce inefficient machines such as cars and unproductive military armaments—tanks, missiles, etc.

Everyone is eager to conserve natural resources, but few even dream of conserving the most critical resource of all: one's own vital energies. The careful harboring of the energy stored within man's seed is a truly rational energy program. Yet this aspect of conservation is entirely overlooked by politicians and health experts.

One reason for this neglect is simply general ignorance of the ancient and highly secret methods used in the past. Taoist Masters gained knowledge of these methods through unknown millenia of relentless searching for the secret principles animating matter. These methods are the fruit of many generations of inspired meditation by sages coupled with my close observations on modern life. This book fashions into a unified whole my personal experience of the teachings.

The Taoist masters felt bound to reveal their potent secrets to only the most select disciples, those who had proven their devotion to the Master's ideals by years of arduous self-sacrifice and service. Why did the Masters feel so strongly compelled to hide their tremendous knowledge from the public?

The reason for this secrecy is not easily comprehended by the western public today. The mass media have fostered a state of mind in which anyone's life is everyone's business: the most intimate details of private sex life are the most greedily lapped up. Advertisers assure their clients today "Nothing sells unless it is sexy." This mentality has made sex, in America, into a disposable commodity, making it harder in our private lives to experience sex as an intimate pleasure that can be cultivated over time to ever deepening levels. Today sex is often consumed and thrown away as soon as the lover becomes old or an inconvenience. Even the women in the harem of Chinese Emperors and aristocrats fared better, being assured of material comfort for life in exchange for their sexual favors. The court society favored the position of men, but at least the female sexual energy was respected for its healing benefits and honored as being necessary for the spiritual development of the male.

A classic Taoist story tells of a woman who learned the process of sexual transformation and exchanged her yin energy with her lover's yang energy and thereby achieved Immortality. She thus became the guide to ancient emperors on the subject of love. There is a recorded historical instance of a palace maid in 690 A.D. becoming the Empress on the death of the Emperor. Empress Wu, respected for her mastery of the art of love, ruled wisely for several decades until her death.

The ancient Taoist masters were not superstitious. They were natural scientists who laid the foundation for amazing technological advances in medicine, chemistry, biology, navigation, and many other fields that would not be discovered by western scientists until 2000 years later. Nor did they crave exclusive possession of their potent knowledge. They had their reasons for secrecy, and their reasons were well-founded at the time. They were custodians of the doctrine taught to them by their masters, and feared the misuse of the great force unlocked by the secret principles. Perhaps, they felt an obligation to protect the public from its tendency to distort the purest teaching to suit its own base instincts. In rural China, which was much less populous then, someone with such esoteric knowledge could easily become a chieftain or a king. A warrior could use his power to defeat his opponents.

The Taoist Masters thus thought it dangerous to spread their teachings too widely, and passed them on to only a few chosen disciples before departing their earthly life. To guarantee that the formulae not be used for selfish purposes, these Masters often transmitted to each disciple only a part of the doctrine. Thus, only if the disciples banded together and shared their learning could the supreme potencies be unleashed. If anyone selfishly withheld his learning, they would never receive the whole doctrine. In the course of many generations, fragments of the innermost secrets came to be regarded as the whole. My attempt is to reunite many disparate parts into an organic whole which I believe similar to the most ancient and complete teachings.

WHY REVEAL THE SECRET NOW?

Why violate the traditional Chinese teaching method and expose to the general public these powerful principles? The simple reason is that the historic moment is already late. The human condition is too desperate to deprive our species of a potentially great infusion of vital energy. If the human race is not quickly infused with a new life energy to render it more harmonious than it has been for most of the last 2,000 years, we are all, earthly Masters and mortals, threatened with an untenably harsh existence, if not extinction.

There are so many wizards of the computer, stock market, test tube, and spectator sport, but so few of the art of life. Our race spends its brief span fiddling with statistics, black boxes, noxious chemicals, and above all, with meaningless words. A majority of Americans daily pass more than six hours in a mesmerized trance induced by a colored shadow dancing in a box of glass. These machines have inadvertently become instruments of our own destruction; a tv programmed mind is not a free mind. Too few devote even one second to entering deeply the great current of life hidden within ourselves. Yet all the technological energy is eagerly sought is an apish imitation of the electrifying ecstasies found hidden within the body and mind.

There are positive signs; in Taoist thinking, any excess eventually leads to its opposite. Despite the current mediocrity of most popular culture, there are tremendous forces driving the race into expanded consciousness. It is clear that the reason for the chaotic state of planetary affairs is the revolutionary advance in human consciousness. In simplest terms, hydrogen bombs hover above us only because we are clever enough to conjure them up. Hatred contains the seeds of love. We have created a crisis in order to force a solution demanding that we restore our balance with one another and nature.

Among the most important implications of this soaring up of consciousness is that the ordinary man will be admitted to secrets of life and mind that were formerly reserved for the chosen few. The French scientist Schwaller de Lubicz elucidated this idea: "It is certain that such a revolution in thought . . . is not the result of whim. It is in fact a question of cosmic influence to which the earth, along with everything in it, is subjected. A phase in the gestation of the planetary particle of our solar system is completed . . . A new period must begin, and this is heralded by seismic movement, climatic changes, and finally, above all, by the spirit that animates man." Not only do troubles press consciousness to evolve, but changing consciousness bursts the constraints of existing order.

I hope that the Taoist practices of cultivating male energy presented here will attain higher perfection when subject to the shock of opposing ideas, scientific study and personal experiment, and the whole race's inventive genius. Today in China, it is formally prohibited to keep secret beneficial practices: one must reveal all knowledge that may improve the general welfare. Henceforth, closely-guarded preparations of medicinal herbs, roots, mineral waters, barks, muds, flowers, gems, venoms, as well as yogic and meditation practices will reach perfection more quickly by serving all.

So the revelation of the Taoist secrets of sex is a contribution to human culture that may take time to manifest its real influence. Where a few great minds once acted, the full race of human genius must now struggle to save our world from the dangers of its own excess.

CHAPTER 2

WHAT IS "CHI" ENERGY?

"Essence, chi, and spirit are the three jewels of life."
—*Book of Changes and The Unchanging Truth,*
Master Ni Hua Ching

Taoist cultivation of sexual energy cannot be understood until the Chinese concept of "chi" is clear. Chi, also known as prana, the warm current, Kundalini power, or the electro-magnetic life force, is very difficult to describe because this life energy is invisible and cannot be seen. However, we can feel it. "Chi" is simply the Chinese word for "breath." On the physical level it is the raw air we breathe in and out, revitalizing us and keeping us alive. Our life hangs by this thin thread of breath every second of our lives, and that thread is seemingly empty air.

   We transform that raw air by mixing it with other nutrients and refining it into a different kind of energy, one that takes a solid form. It becomes our blood, flesh and bones, but never loses an inner rhythm of pulsation that flows through each cell. Our vital organs—heart, liver, kidney, and glands—in turn refine this energy and send chi power to the higher functions of our brain, thus creating our thoughts, dreams, and emotions. From this emerges the human will to live and die, the power to love and ponder this breathing planet suspended in the vacuum of space. As this "chi" follows a self-perpetuating cycle, its rhythm becomes so natural we hardly ever notice it. When was the last time you marvelled at the simple fact you are breathing and your heart is beating?

The ancient Taoist masters spent a lot of time observing the flow of this "chi", which they recognized as the breath of the universe that moves through everything. Chi is the glue between our body, mind, and spirit, the link between our perception of the inner and outer worlds. Living close to nature with few of the distractions of modern civilization, the Taoists were able to map in fine detail the workings of the chi energy both within the human body and in the world at large. Later Taoists made numerous distinctions between the different kinds of "chi" that operate, so that today in China the working heirs to their knowledge—the acupuncturists and herbologists—refer to as many as 32 different functions of chi in the human body.

The Chinese never bother trying to analyze exactly what this "chi" is. Whether it is matter or energy or a process of changing between the two is irrelevant. All that matters is how the chi functions, in short, what it does. When you want light in your room you turn on the lamp, the electricity flows and radiates light. You don't analyze it, you simply flip the switch. When an acupuncturist inserts a needle into a point on a liver meridian, he switches on the liver "chi" so it flows more powerfully.

DIAGRAM 2

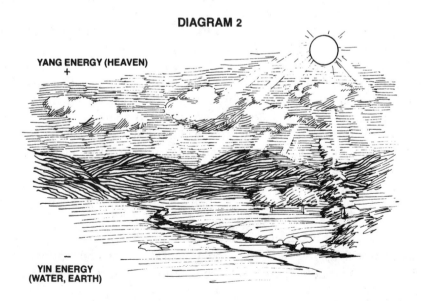

YANG ENERGY (HEAVEN)
+

YIN ENERGY
(WATER, EARTH)

CHI: ELECTRICITY OF THE HUMAN BODY

Modern scientists are beginning to describe the world in much the same fashion that the ancient Taoists described it—as an interplay of positively (yang) and negatively (yin) charged "chi" energies. Here is a recent description of electricity in Time-Life's science magazine:

> "Electricity is almost certainly the most elusive of everyday things: It lives in the walls of our houses, and regulates the lives of our cells. It bolts from the sky as lightning, and sparks from your finger if you touch a metal doorknob after shuffling across the rug. It shapes the structure of matter—making plastic pliable, oil slick, and glue sticky. It runs electric trains and human brains . . . Light is electromagnetic radiation—and that includes everything from visible light to x-rays, microwaves, and radio waves. The magnetism in iron magnets is caused by the spinning of countless electrons twirling in unison, just as the magnetic field of the earth is most probably created by the swirling of electric currents in its molten metal core.
>
> "Your entire body is a giant electric machine: body chemistry (like all chemistry) is based on electrical bonds. It even runs on electricity. The energy you need to see these words comes from the egg you ate for breakfast; the egg got its energy from the corn consumed by the hen; the corn extracted that energy directly from the electromagnetic light of the sun through photosynthesis.
>
> "When you think about it, the universe is positively (and negatively) electrifying. But because of the usually perfect balance between positive and negative forces, most of the electrical power around you is neutralized—and therefore unnervingly invisible, at least in the normal sense . . . Essentially, everything around us is electrically charged empty space."
> K. C. COLE,
> *Discover Magazine*, Feb. 1984

What is curious is that even in China today, ordinary people take for granted that the universe is made up of these charged energies. If asked, they would say a garlic has a very hot (chi) energy. It warms the body: therefore the essence of garlic "chi" is hot, or yang. In the early centuries of China, chi was expressed in written Chinese as a blank in the top portion of the Chinese pictogram and as fire in the lower part. This was done so that no "fire"—no single creative energy might be conceived of as defining chi.

Chi pre-existed before everything in the physical world as original chi, or pure energy. This neatly avoided disagreements about the metaphysical nature of original chi (eg. is God good or evil?) and focused attention on its functional manifestation in the ordinary world, as hot yang chi in fresh garlic or weak yin chi in a diseased liver. As a result, Taoist philosophy tends to be very pragmatic and grounded in observation of the natural organic world. Taoist cultivation of chi energy may extend into what may at first glance appear to be impossibly subtle spiritual realms, but it always begins with down-to-earth and in-the-body practices.

DIAGRAM 3

THE ANCIENT CHINESE CHARACTER FOR CHI ENERGY

derived from the root of fire above
and emptiness below to denote its original purity.

HOW DOES "CHING", OR "SEXUAL ESSENCE" FUNCTION IN HUMANS?

For the Taoists, sexual energy is called "ching," or "essence." It can also be understood as a kind of "human electricity" because like "chi" it is an invisible energy that flows through the body. However in its raw physical form, it is stored in men in their sperm and women in their ovaries. Thus it is a kind of chi energy that has been transformed by bodily process into a more potent form. It is raw matter distilled into a powerful essence that has the ability to recreate the entire human organism. For men, their sperm power is the essence of their "yang" or male energy.

When you feel sexually aroused, this is your "ching" essence expanding at a phenomenally powerful rate. Your whole being is suddenly charged with new energy, your body fired with passion and your heart transfixed with desire. It's like turning on the light switch. Your entire world of touch and feeling is dramatically changed from night to day within seconds. This happens in men when they feel attracted to a woman because their hundreds of millions of sperm cells begin vibrating and generating a larger field of sexual electro-magnetic energy. It also occurs spontaneously in the springtime. When trees are bursting with sap, man's ching is attuned to the cycles of nature and expands as well. What is the relationship of this sexual "ching" essence and the other types of chi energies that form your life force?

MAJOR PHASES OF CHI ENERGY

The following lists in simplified form some of the major phases of "chi" in humans and their relationship to "ching" essence as well as "shien," or spirit, the highest stage of refinement. These three: chi, ching and shien, are known as the "three treasures" because their proper cultivation leads one to enlightenment.

   1. Prenatal Energy: Combines "chi" and "ching" inherited from mother and father, expressed in the gene code and visible as the innate vitality that people have.
   2. Breath Energy: Body absorbs cosmic energy from the inhalation and exhalation of air. Those who breathe properly—relaxed, deep breaths to the abdomen—will receive more energy.
   3. Food Energy: The purity of chi received from food will depend on quality of diet and ability of body to digest and assimilate nutrients.
   4. Meridian Energy: Comes from different types of body cells that produce the energy. It courses through the acupuncture channels linking all the vital organs and glands.
   5. Pulsation Energy: The deep rhythm of your body, felt especially in veins and arteries, also seen in biorhythm energy fluc-

tuations that harmonize our emotional, mental and physical bodies.

6. Sperm (Ovarian) Energy: ''Ching'' is the sexual essence that exists from birth but grows more powerful when fed by other types of chi (food, breath, etc.) Sex essence is the source of all energy available for creative and thinking processes (shien).

7. Spirit Energy: ''Shien'' is the light behind our personality, the ability to discriminate, human self-awareness. At its purest level, it is our very being.

8. Wu Chi: The emptiness, or void from which all chi energies originate and must return. (Original Chi)

DIAGRAM 4

THE CYCLE OF SUBTLE ENERGY

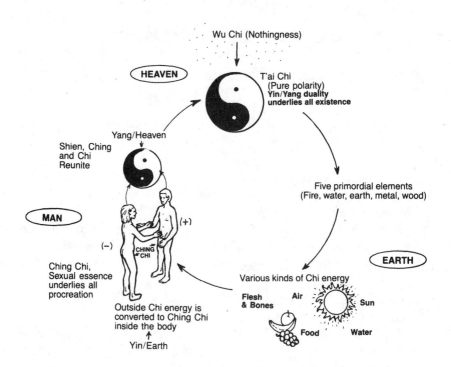

The goal of Taoists is to cultivate the life energy to the highest level possible, bringing good health and deep fulfillment of the human aspiration for wholeness. The early sages observed the natural process of the raw chi of the universal elements—sun and earth, food and air—being transformed into ching, or sex energy, and in the male stored as sperm. The next step is far more subtle and difficult to observe. The sperm energy is mixed with the chi of the human vital organs and refined into shien, or spirit. In short, sex energy offers a link between our biological and metaphysical identities, between the animal and the divine. Sexual ability gives man the divine power to re-create himself, but it also binds him to his animal body and that of his lover.*

The Taoists believe that you can use any substance or force that exists in the universe to feed the process of cultivating your spirit, and thereby free yourself of the limitations of your animal body. Everything has energy in it, and human consciousness can absorb that energy if it so desires. But some substances are easier for the human body to change into a useable form than others. For example, you can absorb the energy from eating a good hot meal more easily then you can from sitting on the beach under the sun. The solar energy is too raw and too powerful to be easily "digested" by the body. Sunlight will burn you severely if you try to absorb too much. But your body can easily assimilate a plate of food and function for a long time on the calories and nutrients digested.

DIFFERENCE BETWEEN HUNGER AND SEXUAL DESIRE

What is the difference between food and sex as energies that our bodies crave to be fed? Many people confuse the hunger for food and sex as being similar biological desires that are both necessary for survival. Clearly they are connected, as many people feeling sexual frustration turn to food for gratification. An imbalance in

---

*If you are interested in a fuller elucidation of the working of chi energy in the spiritual realms, read two books by Taoist Master Ni, Hua Ching: "Tao: The Subtle Universal Law" and "The Taoist Inner View of the Universe and the Immortal Realm" (College of Tao, 117 Stonehaven Way, Los Angeles, CA 90049). There are many volumes in Chinese on this subject, but I feel these are the best translations and commentary on the Taoist canon available in English. Ni's translation of the I Ching is preferred over those of western scholars, who don't understand fully the esoteric aspects of these classic texts. His translation is titled "The Book of Changes and The Unchanging Truth."

ching (sex) energy ranks as a major cause of obesity—when you are sexually frustrated, food is the easiest substitute.

The major difference between food (chi energy) and sex (ching essence) is that sex energy, because it has already been refined and produced inside the body, is much easier to "digest" or "absorb" than a raw substance like food. Food must be broken down and connected before it supplies any useful energy. Sexual essence is already in a state of readiness that is linked within milliseconds to our hormonal and nervous system. The image of sex or the mere thought of it can instantly enter our brain and alter our entire psychological state as well as our bodily feeling.

Thus sexual energy potentially has a far higher value than food as a kind of "nourishment" needed for human emotional maturation and spiritual growth. That is why sex was also considered a department of Chinese medicine and treated so matter-of-factly. A Taoist doctor might prescribe a two week round of love making in certain positions to heal your illness. Human love, expressed through the function of sexuality, was seen as the most potent medicine you could take. It was a kind of "human herb" that could cure most ailments as it restored the flow of chi which governs our organ vitality and general immunological system.

People become obsessed by their relationships as the exchange of sexual energy that occurs is the most important source of sustenance in their lives after food. Relationships invariably get complicated because although your friends and lovers are visible and tangible beings, the sexual energy you are constantly exchanging and transforming into emotion and spirit with them is invisible. It can be known only through your feelings and intuition.

A relationship fails when the spirit of it is not properly cultivated, and you force yourself to "eat" negative, or poisonous, sexual energies without transforming them into positive or neutral energies. When the imbalance in energy becomes strong enough, divorce occurs unless the couple finds another way to correct it. Reading pornographic magazines or masturbation are other examples of negative cultivation of your ching, because they stimulate the "yang" essence in your sperm without balancing it with a real woman's "yin" sexual energy.

The major difference between ching, or sex essence, and food and sunlight energy is that your ching chi is physically manufactured and stored inside your body. This precious substance—

sperm, with its extraordinary power to mate with a female egg and create another life—is manufactured and stored in your testicles for safekeeping. The point is that you are free to tap into your supply of sex energy at anytime by drawing the sperm power from the testicles.

DIAGRAM 5

The modern character for fire can be interpreted as: the primordial element of fire, physical fire, or psychic heat burning beneath the Taoist cauldron.

If you run out of sperm your body automatically makes more. This allows you to be physically ready for your lover at all times. Even if you are alone, without a lover, and never intend to procreate, your body produces the sperm and transforms it into creative sexual energy. So you can always transform this stored sex energy into spirit, your pure awareness, and express it through creative personality at will. So in fact "ching" is internal energy that nourishes us night and day without ceasing. The process of refinement is partly automatic, and partly voluntary. We can either help or hinder the process of transforming our sex energy into creativity depending on how aware we are of our internal process. Yet, like breathing, we draw on this source of energy constantly without being aware of it.

Freud stumbled partially upon this truth many millennia after the Taoist masters had clearly mapped out the role of sex in shaping our destiny. Freud didn't realize that the mental neuroses he discovered could be healed by cultivating the sexual and other Chi energies within the body. When these energies are re-balanced through proper love-making and meditation, the mind is re-patterned and freed of old traumas and habits. Taoist cultivation of one's sexual energy is an extremely powerful tool for self therapy. So powerful, in fact, that it should be used only by those who have achieved a certain degree of integration in the body, mind, and spirit. Severly imbalanced individuals may release more energy than they can safely deal with, and should see a psychiatrist before attempting to learn the Taoist methods.

DIAGRAM 6

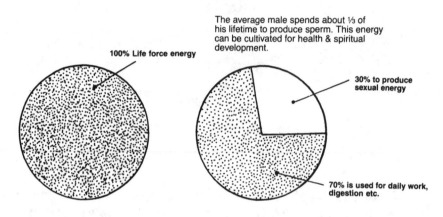

The average male spends about ⅓ of his lifetime to produce sperm. This energy can be cultivated for health & spiritual development.

100% Life force energy

30% to produce sexual energy

70% is used for daily work, digestion etc.

This unique human freedom of utilizing our sexual energy so flexibly does not come without it's price. The price is that we spend an estimated 25% to 40% of our chi energy taken in through food, air, and sunlight just to manufacture this sperm energy and maintain sexual readiness. Why does the body spend so much of its valuable resources to produce billions of sperm cells and regulate them with an accompanying hormonal system? Simply to produce a few children over the course of a lifetime? Nature is not that extravagant. The enormous investment of our bodies in producing this sperm energy is to speed our overall evolution. The more successful man is in transforming his stored energy into higher creative and spiritual energy, the more rapid his evolution. This path of Taoist cultivation of chi energy is simply an attempt to most efficiently utilize the natural gifts every man is born with to evolve the maximum possible in a single lifetime.

CHAPTER 3

THE BIOLOGY OF ESOTERIC SEX

Ordinarily discharge of the seminal fluid completes the act of love. As soon as the fluid is spent, the body strains to replace it. The faster sperm is used, the more the body is forced to produce. Quite obviously, production of this nutritionally rich and psychically superpotent substance requires an enormous amount of raw materials. The reproductive glands receive these raw materials from the blood stream. In its turn, the blood withdraws the precious elements from every part of the body, liver, kidney, spleen, etc., including the brain.

Every organ pays heavy tribute to the glands that produce the sexual seed. Because a single drop of semen houses such prodigious life energies, frequent loss of fluid depletes the body systems of their most precious nutrients and speeds the inevitable physical decline into old age. Retaining the seed within the body is the first step to reversing this cycle in which the male pays an unnecessarily stiff price for sexual satisfaction.

THE VOLUME OF SPERM FLUID LOST IN A LIFETIME

One may conservatively estimate the average American male ejaculates 5,000 times in his lifetime, equal roughly to 4 gallons of fluid. The Kinsey Report provided the following details on the American male's normal frequency of ejaculation:

AGE	AVERAGE EJACULATION PER WEEK
Puberty–15	3.17
16–20	3.3
21–25	4.14
26–30	3.51
31–35	2.9
36–40	2.42
41–45	1.95
46–50	1.8
51–55	1.54
56–60	1.09

More recent studies suggest that it is likely that the vital seed is more frequently lost now than in the time of Kinsey's study because the overall level of sexual stimulation and activity is presently higher. The effects of the sexual revolution, availability of contraceptives, attitudes toward sex in television, film and magazines has been particularly strong in encouraging premarital sex among youth.

But to avoid any statistical inflation, let us use the estimate of 5,000 ejaculations per lifetime made by Kinsey in the 50's. To calculate the flood of fluid normally lost: 5,000 (ejaculations) × 3 cc (fluid) = 15,000 cc.

This is 15 liters or roughly 4 gallons of fluid. The semen spent in an average ejaculation has a volume of 2 to 5 cubic centimeters. These drops contain 200,000,000 to 500,000,000 individual sperm cells.

YOUR BODY HAS ATOMIC ENERGY IN IT!

This is an astonishing statistic: a single male ejaculation scatters two to five hundred million sperm cells. Cast upon two hundred and fifty million female eggs, a single ejaculation could conceivably generate the present population of the United States. Multiplying this figure by 5,000 ejaculations per lifetime yields a numerical indication of the seminal power.

The normal male ejaculates enough semen to generate one

trillion human lives. Within a single man's loins sits the capacity to sire more than two hundred times the present population of four billion on the planet! In a very real sense every man can create a stockpile of sex energy literally more potent than the atomic bomb. If this immense reservoir of psychic energy were to be redirected towards love and spiritual harmony, the possibilities for a peaceful existence seem unlimited.

Some Western scientists may scoff at the idea that semen is an immensely powerful substance. Yet no one can deny the prodigious life-potential in the seed of a single man. By gathering this life-generating force within oneself, one collects tremendous energy.

The effects of conserving this energy would differ with every individual. No man or race produces the same type of energy. Each creates according to its own genius. One group develops enormous physical force, another massive resistance to disease, another clairvoyant powers, still another great longevity. But all men have the inherent ability to substantially increase their active lifespan by creatively adapting to their environment.

Scientists have tried to improve upon Darwin's thesis by focusing on specific genetic impulses behind behavior that lead to increased survival of an individual's gene pool. This correctly gives a lot of evolutionary power to our sexual impulses, but ignores the process whereby this sex energy is transformed into higher creative impulses of the mind and spirit. The evolved man directs his animal body and instincts with his mind and spirit. The scientists maintain the reverse is true. They are right, but only to the extent that man's evolution back to his original self is incomplete.

Man is still bullied about by his biological urges. When man is complete, and has truly integrated his still clumsy body with his mind and spirit, his total freedom of spiritual being is beyond the control of biological instinct. This does not violate the physical laws of the universe; it simply postulates that we are beings with the inherent power to cultivate our energy to a level of power where it allows us to direct our bodies freely. It is not mind over matter, as that implies a battle. It is more mind inside matter. The revelations of mind have allowed us to create nuclear bombs and send man to the moon, so why not use mind to direct its own body which is immediately at hand?

Scientifically minded readers may refuse to accept this. No

proof is possible except in the experience given by daily cultivation of one's chi. Many scientists may have thought it impossible to have an orgasm without ejaculation, yet I and hundreds of my students know it is only a matter of education, of training the mind to control the chi in the domain of its body.

While science may analyze the chemical constituents of seminal fluid, it cannot account for the human seed's life-genius. This is beyond instrumental measure. How can one measure a human life? Only a scientific philistine would try to reduce man to a mechanical theory.

These and other scientific explanations pale before the power of the seed's ability to make 4 billion unique human beings with creative intelligence. Theoretical physics now acknowledges it is impossible to scientifically analyze the ecstatic fact of creation. Quantum physicists have accepted the likelihood that there is no smallest particle, no physical building block upon which the cosmos is built. There are only the multi-universes of space and time linked together by infinite fields of energy. These are currently described as gravitational, weak and strong forces, and electromagnetism. Taoists view any attempt to describe the totality of nature, the Tao, as futile. They found it far more useful to find ways of experiencing deeper harmony with it.

Sexual energy is a field generated within the body and linked to the larger cosmic fields in ways that no scientist can presently understand. But there is no reason to wait 500 years for science to come up with explanations of sexuality, as every man can experiment with his own sexual energy field and draw his own conclusions today. The Taoist masters were ancient scientists with a genius for self-observation and were dedicated to furthering human evolution. Each generation tested the practices taught to them by their masters and tried to improve on it. The methods of chi cultivation may have evolved over the millennia, but the principle has remained the same: The ching or sperm power is a super potent force readily available to men, awaiting only their harvest. Sexual essence is a building block for expanding our personal universe, the foundation for human love and evolution.

BIOLOGICAL IMPORTANCE OF SEX HORMONES TO HEALTH

Modern science has given us the opportunity to study the function of sperm in the body in amazing detail. Each of the sperm cells contains 23 chromosomes, prostaglandins, ions, enzymes, trace elements and other essential parts of human life. Only the elements of the egg and the nurturing environment of the mother are needed to form a living human being of infinite potential.

The seminal vesicles, two little sacks collecting sperm at the base of the bladder, are tied to the vas deferens. They produce a yellow fluid that mixes with the sperm and thickens the seminal fluid. This secretion contains the sugar, fructose, which nourishes sperm cells.

The prostate gland also contributes to the reproductive secretion. It surrounds the urethra (the main duct or tube running the length of the penis) beneath the bladder. In ejaculation the prostate jets forth a thin clear fluid which helps to propel the sperm. Cowper's glands along the urethra supply a few drops of alkaline secretion, which serves to neutralize acid remaining from urination.

DIAGRAM 7

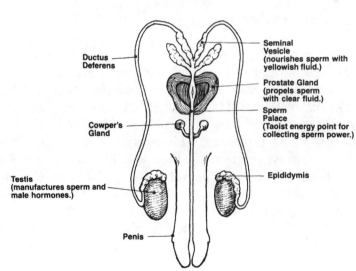

Ductus Deferens

Seminal Vesicle (nourishes sperm with yellowish fluid.)

Prostate Gland (propels sperm with clear fluid.)

Sperm Palace (Taoist energy point for collecting sperm power.)

Cowper's Gland

Testis (manufactures sperm and male hormones.)

Epididymis

Penis

Dr. Beyoihn, a noted endocrinologist, stressed the importance of the hormonal function of semen production: "Sexual hormones are important to our harmonious development. When men abuse the reproductive function, the secretions of the sexual glands are lost . . . resulting in mental and physical weakness, inability to concentrate, and a less tenacious memory."*

Love-making is an internal exercise which helps restore imbalances in bodily chemistry. A moderate amount of sex tends to repair hormonal disturbances, to reduce cholesterol and blood pressure levels. Sexual activity alters the body chemically. The reason this happens is because each gland in the body affects all the others. Thus when sex hormones are stimulated, it stimulates the hormones secreted by the other major glands—adrenal, thymus, thyroid, pituitary, and pineal. The illusion when you are young is that you can stimulate your glands indefinitely, without paying a price for it. Sex seems like a bottomless well of bliss. It is, if you take the trouble to recirculate the sexual hormones within the body instead of repeatedly ejaculating them.

These sex hormones do more than just make you feel good. They literally invade every sphere of your activity and form your personal identity. Recent scientific studies have shown that sex hormones influence the brain's cellular organization. If you are male, then your brain has male stamped on each cell. This is what produces different proclivities in men and women.

Dr. Gunter Dorner, director of the Institute for Experimental Endocronology at Humboldt University in East Germany points out: "The sex hormones . . . don't just suddenly appear out of nowhere at puberty. Nor do they just meander about the body. THEY KNOW WHERE TO GO. The cells that are their targets have already been primed in the womb to respond to the hormones that are now being produced. This is true of the body, of the reproductive organs, heart, lungs, liver, and kidneys. But it is also true of the brain. The tissues, neural circuitry and chemistry of the brain have already been stamped during fetal life by the sex hormones. And the foundations have already been laid for the range of behaviors that will characterize the organism as male or female in adult life."*

---

*E. Flatto, *Warning: Sex May Be Hazardous To Your Health* (Arco Publishers 1973).
Science Digest, September 1983, p. 87.

These hormonal differences obviously determine many of the qualities in men and women the Chinese have called yin and yang. The Taoist goal of total integration of sexual impulse with the mind begins to make sense even to a western intellectual when the connection between sexual activity, hormonal balance, physical health, and personality are examined together. The evidence for health being powerfully affected by hormonal balance has been well substantiated, and is even now a major topic for cancer researchers in their efforts to understand how the mind and emotions control our immune system. The Taoists would say it is unnecessarily complicated to track each individual microscopic hormone receptor and enzyme in the gene code to fight the hundreds of different types of cancers and diseases that result when our immune system fails.

The Taoists contend the critical factor is simply balance—that when male and female chi energies are balanced in the body, each cell will have the energy to function perfectly, and hormones do their job in making the body machinery run smoothly. This balance of male and female hormones produces a happy personality who lives harmoniously with the world. The specific Taoist practice of sexual energy conservation and transformation is one of many designed to insure that the internal equilibrium of the human energy system is so powerful that no outside force can destroy its inner balance. The Taoists thus see everything, hormones, sex, personality, health, and beyond that, your spiritual destiny, linked inextricably together. That is the working of the Tao, which links the finite ordinary world of a Saturday night date to the explosion of a super nova light years away. The principle of the fusion of energy in both is the same.

In olden times the Taoist secret of secrets was the method of being reborn through a process of giving birth to your new self. When I first learned it I didn't understand it, but later, in studying the endocrine system, I was able to see analogies. I realized that both men and women have the makings of male and female hormones and that, in effect, they are each capable of having intercourse within themselves, and giving birth to a new self.

The most important connection in the male hormone system is between the testicles and the pituitary gland located between the eyebrows, behind the forehead. These glands work together in the transformation of sexual energy, a fact that you will experience

DIAGRAM 8

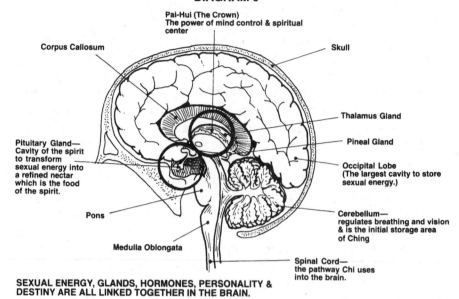

Pai-Hui (The Crown)
The power of mind control & spiritual center

Corpus Callosum

Skull

Thalamus Gland

Pineal Gland

Pituitary Gland—
Cavity of the spirit
to transform
sexual energy into
a refined nectar
which is the food
of the spirit.

Occipital Lobe
(The largest cavity to store
sexual energy.)

Pons

Cerebellum—
regulates breathing and vision
& is the initial storage area
of Ching

Medulla Oblongata

Spinal Cord—
the pathway Chi uses
into the brain.

SEXUAL ENERGY, GLANDS, HORMONES, PERSONALITY & DESTINY ARE ALL LINKED TOGETHER IN THE BRAIN.

when you begin cultivating your sexual energy up. Your testicles and your pituitary gland will begin to pulsate together when the ching is cultivated properly, and is a sign that your glandular system is working harmoniously all the time, not just during sex. The pituitary gland in turn regulates the activity of the other glands. When they are in perfect harmony they secrete an exceptionally fine nectar—a superfine hormonal substance undiscovered by scientists—which floods the nerve centers of the brain and helps create the feeling of bliss described by so many mystics. This is only one phase of spiritual development, but one that is powerfully affected by the balance of sexual energy in the body.

Sexual activity is equally powerful in the more ordinary spheres of health. Sex offers all of the health benefits of physical exercise. Sex reduces the tendency to compulsive eating while burning calories, and thus helps remedy obesity. Sex strains the heart less than driving a car in city traffic, or watching a good football game. Moreover, the heart rate quickly diminishes after sexual action. (For someone on the verge of a heart attack, passionate sex may be sufficient to trigger it. Passive sex is recommended in this case.)

Loving is thus a great natural antidote to stress. Emotional stress especially causes untold harm, as it is a continuous injury to every cell. Life in our urban society subjects us to increasing doses of this potent poison.

Stress directly causes cardiovascular degeneration, such as arteriosclerosis and hypertension. Love restores impaired body chemistry by activating the hormonal centers to defend the physical body and by harmonizing our mental and spiritual faculties.

With frequent ejaculation, the benefits of sex begin to decline, and vitality ultimately plummets. The sexual big spender loses stamina. His vision begins to weaken, hair tumbles from his skull. He grows old before his time. The physical damage caused by expelling the sexual essence from the body is greatly alleviated only in couples or individuals who create and sustain a powerful emotional and spiritual love.

Over years of marriage, couples who consistently find a deeper harmony naturally conserve some of their sexual essence. Insurance studies bear this out: married couples live longer than single people. Two can often share the stress of life better than one alone. A better balance of yin and yang is achieved. The very act of love spontaneously transmutes lower vital chi and ching into higher mind. The Taoist methods of cultivating sexual energy are powerful aids to those following this "path of the heart", but take the path a step further by maximizing the benefits of sex for health and personal growth.

In Chicago a group of elderly people urge couples to practice sex in a ritualistic fashion to preserve vitality. The group, called "Sexy Senior Citizens," is the unconscious heir of many comparable societies flourishing in the Orient for millennia which taught Taoist methods of chi cultivation.

With aging all bodily systems become less efficient. Among these is the hormonal system, which regulates important electromagnetic reactions. If hormonal secretion declines from optimal levels, the body must necessarily weaken.

The relations between the hormones, sexuality and aging have not been fully elucidated. However, many researchers in the vanguard of medical science feel that the hormones regulating growth and sexual development play a critical role in aging. These are produced in the pituitary, thyroid and gonads.

The testes have a double function: besides being the factory for the sperm, they produce male hormones, among which is testosterone. The Sertoli cells in the testes produce another hormone, inhibin. When not ejaculated, these hormones go into the blood stream and are carried to every part of the body.

DIAGRAM 9

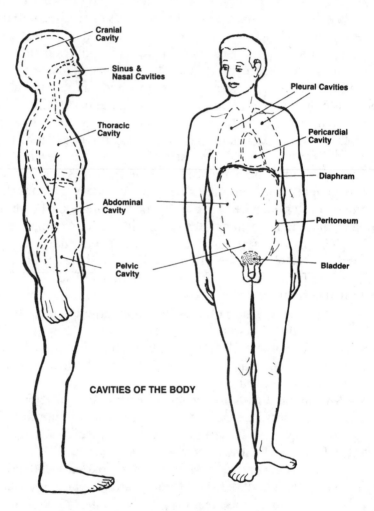

Cranial Cavity

Sinus & Nasal Cavities

Pleural Cavities

Thoracic Cavity

Pericardial Cavity

Diaphram

Abdominal Cavity

Peritoneum

Pelvic Cavity

Bladder

CAVITIES OF THE BODY

Sexual Kung Fu fills the cranial cavity with Chi. This overflows & begins filling other body cavities with life-force, retarding the aging process & strengthening the body's immunity to disease.

Much evidence points to the link between harmonious sexual activity and the retardation of aging. Loving sex stimulates high-quality hormonal secretion. The presence of these hormones in the blood appears to slow the aging process. With Taoist cultivation one produces unusually potent hormones because one focuses energy directly on the endocrine glands, stimulating them to much greater levels of activity. Because the hormonal energy is constantly circulated within the body instead of being ejaculated, a successful student of Taoist loving finds himself with ever-increasing amounts of energy as he grows older.

This increased circulation of sexual energy also redistributes the chi within the body's storage system. As we grow older and our life force is depleted, our body cavities increase in size and are gradually filled with fat or various kinds of pollution that speed the aging process and lower the quality of our final years. The Taoist method draws sexual energy up from the testicles and fills the spinal and cranial cavities with ching. When full, this overflows and begins to fill the chest and abdominal cavities with rejuvenating life force.

These reservoirs of chi within the body supply the raw material used to make the body virtually impervious to disease in the method known as "inner alchemy" to the ancient Taoists. This process of refining the "Elixir of Immortality" or the "Pill of Immortality" may be described in biological terms as storing the body's life-force and then returning it to its source. The chi is moved from these reservoirs within the body cavities into the deepest centers of the brain and bones. The secret of packing chi into the bone marrow is well known to highly achieved masters of Tai Chi Chuan and other internal martial artists. They know that muscle power cannot survive the aging process, but that bones survive for thousands of years. This practice which I will describe in an upcoming book on Iron Shirt Chi Kung, is dependent on retention of sperm power.

Recent scientific studies show the importance of bone marrow to the production of disease fighting white blood cells. These scientists will eventually catch up with the ancient Taoist masters and figure out the full connection between healthy sex, hormones and bone marrow and the prevention of aging and disease.

DEATH AND SEX IN THE NATURAL WORLD

". . . When the living organism, whether vegetable or animal, achieves its aim, which is a new seed, its organism deteriorates."
—*Schwaller de Lubicz, The Temple in Man*

Nature perpetuates its species through sex. In the male seed she concentrates the parent's essential elements. The theme of parental sacrifice for the offspring is repeated in all life forms, from amoeba to walrus, praying mantis to orchid.

One may readily glimpse the death in generation by considering the Emperor Moth's brief span. This large moth travels many leagues across the countryside in quest of his female: "The famous principle of the struggle for life is here the struggle to give life, the struggle to die. Although they can live three days in quest of the female, they perish as soon as the fertilization is complete."[*]

Plants, too, are subject to these laws. After a plant goes to seed or bears fruit, it dies or enters a period of dormancy. Gardeners know that a plant prevented from going to seed outlives its more precocious brothers. Most fruit-bearing trees do not produce fruit until they are five or ten years old. During this period they devote their entire biological force to the growth and strengthening of tissue.

Later in their life, plants split their vital force between reproduction and tissue maintenance. When they grow old they need all of their remaining energies for survival: they withdraw power from the sexual sphere and bear no more.

Some male insects may increase their lifespan several fold simply by not spending their seed. One may object that an insect's sex life has no relevance to ours. Yet the insects excel brilliantly in sexual invention and effectiveness. They comprise more than half of the total animal weight on earth. They far surpass human erotic variety. The insects make D.A.F. de Sade, Saint Anthony, and David Bowie look like a troop of boyscouts discovering sex for the first time.

Insects work the web of material life with particular intensity. Their power to impose their definition of life is manifest in their

---

[*]Carlos Suares, *The Cipher of Genesis* (Shambhala 1978).

numbers, gigantic age and breadth of habitat, garb and custom. Marxist-Socialist deification of the State but weakly mimicks their pitiless genius for collective organization. Rather than staggering them, nuclear war will offer a rare occasion to spin new organs to create an abundancy of new life forms.

In all forms of life the reproductive act exhausts essential energies. The offspring consume bodily stores of nutrition to get a grip on their new life. Vital organs suffer the most depletion because they contain the densest concentration of nutrients. Among humans, the female sacrifice of her bodily energy is unavoidable in the passage to birth. The male, likewise, must surrender the potency of his seed at least once to fertilize the female ovum.

Nature warrants the sacrifice worthwhile, for it fulfills her goal of multiplying life. She intends the old to make way for the new. But amongst all material creatures, only man has the force of will to oppose Mother Nature. "Not distance, not the difficulty of the journey, not the danger of approach foils instinct (in the animal kingdom). In man, who sometimes has the force to escape the sexual commandments, disobedience may have fortunate results.

Chastity in a human being can function like a transformer, changing unused sexual energy into intellectual or social energy. Among animals, this transformation of physiological values is impossible."*

It is the very possibility of transforming our instinctual and essentially animal sexual energies into something higher that makes us human, and potentially divine. The failure to direct our sexual energy upward is a failure to fulfill our deepest human potential. That is why unconscious sex with ejaculation of the male seed is a kind of mini-death seen so often in the plant and animal kingdoms. Two hundred to five hundred million sperm die upon a single ejaculation. The expenditure of subtle energy is even much greater than these huge numbers suggest.

If this spent seed leads to any kind of rebirth in the man, or in the woman, receiving new life, this loss or death is in harmony with nature. But without transforming these mini-deaths into a sharing, a love, a child, or a higher awareness of some sort, this act of sex becomes a mere killing of the potential life energy stored in the seed. Perhaps that's the connection between sex and violence.

---

*Suares, *op. cit.*

Those radically opposed to abortion and contraception might as well begin their campaign against men who kill their potential life-force by ejaculating needlessly.

Although the Taoists have no concept of sin, they might say that man has fallen to his current weakened psychic state in large part because he has squandered his sexual energies over the last several millennia. The Chinese legends speak of a golden age when all men lived in harmony with nature and transmuted their seed up as naturally as you or I breathe. Whether or not this is literally true is irrelevant—the kernel of truth in the story is that man is capable of a much higher existence than what he now accepts. The story bears a striking resemblance to the Biblical story of Adam and Eve's fall from grace after tasting the forbidden fruits of sexual love. In this sense, the end of the Taoist cultivation is to regain the lost paradise which still exists within every man and woman, their original nature.

The major function of sex in nature is to create new life and to perpetuate the species. Yet in our time humanity has been fruitful and multiplied itself to the brink of overpopulation and its attendant ecological horrors. The abuse of sexual power through indiscriminate procreation has brought humanity to a global crisis. It has accelerated the danger of a war which might result in the extinction of the species.

Apart from certain insects and higher apes, animals engage in sexual intercourse for reproductive purposes only. The female receives the male only at definite mating periods, that overall compromise a small part of the animal's lifespan. It is clear that sexuality plays a different role for humans than it does for animals, and it is critical that men and women become educated as to the possibility sex can play in their own evolution and thus affect the balance of nature as well.

CHAPTER 4

THE SEXUAL ECONOMY

"Man cannot be without woman and woman cannot be without man. If you think intercourse is an isolated or separate act, longevity is threatened and every illness arises."
—*from the Recipe for Making Priceless Gold*
Sun S'su-Mo, physician who lived 101 years

Every man is born with a certain amount of priceless vital chi energy. Some begin with more than others, but for the sake of simplicity let us assume an average man is born with a sum of vitality likened at $1,000,000. Over one's life span this million dollar's worth of life force is spent. Some spend wisely and live heartily into the 80's and 90's. When you are young you spend it faster because it seems like such a huge amount it could never run out.

Most people in our consumer society spend more money than they earn. They borrow themselves deep in the hole, assuming they will earn enough to pay it back later. If they fail, they face bankruptcy or a corrective period of lean living. Through poor habits the same thing happens with life energy, only the penalty is loss of appetite for life, sickness, and death.

Let us say that someone earns an additional 100 units of life force daily through breathing, eating and resting. Yet he may spend 125 units of life through poor diet, smoking, gluttony, overwork, anxiety, constitutional weakness, drug abuse and frequent loss of the vital sex fluid. To spend the extra 25 units he must continuously borrow vitality from the brain and organs. This theft of vital energy from one's own million dollar reserves gradually induces mental and physical sickness and premature aging.

Conserving sexual energy is a practical way to earn 125 units and spend 100 units or less. It's an investment in one's physical, mental, and spiritual growth. The imbalance of one's personal economy can be corrected by reducing the disastrously wasteful expenditure of ejaculation. A "profit" of 25 units of vitality is then made by transforming the conserved sexual fluid into higher mental or spiritual energy. Eliminating other bad habits will reduce the loss and increase the profit, but no other single factor in life is so potent as sexual energy.

If you work hard all day, you've already used up much energy. If you then have a few drinks, eat a heavy dinner and later have sex in which you ejaculate the vital sperm fluid, you are overspending your life's provision prematurely. Some people would call it a day well spent, as they cannot envision anything better in life to spend their energy on. If you continue to overtax your resources, you may wake one morning fatigued with life, sick with arthritis or cancer, or maybe you won't wake up at all. You will have prematurely exhausted your vital capital and may have to die at an age that you feel is somehow "unfair" or possibly worse, suffer through your final years in life with your creative powers and physical faculties greatly diminished.

I am a Taoist living in the twentieth century near New York City and lead an extremely busy life. I have a wife and an overly energetic young child. I own a computer, drive a car in city traffic, deal with teaching hundreds of students, and maintain a heavy travel schedule flying around the U.S. I know it is possible to lead a rich and rewarding life without exhausting oneself, and have seen my students do the same. The more you cultivate your chi energy with daily practice, the easier it becomes to replace energy spent and still end up ahead.

Of course, if you choose a simpler lifestyle you can progress much more quickly. That's why many Taoists choose to live up in the peaceful mountains. But you can live by the same Taoist principles anywhere. The universe is bountiful if you know how to live with it. Sexual energy is one of the most abundant gifts given to us by nature, yet most people casually toss it away without realizing the full value of its treasure.

As Americans become more aware of the importance of personal health they are seeking to change their lifestyles. Many people are now realizing that they have been living destructively. Fortunately, they have grown conscious before it is too late. Whether they are jogging or taking a dance class, they wish to begin a life-energy conservation program. First they must pay the interest on the vital sums they have overspent from their mind and body. After a while they may repay both interest and principal as they begin to produce and conserve more energy. At that point they can take the path of cultivating their chi energy into its original spirit.

Have realistic expectations. You may have spent more vitality than you had to spare. Concentration and patience are necessary to recover it. You can spend $100,000 in an hour, but you may need one year to earn it back. Serious physical and mental trauma, heavy use of drugs, and frequent ejaculation all involve grossly excessive spending. Many young people seem to have unlimited energy. But these youths are toying with the sources of life as if on a wild spending spree.

Many older people apparently in good health are, in fact, tottering on the brink of serious breakdown. Only the strength of habitual self-will allows them to continue to function. When they have a check-up—often prompted by unconscious awareness of their condition—the doctor may order an immediate halt to strenuous exertion. Often these people collapse in the first days of their enforced rest because the flimsy strand of willpower which kept them going has been cut. Friends will say, "I can't believe it. Yesterday he seemed strong as an ox." If you learn to balance your account in the sexual economy, you will be taking the most prudent steps possible to avoid such a scenario in your own life.

THE YOUTHFUL FURY OF SEXUAL FRUSTRATION

One of my main concerns is the frustration of youth in our society. Upon the quality of their thoughts and acts civilization will endure or crumble. Most male youths are more interested in sex than almost any other subject. This is natural, as their bodies are working overtime to produce billions of sperm cells. Women cannot imagine what an intense experience this is, as their energy cycle is more evenly distributed over the fluctuation of a monthly menstrual cycle.

This build-up of male energy is a natural manifestation of universal Yang energy. The development of traditional romantic love at this stage is natural. If this expanding Yang energy finds a receptive female to nourish it the love between them can mature and spiritual evolution gradually awaken. The problem of obsessive sex arises from a material society that stresses the value of physical sex so highly that people remain immature all their lives seeking to sustain a lusty image of sex that exhausts them and ultimately blocks their evolution by stimulating them to rapid loss of their seed.

The harder youths try to grab pleasure, the more surely it eludes them. In their frustration, many seek pleasure with increasing fury, a quest for identity that leads to frequent masturbation and promiscuity. The more often they spill out their vital seed, the more empty they gradually become despite the temporary feeling of gratification as the life force passes out their loins. Unrestrained sexual frenzy can destroy a young man's fragile identity and melt him into the mob mind cultivated by sex-for-profit industry and sexually exploitive media shows. Higher vital energy which should nourish the young person's true center serves instead to grease the empty fantasy of his bed of lust. Afterward he is left with nothing. This spells spiritual disaster if the excesses are not corrected in time. This type of young man may have difficulty in his relationship with women and ultimately this leaves a vacuum in his understanding of himself and the female pole of his own male energy.

For this same reason adolescents tend to fanaticism, political, religious, or otherwise. Mao's Red Guard is but one youth group that has propagated its reigning tyrant's brand of fascism. The proliferation of various cults in the U.S. is strong evidence that the young are not able to fill the void in their lives with the physical pleasures that have become standard. If the fragile link with his newly forming adult identity is frayed or broken by lack of love or social nurturance, a youth has only the group psyche to animate his life. The group mind provides the fullness their hollowness craves. As Nature abhors a vacuum, their own emptiness despises itself.

These remarks apply to adults in our sex obsessed society as well; many are desperately questioning for an identity that is their own by natural right, if only they knew how to claim it. The proper understanding of the function of sexual love in their personal evolution would go far to correct these excesses. Education about methods of chi cultivation of all types, but especially of the sexual energy is the most direct solution. Teenagers will never give up their sexual desire, but it is not far-fetched that many of them would be interested in improving it if they knew how.

SEX AND THE SUPER ATHLETE

There is a widespread belief among many professional sports coaches that an athlete who makes love the night before a big game loses his competitive edge. This is a controversial topic and a survey of existing opinion on the subject is inconclusive. Clive Davis, editor of the Journal Of Sex Research, looked into the effects of having sex before competition and concluded "You can always find anecdotal reports to support any position you want to take, but certainly you couldn't support either side medically."

Top-ranked prize-fighters are the most vociferous in contending that they cannot violate natural laws without paying a stiff price. Ken Norton publicly stated that he gave up sex for eight weeks before his first fight with Ali and abstained for a similar length of time in subsequent Ali fights. "A couple of times in my first 10 or 11 fights, when I didn't abstain from sex, I think it hurt me." Norton said that he believed that "9 out of 10" fighters give up sex while training for a bout. Joe Frazier, who also fought Ali, felt very strongly about the damaging effects of ejaculatory sex: "If you mess around before a fight you don't have any reserve energy left."

It is rumored that the great Muhammed Ali observed strictest sexual continence for as long as one year before his bouts. He didn't publicize this because he keeps his training methods secret.

The Taoist approach to sexuality resolves the dilemma facing a male athlete who is forced to choose between losing his competitive edge or his woman. An athlete can have the best of both worlds by learning the secrets of conserving and transforming sexual energy. There is a substantial increase in available energy reserve after Taoist lovemaking, as the male has not only conserved his own super potent seed power but also absorbed a high dose of equally potent yin/earth power from his lover. Any athlete who can master the urge to ejaculate his life-force will have taken a step in the life-long process of mastering himself and his chosen sport. He can awaken from a night of ecstatic lovemaking feeling light hearted and energetic, with his batteries fully charged. This is quite different from the pleasant exhaustion that often follows ejaculatory sex.

Some male athletes claim that ejaculatory sex the night before is beneficial to their sport. The reason for this is usually simple— the athlete has too much nervous energy and lovemaking relaxes him. His excess energy impedes his performing ability, and ejaculation relieves that tension. This improves his coordination and attention in the field the next day and thus helps him to win. This is entirely in line with the Taoist idea of the function of lovemaking to harmonize the mind, body, and spirit. Huge quantities of raw chi energy in the physical body are useless until they are harmoniously integrated with the mind and spirit.

University of New Mexico Professor Mark Anshel did extensive research on sex and the athlete. He found that many coaches were intentionally creating sexual frustration with the hope that their athletes would redirect their drives against an opponent. "All people don't react to frustration the same way," Anehel points out. "By preventing sexual activity, these coaches (or the athlete himself; Guillermo Vilas, the Argentine tennis pro, once admitted staying celibate for a year to improve his game) may actually bring about negative personality manifestations such as anger or feelings of isolation."

The Taoists have used sex since ancient times to heal physical, emotional, and mental imbalances, a practice very much in line with helping athletes maintain maximum fitness. The Taoists were martial artists as well, and knew the secret of defeating an opponent was a combination of physical discipline and maintaining a superior degree of self-awareness. For this reason they cultivated their chi energy and guarded against the loss of their seed to women. This Taoist practice of "Sexual Kung Fu" is kept a closely guarded secret amongst martial artists lest their opponents learn it and grow stronger. The modern athlete can enjoy the same benefits today as the Taoist fighters, swordsmen, and Tai chi chuan players have for hundreds of years—the full freedom to love without losing the competitive edge.

SEX, COMMITMENT, AND MARRIAGE

This subject of marriage is too vast to be generalized by any fixed rules. Marriage may suit some men and not others. One man may marry and be happy for a lifetime and his brother find it torture. In the Tao, nothing is ever forced; alignment with the natural is sought, and from this comes lasting balance of yin and yang.

The Taoist sages would never say that a celibate man is higher or more pure than a married man. Both men have equal opportunity to adapt their daily practice of cultivating their chi energy to their life situation, and thus, to achieve union with the Tao. If all spiritually inclined men were to remain celibate, society might suffer from the lower quality of parental guidance offered to children, and result in disharmony in the world.

Practically speaking, a marriage, especially with children, consumes an enormous amount of time and energy and should not be entered into lightly or for the wrong reasons. The wrong reasons include marrying because of outside cultural pressure or to satisfy someone else's desire, such as parents.

The decision should come freely from within you or else later you will have trouble accepting the responsibilities which arise from your choice. Many men marry because they are emotionally insecure and hope a woman will offer that security. This emotional insecurity can often be traced to insecurity in the male sexual role. So, if you have not yet married, I suggest you master the sexual energy cultivation methods in this book before making that deci-

sion, and if possible learn the Fusion of Five Elements meditation for balancing emotional energy (see Chapter 18 for a description).

Even this is no miraculuous overnight cure for emotional insecurity. If you spent decades feeling and acting insecure, it will take a while to change. Cultivate and balance your internal energy constantly, and you will be surprised at how your emotions will lose their power over you, and be replaced by a continuous feeling of inner connectedness. You won't need to seek your emotional understanding from a woman, which is a dependancy trap many men fall into. When you understand the source of your emotions in the movement of the chi energy in your body, you will be in a position to maintain inner balance and help your lover to achieve the same.

Once you are free of sexual and emotional compulsiveness you will find yourself a very changed man in your relations with women. Ideally, you would get to know a woman for several years before having children with her. This allows you both to learn the subtle energy rhythms of the relationship before your attention is focused on child-raising. If, by then, you have practiced dual cultivation to a high level, the deep bond will go far in getting you through the inevitable difficulties that lie ahead.

For many American men, sexuality actually remains on an infantile level. It is often no more than an extension of feeding. It is an attempt to take in love from outside themselves and childishly demand the certainty of continual gratification. This leads necessarily to the jealous dependency that plays havoc with so many relationships. People spend years watching to see if they are loved: in this way they annihilate even the possibility of what they seek. This type of destructive sexuality is a constant looking outside oneself for assurances. This insecurity can generate negative emotions we are often unconscious of, such as jealousy and guilt, as well as acts that consciously violate our own integrity, such as adultery. One ceases to live in the present moment, creation stops, and life becomes slavish rehearsals of lust broken by long periods of boredom.

It's easy to observe that after a time the life of many couples seems weary, stale, flat and unprofitable. One reason for this is because when they embrace intending to make love, the man ejaculates and thus excretes his deep vitality and depletes his yang charge. Nature is abundant and forgiving, but after years of ejaculation the difference shows up as weakened sexual desire.

Unless the couple has spontaneously found the will to transform their life energy into a higher love—a process of spiritual attunement that balances the daily losses of vital energy—the relationship is in danger of becoming a ghost of its former passionate self.

Energy that could become genuinely joyous is spasmodically thrown out of the body by ejaculation. This loss occurs every time you ejaculate. Eventually a man can develop feelings of indifference or hate for his sexual partner because he subconsciously realizes that when he touches her, he loses those higher energies that could make him a truly happy man. This produces a deep crisis, because during the years of love-making and sharing their lives, a powerful emotional bond has developed. A lot of his sexual energy has gone into making that bond and he can't understand how the bond could exist and yet he feels bored, resentful, and fatigued.

This flattening of sexual desire between regular partners is due largely to depletion of polarity or sexual-electrical tension. You can increase the attraction by charging the positive and negative poles of the male-female battery. Some couples achieve this temporarily by taking seperate vacations or sleeping in separate beds, or they find other ways to naturally keep the balance of energy through outside friendships and activities. With polarity restored the current of life flows between the lovers ever more swiftly and powerfully. Dual cultivation allows a couple to remain together and keep this polarity of their relationship fully charged.

Dual cultivation is designed to promote the happiness of couples, to teach the partners to discover inexhaustable pleasures in each other. There is no inherent reason for love to grow old. The practice of conserving and exchanging sexual energy without loss of the seed will help remove a major cause of promiscuity: incomplete satisfaction with one's lover.

It can also alleviate a common problem in marriage: not enough energy to work things out. With the stress of both parents working and modern fathers trying to share in the child-raising tasks, many couples simply burn out. They never have enough time to make love; if one is aroused the other is exhausted or asleep. Using the Taoist Secrets of Love, both husband and wife will find sex rejuvenating and an endlessly fascinating journey into the subtle realms of chi exchange. They can return to the routine of daily drudgery with renewed vigor and light heart; when your chi is full and running in all your meridians, the most ordinary things become interesting again. Your chi is the glue between your body, mind, and spirit; until it is completely integrated you will feel incomplete.

The Tao teaches there is infinite pleasure and limitless potential within every human being. The addiction to sex as emotional food can gradually be changed from within the male body through chi cultivation. One grows to appreciate this fact with the retention of the seminal fluid and its transformation into the higher center of the heart. One experiences the fullness of life long after the lovemaking has ceased, and a delicacy that more easily moves beyond temporary sensory stimulation, to a continuous connection of feelings with the lover.

The man who diligently studies the Tao learns that the source of all emotions as well as the source of a woman's allure is also within himself. However, when difficulties arise, the first question to arise is always, "What does my commitment to her mean?" This self-questioning can raise its head at any stage of spiritual accomplishment or emotional maturity in your marriage.

The highest commitment a Taoist can make is to the marriage of yin and yang in the universe. In fact yin and yang are always married, as they are just two poles of the same subtle energy field. Thus, the real commitment a Taoist makes is to consciously realize their union in his life and thus empower himself (single cultivation) and his lover (dual cultivation) with his awareness. When the level of chi and ching chi cultivation reaches a very high level and is integrated with shien, or spirit, the awareness extends to an even wider field and might be likened to the Christian universal love or Buddhist sense of compassion for all sentient beings.

The difference is that a Taoist cultivates this universal sense within his body, so it remains as a tangible experience of his subtle chi energy field. This insures it does not become a conceptual or theological idea of love into which a man is trying to fit his behavior. This is an impossibility, as no whole human being with an integrated body, mind, and spirit can fit into the shoes of an abstract idea, even a noble one like love.

The Taoists in China traditionally cultivated themselves in pairs or small groups, whether it be two friends, a master and student, a man and woman, or a small community of adepts. There were many different approaches used by these different groups;

some were strictly celibate, others quite openly favored dual cultivation between man and woman. Because of the strong emphasis on sexuality in America, and the freedom from social restraints, I'm certain that the method of dual cultivation will become a major path for growth among couples. Americans are raised with the idea that they can do anything they want to do, and don't like being told by priests or gurus that their love of sex is dirty, sinful, or blocking their path to enlightenment. So, let them enjoy sex and take the best from it. It's all part of the Tao, and their marriages will be all the better for it as long as the sexual energy is properly used.

Some men and women will choose to love outside of marriage, and if they cultivate a harmonious balance of yin and yang their union is as holy as one with an official state seal stamped on it. A word about the virtue of a lengthy committment. It normally takes decades to fully cultivate one's chi energy to the highest level of shien. It will likely take years to appreciate the subtle energies your woman is capable of creating and making available for your own cultivation. It is said it takes seven years to know the rhythms of a woman's body, seven years to learn her mind, and seven years to understand her spirit. Don't be a promiscuous fool who is never patient enough to learn the true depth of the Tao.

THE MORAL EFFECT OF SEMEN LOSS

There is a distinct tendency for strengths and weaknesses to propagate themselves. The weak grow weaker, the strong strive to increase in strength still more. Taoist Cultivation helps curb self-destructive tendencies which are worsened by weakness itself. The Taoist treasures the energy stored in his vital fluid. The vital power within him slowly begins to resist abuse of any sort to both his body and character.

The loss caused by ejaculation is not limited to the physical sphere. Mental and emotional functions are profoundly influenced. Hormonal fitness directly effects personality and capacity for creative thought. The mind suffers from the loss of testosterone, the hormone secreted in the testes and spent in ejaculation.

Chinese medicine long ago observed that vicious crimes are often committed soon after seminal loss. Courage is usually at low ebb after ejaculation. One scares easily and reacts violently. This is one reason murder and mutilation often follow rape.

Thus there is what may properly be called a moral effect of cultivating one's sexual essence or ching chi. The yang fire within the seed burns up internal poisons at the same time it generates an essential life-supporting substance. One who retains his seed increasingly respects every form of life.

Everyone has experienced discomfort when watching someone abuse their child in public, or felt the stare of a starving bum. The anger or despair of others actually spills over to us and influences us whether we like it or not. In like manner, each of our thoughts and acts beams to the far reaches of creation.

The man who cultivates his subtle energy eventually experiences in his body the fact that all living beings are part of one life. He and his lover flow into each other. He knows that across the web of consciousness one living thing constantly nourishes another. In becoming highly aware of the interconnection between all creatures, he strengthens his tendency to be unselfish. He may suddenly find himself asking: why pour negative thoughts into the single stream from which we all must drink? In this sense all loving energy is cosmic, or divine energy. When two people love each other consciously their energies are intentionally consecrated to the good of humanity. This kind of love offering develops a special egolessness in the lovers and will inspire others whom they meet.

While this approach to loving is not limited to the esoteric Taoist cultivation, the use of its methods of transforming sex energy vastly increases the amplitude of loving power which is emanated. In the Taoist view, man cannot direct the heavens, but if he behaves in harmony with the laws of heaven and earth he can guide the larger course of events by becoming harmonious within himself. Thus, Taoist philosophy does not preach any specific moral guidelines. It simply posits that morality is innate within man; if he cultivates his subtle energy and experiences his true self, he will act in a moral fashion among men.

THE CONTROVERSY:
IS SEX GOOD FOR YOUR HEALTH?

Man appears to be the only higher creature naturally endowed with the power and inclination to perform sexually regardless of the possibilities of spreading his own kind. There is no falling off of

sexual appetite in the pregnant female or her mate. The human
begins sexual activity soon after reaching puberty. Most people
spend a lifetime performing and dreaming of sexual intercourse for
the sake of pleasure and emotional fulfillment. It seems clear that
sexuality serves a higher function in humans, but doctors, scientists, psychologists, priests and artists cannot even begin to agree
on what this higher function is and how or if it should be regulated
to improve human well-being.

Western scientific texts are curiously contradictory about the
healthfulness of sexual intercourse. Many sex manuals today
praise the restorative qualities of extensive sexual activity. Others,
equally authoritative and based on psychiatric studies, caution
against sexual overindulgence. Which school of thought is correct?
When does too much sex become unhealthy?

To complicate matters still more, there are similar inconsis-
tencies among Oriental sages. One renowned Indian holy man
counsels the male to see every woman as a sack of shit and piss in
order to resist the temptation of losing the precious male seed to
her.

Yet the Lord Buddha himself is held to have said: "Women
are the Gods, women are life . . . Be ever among women in
thought."

The Taoist teaching of sexual yoga reconciles these view-
points because it accepts the middle way, recognizing the truth in
both extremes. Their solution is of utmost simplicity: joyous and
loving sexual intercourse without the loss of the male seed is
healthful in the highest degree.

Much depends, of course, on the path you are taking through
life. At a certain time in your life celibacy may be best for restoring
your health or for achieving rapid spiritual progress. Celibacy can
be an extremely powerful means of conserving all your vital energies freeing you to work with greater intensity in cultivating yourself. But most Westerners are focused on finding the right mate,
and working out their sexual and emotional desires with a partner.

The Taoist principles of energy cultivation work equally with
both cases, the single or the dual cultivation. For a Taoist, all paths
must ultimately move beyond a focus on sex energy and towards
attunement to all the subtle energies of the Tao.

But no one can take more than one step at a time. If part of
your mind is fixed on sex, you must live out that impulse, study it,

and know its source before you can transcend it. Taoists are always flexible; your energy can be cultivated no matter what your situation in life is. But the basic principles remain the same. Sexual activity without love and with frequent loss of fluid is physically and mentally destructive to any path. Engaging in sexual love with a partner—but without any esoteric practice to cultivate the chi—is an incomplete path to transforming oneself.

Love will spontaneously transform any couple to a higher level of awareness, but at the same time the repeated loss of seed will hasten their physical decline and slow their progress. It's like climbing a mountain slope with loose rock scree—you take three steps up and slide back down one. This pace may lead to emotional and mental happiness found at the top of the first ridge. But it may deprive you—for the lack of time and energy—from seeing the valleys, mountains, rivers and ocean beyond. This is the fullness of the Tao, the attaining of a lasting experience of your higher spiritual self.

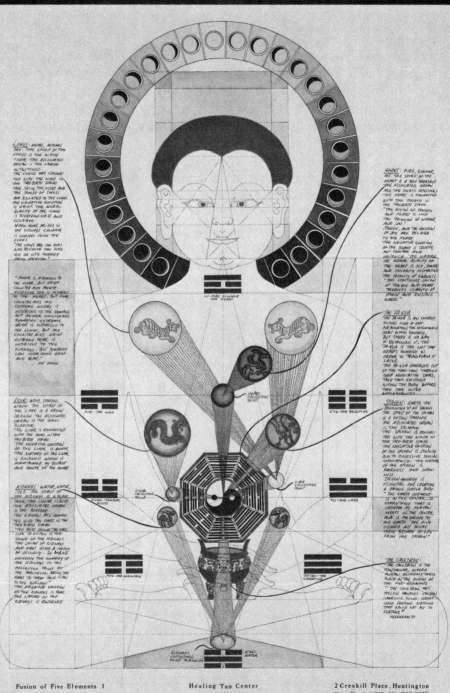

Fusion of Five Elements I
Cleansing, Clearing and Harmonizing
of the Organs and the Emotions
as taught by Master Mantak Chia

Healing Tao Center
of
Taoist Esoteric Yoga

2 Creskill Place, Huntington
New York 11743 516-549 9452
Poster and Design by Juan Li
©Mantak Chia & Maneewan Chia

CHAPTER 5

SEX IN THE ESOTERIC TRADITIONS OF THE WORLD

". . . It is impossible for us to learn elsewhere what we are incapable of learning within our own bodies."
—*Schwaller de Lubicz, The Temple In Man*

Religions have nearly always tried to control the sexual habits of their followers. Their success seems to swing in cycles of the public submitting and rebelling, but I would guess that ultimately they have failed because for most people the experience of sex is more powerful than their experience of religion. As a biological impulse, sexual drive so completely permeates our actions and desires that it is not easily harnessed by any system of belief, however dogmatic. Hence the adage that prostitution is the world's oldest profession.

In my travels I have noticed that prostitution seems to flourish side by side with the most fanatic religious communities. Sex is like an inflatable ball floating on the surface of a pool—the deeper you push it down into the water, the more strongly it presses back up. If you lose control of the ball for even a split second, it will shoot up into the air out of control.

The attempt by religions to publicly dictate sexual morality is actually a vestige of an earlier, less material era when spiritual experience was more intense than the fleshly pleasures of sex. The

founders of the earliest religions—then known as Mystery Schools
or Fertility Cults—understood the role of sexuality in spiritual development, which is why their practices and rites held such powerful experiences for converts. Many modern spiritual leaders,
whether Catholic, Jewish or Hindu etc., have forgotten the link in
their religious rites connecting sexual power and spirituality. Cir-
cumcision rites, Spring fertility festivals (*e.g.* Easter), and communion ceremonies are all remnants of a time when the esoteric and
hidden meaning of sexuality was understood and incorporated into
religion.

The task for twentieth century man is to peel off the layers of
his outer or "exoteric" religious beliefs and free his mind to experience the ecstatic core of his existence in his body. Then the outer
ritual and the beliefs of the old religions will either fall way, or take
on a new and profound meaning. By accepting sex as sacred, the
role of religion will be revitalized in society and made more meaningful in ordinary personal relationships.

Taoism is different from the major religions in that it is a
spiritual philosophy and not an organized religion with a body of
believers obeying a holy scripture. Faith in God (or the Tao) is not
enough for the Taoist; devotion to higher harmony must be accompanied with the self-knowledge that comes from cultivating one's
own energy. In a sense, a Taoist must "grow" his soul in order to
fully gain knowledge of it. Every human has the same seed within,
but unless it is properly nourished, its bearer will never see its fruit.
The divine world within man is patterned after the natural world—
as a child will never know its full self until adulthood, so must a
man cultivate to maturity his subtle spiritual energy if he wishes to
enjoy and participate in the fullness of the Tao.

There were some folk cults with Taoist priests that rose up to
compete with the arrival of Buddhism in China, but I am concerned
here only with the original esoteric teachings of the Taoist masters.
These Taoists are famous for permitting the use of sex on their
spiritual paths. There were many Taoist sects which sprung up on
the five holy mountains of China, and each emphasized different
aspects of chi cultivation in their spiritual development. A few
sects taught the path of "single cultivation", which utilizes the
Taoist principle of mating male and female subtle energies withn
one body, but strictly forbids physical sexual intercourse as either
unnecessary or too risky.

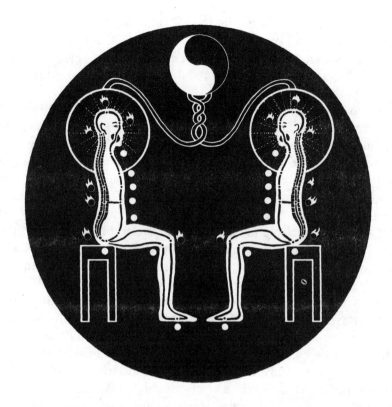

The practice of "dual cultivation" was widely accepted by most Taoists for both its hygienic and spiritual virtues. Even in these schools the danger of becoming deeply attached to one's lover was acknowledged as a possible stumbling block for those seriously aspiring to become immortals and enjoy full union with the Tao. This sexual attachment was never viewed as sinful, and no sense of guilt was encouraged as in the Christian tradition. Becoming sexually attached to one's partner simply means that the aspiring yogi might experience only the union of a man and woman in this lifetime instead of the greater union of Heaven and Earth. This is no condemnation of the couple, as such a union might be a high accomplishment for them.

The Christian religions have a strong tradition of a sacred marriage, but church politics—mostly male priests afraid or jealous of women's earthy, "dark," yin power—led the Christian world into periods of woman-hating witch hunts that alternated with woman-worshipping cults of the Virgin Mary. China, whose culture was molded by a blend of Taoism and Confucianism, was spared this vicious cycle. The yin energy of the universe—personified by woman—was always viewed as necessary to its functioning and to the well-being of man.

Even when the original Taoist teachings on the perfect balance between yin and yang fell into periods of decline after the Manchu reign in the Eighth Century A.D., women were not subjected to the same abuse seen in some other cultures. Chinese society became increasingly paternalistic and women were viewed as a kind of male property, but at least the general cultural sentiment favored treating this female "property" with respect. Many of the Taoist sexual manuals which survive today come from this period, and are somewhat lopsided in advising the aristocrats who read them on how to get healing yin energy from the woman.

These manuals totally ignore how men can help to heal women with their powerful yang energy. They do correctly advise men to conserve their seed while suggesting that a man make love to as many as eleven concubines a night. The manuals are really medical textbooks, with a very cut-and-dried clinical approach to sex that treats it solely as a means to harmonizing one's health. Although these manuals fail to stress the higher path or teach meditative practces for exchanging energy with the women they do reflect the basic esoteric Taoist teachings that sex, when properly practiced can be incorporated into daily life with tremendous benefits to health.

The Taoists may have one of the oldest esoteric traditions of cultivating sexual energy in the world, but they certainly were not alone. The idea for transforming sexual energy for spiritual purposes is well known in all the esoteric traditions of the world, both Eastern and Western, although generally it has been guarded as a great secret. Whether in Egypt, India, Tibet or Europe, the information that was revealed to the public was usually kept to a vague or abstract theoretical/theological level. A practical method to hold and transform the sex energy in the body was never taught to the public.

The best place to begin a brief historical survey of this field is with Theophrastus Bombastus Paracelsus, the famous 16th century physician and alchemist extraordinaire. Paracelsus' credentials as a medical scientist are impeccable; more than 400 years ago he discovered the mercury cure for syphilis. Yet, he came to the same conclusion as the Taoist masters of what was known as sexual alchemy—the seemingly magical but entirely natural transformation of the sexual seed.

Paracelsus experienced the seminal fire with as much reality as an ordinary person feels when his hand is burned in a hot oven. Regarding the constituent elements of the substance, he wrote: "All the organs of the human system, and all their powers and activities, contribute alike to the formation of semen . . . The semen is, so to say, the essence of the human body, containing all the organs of the latter in an ideal form." This position is strikingly similar to the Taoist description of "ching chi," or sexual essence. Taoist cultivation also emphasizes balancing the subtle energies of each organ, which one then fuses into a single higher spirit.

Paracelsus distinguishes between the sperm fluid and the "aura seminalis", which is the light or energy of the sperm. Scientists today might call the "aura" the biophysical energy of the seminal fluid. Paracelsus claimed energy could be distilled from the physical fluid: "This emanation or separation takes place by a kind of digestion, and by means of an interior heat, which during the time of virility may be produced in man by the proximity of woman, by his thoughts of her, or by his contact with her, in the same manner a piece of wood exposed to the concentrated rays of the sun may be made to burn."

This statement rudely translated into modern language means that contact with an attractive woman may stimulate the production of high quality biophysical energy. Taoist alchemists realized a thousand years before Paracelsus practical ways to retain these valuable energies in order to profit from them.

If we turn from the Renaissance alchemist to the great British authority on Indian Tantric practice, Sir John Woodruffe, we find the same principles. In his classic work, *The Serpent Power*, Sir John speaks plainly to those who know how to hear: ". . . the force of the latter (sexual centers), if directed upwards, extraordinarily heightens all mental and physical functioning." He notes that mind, breath and sexual function are interconnected. The spiritual aim of the yogi is to "carry his seed high." This seed releases pranic energies, also known as the Kundalini power, rising up the spine to higher chakras or centers of spiritual function.

Another great modern spiritual authority, attuned to the

power within semen was Gurdjieff. According to this master, certain peoples understood that ". . . by means of the substances 'Exhioehary' or sperm formed in them, it was possible to perfect oneself." He adds that ". . . this self-perfection could probably be actualized by itself, by abstaining from the ejection from oneself in the customary manner of these substances formed in them called sperm."

Gurdjieff maintains that this self-perfection usually cannot be attained simply by retaining the semen, but requires a technique to release the energies of the seed. He is in perfect agreement with Paracelsus and the Taoists on this point.

Without exception authorities on the occult know of the seminal power, and that this substance must be stored and transformed to accomplish higher deveopment. The distinguished magician, Kenneth Grant, writes: "Thus the function of the semen—in the Tantras—is to build up the body of light, the astral body, the inner body of man. As the vital fluid accumulates in the testicles it is consumed by the heat of the Fire Snake, and the subtle fumes or 'perfumes' of this molten semen go to strengthen the inner body."

Most authorities agree on the necessity of collecting seminal fluid and transmuting it by application of inner heat. In the Chinese practice we refer to this as "cooking" the seminal fluid to obtain its "steam." The first step to release this tremendous vitality is conservation of the semen in the act of love.

The modern American spiritual master, Da Free John, also stresses the necessity of conserving the seminal force: "We must find a way of enjoying sexual intimacy whereby Life is not lost, we do not discharge Life in order to achieve pleasure, and we love one another, completely happy and free in our life together."

The "loss of Life" Da Free John refers to is ejaculation. He considers proper use of the sexual force—without ejaculation and with truly loving feeling between partners—as a key to human evolution. He stresses the importance of love in aiding the spontaneous transmutation of the seed to its higher centers of divinity. In this he is in complete accord with other spiritual authorities. Alchemists, yogis, magicians, and mystics agree unanimously on this fundamental point.

Another perspective on the vital seed is found in the works of an eminent Kabbalist and poet, Carlos Suares. The esoteric Kabbalist tradition originated in ancient Egypt. He emphasizes that development of the will to retain the seed is identical with development of one's true self: ". . . man, endowed with his self (which, though static by nature, shelters living seed) must struggle against and overcome the centrifugal sexual movement which tends to lead him into the abyss of the female. . . . Instead of being carried away, his mind rules."

Suares here alludes to the degenerative role played by woman in unconsciously luring the seed out of man. She profits very slightly from his great loss, since she usually doesn't have the yogic skills to absorb it. Woman is a bottomless pit for the man who incessantly gives his seed to her, although she can attempt to compensate this loss with her nearly inexhaustable female energy and love.

This chapter could be expanded to include the entirety of initiatory writing. There are many works by Masters who have felt the powers of semen transmuted by vital heat. When Moses is wandering in the desert for forty years, he speaks in the Bible of experiencing "a serpent fire." Since the Bible also declares Moses was "trained by the Egyptians in all their mysteries," it seems likely that this fire refers to the transmutation upward of his psychic energies. Bodily experience of the subtle realm is the final criterion in these matters.

THE DIFFERENCE BETWEEN TAOISM AND TANTRA

The principles of Tantra from India and Tibet have received wide attention in the west in recent years, especially by seekers interested in integrating their sexual impulses into their spiritual growth. The principles behind Tantra are nearly identical to that of Taoism. Both seek to reconcile the opposing dualities of life as symbolized by male and female and both accept any moment or experience in life as a starting point for spiritual growth and as an end point for insight into truth.

Keith Dowman, a western scholar and practitioner of Tibetan Tantric Buddhism put it succinctly: "Strip the (tantric) yoga of its arcane terminology and there is a simple meditation technique: stimulate the desire and then use it as the object of meditation and it becomes awareness—a field of Emptiness and pure Pleasure." A Taoist would agree, only he might phrase it differently: "Within every moment there is only the Emptiness of yin receiving the

Fullness of yang.'' This is the eternal marriage of man and woman, of spirit and matter, of Heaven and Earth.

The Taoist path and Tantric path differ mainly in their language and in the practical yogic methods taught to achieve the same union of mind, body, and spirit. Both fully accept the mastery of one's sexuality as not only a legitimate but necessary means to attain the highest enlightenment possible in the body. Dowman describes the importance of semen in the inner tantric path:

> "Refined semen in the heart center permeates the body as awareness. Loss of semen, by any means, causes life-span to be shortened and causes a pallid complextion. In Anuyoga (fulfillment yoga, or Kundalini yoga) loss of semen is equated with killing of the Buddha. . . . After initiation, intensity of desire is essential to force the bodicitta (seed essence) up the medial nerve (of the spine); not only is desire vitiated by orgasm, but the will to enlightenment itself is temporarily lost.''*

This accords perfectly with the Taoists view of retaining semen and transferring it upward, only the Taoists do not personify the subtle energies with a pantheon of divine beings. So I would say that the Tantra is for someone who is fascinated by or is attracted to the religious archetypes of the Tantrics—the gods and goddesses, the Bodisattvas and demons—and their elaborate secret rituals, initiations and invocations using mantra. If you have the patience to follow the rigorous path set out by a lama or guru who understands the true esoteric practice and is not merely a faith worshipper, you should eventually be successful with it.

I myself was raised near a Buddhist temple in Thailand and hung out with monks from an early age. I later decided the external rituals were not so effective as the internal methods of cultivating I learned from my Taoist teachers. These rituals are a blend of the esoteric and local culture. Many westerners may not respond deeply to the archaic imagery of the religious deities or will be confused by the different states of mind to be invoked, as the traditional descriptions of these states of mind do not translate easily from Sanskrit or Tibetan into English.

Certainly the acceptance of Taoism here in the west has been slowed by the difficulty of translating Taoist philosophy from Chi-

---

*''Sky Dancer: The Secret Life And Songs Of The Lady Yeshe Tsogyel'' (Routledge and Kegan, Paul 1984).

nese into English. But the archetypal images of the Taoists—principally images from nature, but including the yin and yang symbol—became globally accepted archetypes long before myself and others began teaching out the esoteric practices. The Chinese form a quarter of the world's population, and our civilization has been around for the last 5000 years, so our basic teaching models are already well known throughout the world.

Perhaps most important is the fact that the esoteric yogic practices of the Taoists were not buried in the rituals or lost on the changing doctrines of religion. They were kept secret and passed on orally for many thousands of years, and when they were finally written down beginning in the second century A.D. they were disguised with arcane poetry to prevent the uninitiated or unvirtuous from learning the meditative practices. But much of this esoteric knowledge was preserved and further developed by Taoist acupuncturists and herbologists, which helped to keep the mystical teachings practical and grounded in using the chi energy to heal bodily functions. Another example of this is the Taoist art of Tai Chi Chuan, a wonderfully multifaceted form that is simultaneously a means of self-defense, a playful dance, a metaphysical meditation on yin and yang, a physically healing exercise, and a ritual invocation of the cardinal energies that can be experienced by anyone watching a master perform.

The actual Taoist practices themselves are as simple to understand as the sun and the moon, because the ancient Taoists used the natural elements of the universe as their teacher. They watched the way plants and animals lived and died, how the weather effected their own metabolism, and how their subtle energies varied with the seasons, the earth's tilt toward the sun and stars, and the phases of the moon. Before language was even invented the sages observed the balance of forces in nature and then found that same harmony within themselves. Life is simple and natural if you keep it that way. No extraneous cultural images or religious concepts are needed to decorate the original and natural vision of the Tao as harmonious nature.

Anybody familiar with the qualities of water, fire, metal, earth, and wood—the primal elements—and has lived through the four seasons of the year—spring, summer, fall, and winter—is a candidate for beginning the Taoist practices. For example, to balance the sexual relationship you basically need to know that woman is water and has the power to regulate man, who is fire. On a deeper level you would discover that man has both fire and water in his body and can achieve a perfect internal balance by harmonizing his fire (thinking mind) with his own water (sperm fluid, or sexual "waters").

These symbols of fire and water, often expressed as yin and yang are simple to identify with and work with once you are given the specific details of what to do—how to hold your seed in, how to move your energy in psychic channels, and exchange it with the woman, etc. Of course, the experience of more subtle levels of chi energy takes time and cultivation of physical and mental purity. Thats why practice of tai chi, chi kung, meditation, and virtuous living enhance the speed with you gain clarity, and thus compliment the sexual practices.

KAREZZA AND COITUS RESERVATUS

There are other methods of sexual intercourse which should not be confused with the Taoist practice. Most widely known is the simple act of coitus reservatus, which is making love without orgasm. While this conserves the valuable male seed, it does not teach how to circulate the sexual energy upward or store it in the body's higher centers so it can be exchanged with the woman or put to other creative use. Coitus reservatus can also create severe pressure on the prostate gland and lead to its eventual malfunction since the orgasmic tension in the prostate is never released inwardly (as in Taoist sex) or outwardly through ejaculation. I specifically recommend that you avoid coitus reservatus for this reason—too much heat builds up in the genital area without any means to cool it.

Karezza is a love-making technique said to have originated in Persia. It involves long periods of passive sexual intercourse—lying still for half an hour or more while waiting for the male and female energies to build up. The Taoist method differs in that it encourages as much loving physical movement that the couple can handle without genital orgasm. This dynamic aspect of sex is normally important to westerners raised on a romantic role model of passionate love. To a Taoist, movement is life, whether in the physical body or in the subtle energy, and should be thoroughly enjoyed for the good health it brings. Karezza also fails to provide a method for transforming the sexual energy upward into a transcendent internal orgasm, and is satisfied with simply increasing and prolonging physical pleasure. It was originally intended to help any royal male survive a long night of love-making with his harem. Later it was popularized in America in the utopian Oneida colony in 1866 as a form of mandatory birth control. Certainly it is an improvement over hasty ejaculatory sex, but ultimately lacks true depth.

PART II

TAOIST PRACTICES FOR
MASTERING SEXUAL LOVE

CHAPTER 6

THE DANCE OF THE TESTES: EXERCISES FOR PELVIC STRENGTH

"If a man has intercourse once without spilling his seed, his vital essence is strengthened. If he does this twice, his hearing and vision are made clear. If three times, all his physical illness will disappear. The fourth time he will begin to feel inner peace. The fifth time his blood will circulate powerfully. The sixth time his genitals will gain new prowess. By the seventh his thighs and buttocks will become firm. The eighth time his entire body will radiate good health. The ninth time his lifespan will be increased."
—*from the Canon of Taoist Wisdom collected by Emperor Tang*

All of us are familiar with the shoot-out scene in which someone in danger pulls a gun which doesn't fire. If it's a good guy, he usually finds some heroic way out of his predicament. But when the "weapon" is the male penis, a "misfire"—a failure to erect—is a fiasco for the simple reason that no heroic alternative is easily found. Repeated and chronic misfire is impotence, the incarnation of male misery and the ruin of many relationships. In this chapter we study two excellent pelvic diaphragm exercises that build your urogenital and anus ring muscles and thus greatly strengthens your control of your erection and reduce the likelihood of misfire. Careful practice of these exercises will also prepare you for learning to retain the vital seed during intercourse.

America is presently exercise-crazy. Yet, except for sexual activity, few exercises strengthen the crucial pelvic muscles. There exist pelvic exercises which greatly strengthen the reproductive organs and the complex network of tendons surrounding them. Strength in this department is of inestimable importance—it is the root of man's health. Leading into the pelvis are a vast number of nerve endings, and channels for your veins and arteries. Here terminate tissues communicating with every square inch of the body. All of the major acupuncture meridians carrying chi between the vital organs pass by this area. If it is blocked or weak, energy will dissipate and the organs and brain will suffer. This is what happens to most men in old age—their rectal and pelvic muscles become loose and their vital chi energy slowly drains out, leaving them weak and feeble.

It is important to remember that the foundation of penis strength is seminal retention. Without this nothing permanent may be accomplished, even with exercise. Spending the semen brings about premature impotence and decay. No one, no matter how strong or brutish, can ejaculate often without ultimately paying a stiff price. These exercises massage and stimulate the pelvic region. Life energy is driven down into the testes, filling them with extraordinary vitality. These exercises, combined with the "Big Draw" method of semen retention in Chapter Seven, will allow you to create a permanent store of sexual essence in your body. Only then can you begin to refine it into a higher state and combine it with your chi and spirit to regain wholeness.

THE PELVIC AND UROGENITAL DIAPHRAGMS

The body possesses not one but several diaphragms. Everyone is familiar with the thoracic diaphragm in the chest that causes it to expand on inhalation. Lesser known is the pelvic diaphragm and the urogenital diaphragm which separates the pelvis from the perineum. To practice Sexual Kung Fu properly you must use not only the chest diaphragm but also the pelvic one. Real deep breathing issues from this lower diaphragm. They are exceedingly important in transmitting energy during love-making in the Taoist practice of dual cultivation.

The pelvic diaphragm is a muscular wall that extends across the lower part of the torso. It is suspended concavely downward from the level of the symphysis pubis in front and the sacrum in back. There are several organs that penetrate this muscular partition that lies between the pelvic cavity and the perineum. These organs are the urethra, the vagina and the rectum and they are supported by the pelvic diaphragm and allow you greater control over them. In fact, the pelvic diaphragm is the floor of the pelvic cavity which contains large intestine, small intestine, bladder, and kidney. It lifts up and helps shape these vital organs.

DIAGRAM 10

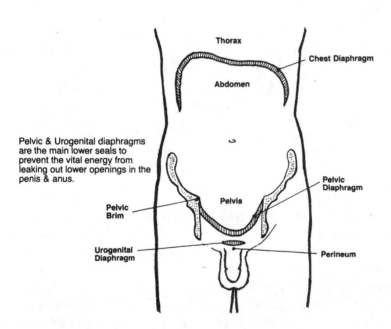

But in the perineum, which is a point midway between the anus and genitals below the pelvic diaphragm, is another muscular diaphragm called the urogenital diaphragm. This is penetrated by the urethra, and to its underside is attached the root of the penis. The pudendal nerve in the penis controls the muscles of the urogenital diaphragm, which in turn holds up the prostate gland, seminal vas deferens, cowper's gland, penis and the anus. Part of this lower-most diaphragm comes forward to engulf the scrotum (which also contains muscle) and the penis and then joins to the abdominal wall.

DIAGRAM 11
PELVIC & UROGENITAL DIAPHRAGM

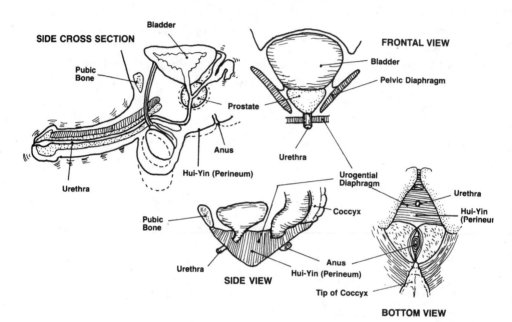

These two diaphragms are the lower seals to hold the life force—the chi energies—from escaping out through the lower openings in the body. When tightly sealed they will increase the chi pressure in the abdomen. When chi pressure strengthens, it will invigorate the vital organs and move the chi and blood flow better. The importance of these anatomical structures will become apparent as you study the larger system of Taoist Yoga. The Iron Shirt Chi Kung exercises also help develop power and strength in these areas, and are a perfect complement to anyone seeking a daily regimen that will aid the practice of Sexual Kung Fu. (See Chapter 18 for a course description)

THE SCROTUM PUMPS COLD SPERM ENERGY UPWARD

Taoists regard the scrotum as the lowest diaphragm, one that functions like a pump. The scrotum is tight during youth and after a refreshing sleep. It is loose in old age or after fatigue. Strong flow of life energy tightens the skin. Scrotal breathing floods the region with energy, and the scrotum begins to tighten almost immediately.

The scrotum is the factory that produces the sexual energy, sperm, and male hormones. So there is a tremendous store of "yin" chi (cold life force energy) in this area. All sexual energy, whether male or female, is "yin" in its latent or resting state. Sexual fluids belong to the water element in the Chinese system of classifying the qualities of different types of chi. Water-rivers, lakes, and oceans are yin. However, yin energy can rapidly change its nature and become more "yang", or hot, when sexually aroused. This can only happen if the sperm is already manufactured while the testicles are still cool. In fact, western scientists have determined the male sperm count goes up dramatically when the testicles are put on ice and several companies are already selling special devices like a "freeze-pak" jock strap to aid infertile men. The cold quality of sperm energy means it must be circulated upward to harmonize with the hot mental energy in the head and the chest area and vice versa.

The testicles are constantly involved in producing sperm, hormones and, though it might presently be debated, or even denied by scientists, in creating ching chi, the life-force essence. The ancient Taoists, who had extraordinarily astute powers of empirical observation, noted that the energy of the sperm cells are of prime importance in that all of the vital organs must contribute some of their own reserves to create and maintain the potency of the sperm. Amongst those organs is the brain. The vernacular expression, "I screwed my brains out last night," suggests a common wisdom that bears out this connection between the balls and the brain.

The records amongst the Taoists on the subject of sex were surprisingly consistent over long stretches of time, which in China meant not hundreds but thousands of years. This is significant because many groups didn't even know of each others abilities or whereabouts or even existence, because these esoteric practices were very hidden. Their records point out that when the energy in the testicles is cold or mostly yin, that this is a sign of strong and youthful sperm energy. This experience of cold gives way to what has been described as a mildly warm quality when the sperm is moved into the body from its exterior scrotal sac and stored in the epidedymis and vas deferens.

The (cold) yin sperm ching chi is more dense than the hot (yang) ching or sexual energy. Most people experience their sexual energy only when aroused and the ching chi is hot, although certainly it is always present. This means the cold energy, since it is thicker and slower to move, needs all the help it can get on its path up to the higher center. If you can open the Microcosmic Orbit first it will make it much easier. This channel, which loops up the spine to the head and down the front to the navel, genitals and perineum, is recognized by acupuncturists as the main energy channel in the body linking the various organs, glands, and brain.

DIAGRAM 12

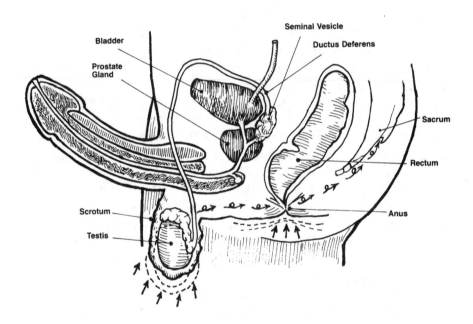

The testicle breathing exercise that follows will also help you to open these channels and complete the microcosmic orbit, a process more fully described in Chapter Seven.

In the "testicle breathing" exercise you use your mind to draw the "cold" (yin), youthful sperm energy up the spine to your head. You draw not the sperm itself, but the energy generated by the sperm. At first it's slow going, but the energy is easy to deal with since it's still cool. Later just a thought will send a refreshingly delightful cool wave of energy up your back to your head.

The second exercise, "scrotal compression," trains you to build up "warm" ching energy in the scrotal sac and move this energy safely upward. The third exercise, the "Power Lock," shows you how to deal with the ching when it is sexually aroused and very "hot." It is like a wild mare, and the most difficult to control. It is recommended you practice this alone (using self-arousal) before attempting to tame your sex energy at its most explosive, during love-making with a woman.

SACRAL PUMP AND CRANIAL PUMP

Contained and protected within your spinal column and head is the very heart of your nervous system. Cushioning it is the cerebrospinal fluid, cerebro for head and spinal for the vertebrae. This fluid, as it turns out, is circulated by two pumps. One is in the sacrum, and is known as the sacral pump. The other is in the region of your upper neck and head, the cranial pump. Many people who got these pumps working have reported feeling a "big bubble" of energy travel up their spine during testicle breathing.

DIAGRAM 13

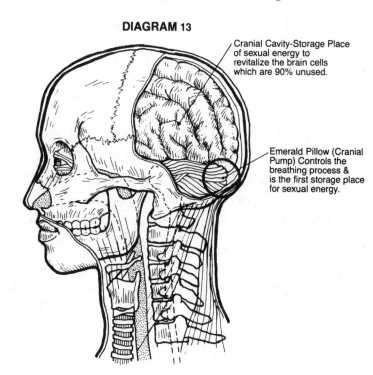

Cranial Cavity-Storage Place of sexual energy to revitalize the brain cells which are 90% unused.

Emerald Pillow (Cranial Pump) Controls the breathing process & is the first storage place for sexual energy.

Taoists regard the sacrum as a pump which will help to hold the sexual energy coming from the scrotum and transform the energy at the same time it gives it a push upward. It's like a way station that refines the ching chi as circulates in the body. If the opening of sacrum, the Hiatus, is blocked, the life force cannot enter and flow back to the higher center.

The cranium of the skull has long been regarded by Taoists as a major pump for the circulation of energy from the lower to the higher centers. Medical research has recently confirmed that minute movements at the joints of the eight cranial bones occurs during breathing. Cranial movement is responsible for the production and function of the cerebrospinal fluid surrounding the brain and spinal cord and this is necessary for normal nerve and energy patterns in the entire body. Strengthening the cranial joints can increase energy and alleviate symptoms, such as headaches, sinus problems, visual disturbances and neck problems. In Taoist cultivation the pelvis, scrotum urogenital diaphragm, sacrum and cranial pump are very important to help move the sexual energy up to the higher center.

THREE POSTURES OF TESTICLE BREATHING: SITTING, STANDING, LYING

Sitting: I generally recommend sitting on a chair. I prefer this position for its simplicity and comfort. Sitting lends ease to a practice that favors relaxation and good concentration.

Sit on the edge of a chair with the buttocks and legs supporting your weight. The scrotum hangs free in the air. This point is important because the testes must be freely suspended in order for you to push a maximum of air energy down into them. Raise the tongue to the roof of the mouth as this is essential in circulating the chi, completing the loop between the front and back channels of the microcosmic orbit.

The feet are firmly planted on the floor with hands resting palm down on the knees. The back should be quite straight at the waist but slightly round at the shoulders and neck. This very minor forward curvature of the upper back tends to relax the chest and helps the power flow through the neck, chest, and abdomen. Keep the chin slightly tucked in. Military posture, with shoulders thrown back and head held high, tends to lodge power in the upper body and prevent its circulating back down to lower centers.

A variant of the sitting position is to sit cross-legged, either in lotus position or American Indian style. We appreciate the esoteric virtues of the lotus position, but Chinese practice attributes to the lotus serious disadvantages. Some Buddhist monks have been crippled by lengthy meditation in lotus position. Also, turning the soles of the feet away from the ground prevents one from directly drawing in through the feet the earth's yin power. The human body is designed to absorb earth energy through the kidney (K-1 point) and other meridians in the feet and filter it before passing it up to the coccyx and brain. Some people can develop problems if they absorb too much "raw" earth chi directly into their sacrum, as occurs in lotus position. Eventually they become allergic to this undigested energy and go crazy.

Nevertheless, the lotus may be used by those accustomed and devoted to it so long as they are comfortable and can apply their whole attention to the exercise. Few cross-legged positions afford such freedom of scrotal movement as sitting on the edge of a chair. If you sit cross-legged, you should wear very loose pants and remove your underpants to prevent resistance to full inflation of the scrotum.

Standing: Another good position is standing. The above instructions on raising tongue tip to palate and maintaining correct posture apply equally to this position. Standing is particularly favorable for scrotal breathing because the testes hang quite freely. Standing up straight in a relaxed manner encourages good posture. The hands are at the sides and the feet at shoulder width. Discipline yourself to relax if you get too tense, or the chi power may stick in the heart region and make you irritable.

Lying: Never lie flat on the back when performing these exercises. In this position the chest sits higher than the abdomen and receives too much energy. Nor should you lie on the left side. Both incorrect positions unduly stress the heart.

The proper lying position is on the right side. A pillow placed beneath the head should raise it about 3" to 4", so that the head sits squarely on the shoulders. The four fingers of the right hand area are placed immediately in front of the right ear, while the thumb sits behind the ear and folds it slightly forward to keep it open.

The ear must stay open to permit air flow through the eustachian tube. The left hand rests on the outer left thigh. The right leg is straight; the left leg, which rests on the right one, is slightly bent. This position allows the scrotum to hang free of the thighs.

DIAGRAM 14

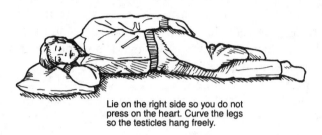

Lie on the right side so you do not
press on the heart. Curve the legs
so the testicles hang freely.

You may have noticed that lions often sleep in a similar posture. The animals are informed by wise instinct. The position frees the spinal column of the oppression of gravity and allows it to assume its natural curvature. Lying on the right side relieves the spine from stress.

TESTICLE BREATHING: STEP BY STEP

1. Sit erect on the edge of your chair with your feet flat on the floor about shoulder width apart. Wear loose pants or wear nothing from your waist down, so it can literally all hang out.* Do not practice naked in a cold room, or you will lose a lot of chi. With the air circulating around your bottom you'll naturally become more aware of your "privates." Allow your attention to center around your scrotum between the two testicles and you might be surprised to discover that it really is cold, or yin, down there. Make sure you feel very relaxed. If you are tense, do some stretching exercises or take a walk first to disperse tension.

2. Inhale slowly and pull the testicles up. Hold for awhile, then exhale slowly and lower the testicles. As you inhale, think of the breath going down into the testes and filling them up. At the same time raise the testes with the breath. Gently continue inhaling and

---

*If a woman performs any of the exercises in this book, substituting her ovaries as the source of energy, she should keep her panties on to prevent any chi from draining out.

exhaling with the testicles until you feel a lot of cold energy in the scrotum. You may do this in a round of 9, then rest and practice again 3–6 sets.

Draw the life-giving air to the very root of the body. Breathe out the accumulated wastes as the testes sink downwards. Generate a strong flow of energy to swiftly circulate the pelvic blood. Use the mind alone to cause the movement of the testes up and down—don't flex your penis or anus muscles.

After exercising for a week or two, you may observe the actual rise and fall of the testes during practice. This movement confirms that you are breathing properly. At a more proficient level, the lower abdomen will appear to move less: nearly all visible action will be in the scrotal sac itself. The dancing movements of the testes may be noted in the mirror and have a rather humorous aspect.

Unless specifically indicated otherwise, all breathing is to be done through the nose. Nasal breathing affords better control of the air inhaled. It filters and warms the air and supplies life force of well-balanced quality.

The whole body must relax. Allow all tension to flow out of you as if you were in meditation. Use the mind alone to raise and lower them. With practice you will learn to identify the cold ching chi stored in the scrotum area.

DIAGRAM 15

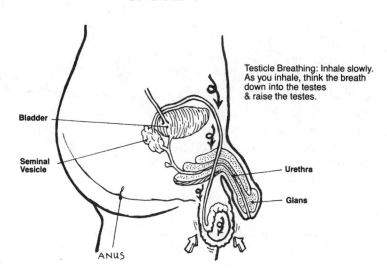

Bladder

Seminal Vesicle

Testicle Breathing: Inhale slowly. As you inhale, think the breath down into the testes & raise the testes.

Urethra

Glans

ANUS

3. Guide that "cold" feeling from your scrotum to your perineum by inhaling and pulling up slightly on your testicles. At the same time feel it coolly flow the few inches to the perineum, an action induced by putting your mind at the perineum and holding it there. Inhale and exhale several times at the testes to build up more energy. The retention of the ching chi at the perineum is very important, for if you release your attention the cold energy will drop down to the scrotum or leak out. It is just like you are using a straw to draw up the fluid. When you are out of breath and pause for a while you need to keep the attention by holding your finger over the straw. If you release it it will drop down and you'll have to start again. Do this for several days or until you get it.

4. Begin to draw the sex energy from the testes up the back channel, as if sipping on a straw. Always start with testicle breathing, inhaling and exhaling till you feel the ching energy is ready. Inhale, draw the "cold" from your testicles to the perineum and then draw it up to your coccyx, the very bottom end of your spine. There's an area a little up from the tip of your spine, mostly bone, that's called the hiatus opening of the sacrum.

When you pull the cool ching up to the perineum and then to the sacrum, slightly arch your lower back outward, as if you were standing with your back against a wall and flattening it against it. Tilt the sacrum downward and hold it down in order to help activate the pump action, which will be further accentuated if you gently tighten the back of your neck and skull bones. Hold the energy at the sacrum for a while, then exhale but hold your attention at the sacrum.

Then let your sacrum and neck relax back to their normal positions, this will help to activate the two pumps, sacrum and cranial pump. At the same time do the testicle breathing. Bring the energy up to the sacrum again, hold it there till you can feel the sacrum open and the energy gradually move up. You can actually feel the cold energy move up a little at a time. If you're having trouble feeling this, try rocking your sacrum back and forth and then hold still and observe the effect of this pumping.

There's an indentation in the sacrum bone and that's where you draw your testes' "cold" energy. This particular area is usually a little difficult to work because sperm energy is denser than chi and has to be pumped up. So that's where that pump comes in.

Some people experience pain, or tingling or pins and needles when the "cold" enters the hiatus, so don't be upset if it happens to you. You can help get through the coccyx if you're having trouble by gently massaging the area with a silk cloth from time to time.

5. If you've managed to go up through your coccyx, spend the next week drawing the cold to T-11 in your mid-back (the 11th thoracic vertebra). Do it in the same manner, with an inhale-exhale at the testes and sucking it up your spinal "straw" to the perineum, sacrum, T-11 (opposite your solar plexus, at the last "floating" rib). Pull up and retain at T-11 till it feels full and continues to open and move up by itself. Again, because sperm energy is denser than chi, you have to accomodate to it by flexing that part of your back in and out to straighten it. That loosens it for freer passage of the "cold" energy.

At the T-11 adrenal glands energy center, sitting atop your kidneys. In Taoist practice we regard this as a mini pump, where your arch will create a vacuum to push up the energy higher.

6. Your next stopping place is at your jade pillow. This is at the back of your head, between C-1 and the base of the skull. Do it in the same manner as discribed by inhale-exhale at the testicle and keep on pumping up the energy up to perineum sacrum, T-11 and the base of skull. In this area is a place to store the energy for further use.

7. Your next stopping point is Pai Hui, at the crown of your head. Do it in the same manner only this time fill the straw to the top. Tilt the sacrum to the back in order to straighten the curve out a little bit to help activate the pump action. This gets the lower pumping going. At the same time you tuck in your chin a little and squeeze the back of your skull, it will activate the upper cranial pump. Keep on pulling up to the point dead center on top of the head.

8. When the energy finally goes up into your head, men will have the very distinct feeling that it's spinning and usually in a clockwise direction, as you look up. If you're alert you can count 36 revolutions. It should feel good and refreshing; the extra energy should help your creative power and improve your memory. You can think more clearly, and are at the beginning stage of controlling your sexual urges or frustrations. This sperm energy is later converted into chi, the original life force, in the spiritual levels of Taoist yoga. When people get older they've used up so much of their chi that the brain energy and spinal fluid gradually drain out and dry up, leaving a cavity. The testicle breathing transports the sexual energy to fill the cavity and vitalize the brain. Taoists regard the sexual energy as very close to the brain energy.

9. Finally you can bring the sexual energy from the testes up to the head in one sweet draw up the straw, a single clean inhale. In the beginning you can just go from station to station, till you feel the back channel (governor channel) is more open. Eventually you will be able to put your mind in the testicles and the crown of the head and just mentally move the sexual energy from the testicles up all the way to the brain.

10. Take your time to really feel the "cold" when you practice. Don't rush it, and always keep those pumps going as you breath in and out. Use more mind than physical pull when you do all this. Let the "cold" feeling be your guide. Work at it too hard and you'll heat up the "cold" ching. You won't be able to safely store this hot energy in your brain.

DIAGRAM 16

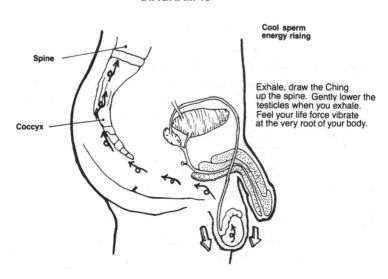

Spine

Coccyx

Cool sperm
energy rising

Exhale, draw the Ching
up the spine. Gently lower the
testicles when you exhale.
Feel your life force vibrate
at the very root of your body.

THE GOLDEN NECTAR

When your head is filled with sperm energy the excess ching may spontaneously combust with the chi in your higher centers and spill over into the Microcosmic Orbit and flow down through your palate and down the tongue. This will taste different to different people. It's generally called the Golden Nectar but it can taste like champagne, honey, coconut juice, or fragrance of all kinds of things, or it can simply feel like a warm tingling sensation on your tongue.

This exercise, the "Dance of the Testes", may be performed anywhere: in the subway or car, at your desk or television, in bed, etc. The main consideration is that the back be properly straight, chest relaxed, and scrotum hanging freely.

It is highly desirable to use the testicle breathing to tone the pelvic diaphragm. The whole lower abdomen is deeply massaged each time the pelvic diaphragm flexes. Life force flows into the region through periodic waves of breath which stimulate the glands and vital organs.

COMPRESSING THE AIR INTO THE SCROTUM INCREASES SEXUAL POWER

Many benefits of the Testicle Breathing are magnified when performed in conjunction with the Scrotal Compression exercise. This exercise reduces the incidence of nocturnal emission and premature ejaculation. It lessens the chance of hernia. It helps you calm down when sexually over-excited by teaching you to consciously direct energy into and out of the pelvic region. It builds your sexual power dynamically by using the vital chi taken from air and packing its charge into your ching chi.

Of the three suggested positions, sitting or standing are preferable. Inhale a fairly large amount of air into the throat and swallow the air. Swallowing drives the air down to the solar plexus. From this center it will be driven down to the testes. This is accomplished by contracting the abdominal muscles downward in a slow wave.

From the solar plexus the air is rolled down into the pelvic region. From there it is compressed into the testes. When the air is driven into the testes you experience a flush of heat. The testes seem to expand, and after a short time the power driven into them flows up the spine to the head, which also becomes very warm.

SCROTAL COMPRESSION EXERCISE: STEP BY STEP

1. Sit on the edge of your chair with your feet flat on the floor about a shoulder apart. Wear loose pants or wear nothing from your waist down, so your testicles literally hang out.

2. Inhale through the nostrils into the throat. From there swallow the air down to the solar plexus, midway between your heart and your navel. Imagine the air as a ball.

3. First the ball sits behind the solar plexus. From this point roll it down to the navel. Then into the pelvis and scrotum.

4. Forcibly compress the air into the scrotum for as long as you can do so. The minimum period for each compression should be 30 to 40 seconds. Slowly work up to at least one minute. Every single scrotal compression shoots tremendous energy into the testes. With compression of an entire minute the exercise takes full effect. The anal sphincter and perineum muscle must be squeezed tight during this exercise to prevent leakage of energy.

5. When you have finished the compression, exhale and relax completely. If saliva accumulates in the mouth during compression, swallow it before exhaling.

6. After complete exhalation take a number of quick, short breaths to recover your wind. Dart the air in and out of the nostrils to quickly regain capacity for another compression. Remember to breath through the nose, and do not inhale unduly large quantities of air. This is called "Bellows Breathing", because you must pump your lower abdomen in and out quickly in order to do it.

This exercise quickly charges the whole body. If you feel ill or out of sorts, several scrotal compressions will restore you to good form. Perform the exercises in the following sequence: First do one scrotal compression. Then rotate the waist with the arms at shoulder level. Rest for a moment and repeat the exercise. Remember to keep the tongue up to the palate when compressing the air. Perform 5 contractions.

When you have grown stronger, you may do five compressions in succession and then rest with waist rotation. Then begin a second series of five compressions. Keep the breathing between compression short and shallow to not lodge power high in the body.

DIAGRAM 17

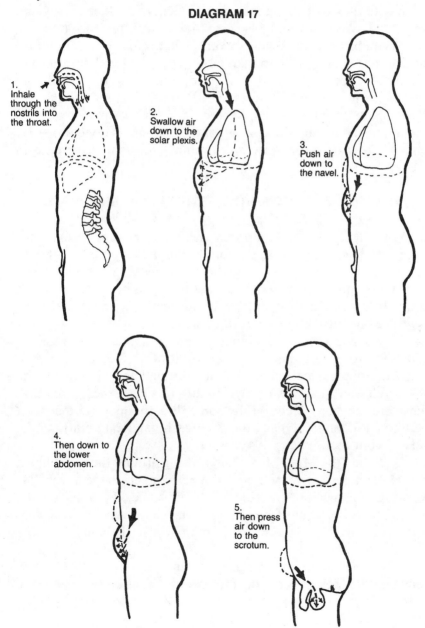

1. Inhale through the nostrils into the throat.

2. Swallow air down to the solar plexis.

3. Push air down to the navel.

4. Then down to the lower abdomen.

5. Then press air down to the scrotum.

Practice testicle breathing and scrotal compression twice a day for about fifteen minutes in the morning and fifteen minutes in the evening. This method alone yields real benefits. In addition to those benefits already mentioned, it also helps cure impotence or deficient virility. Insomnia and nervousness often radically improve with these breathing techniques. General lack of energy and associated symptoms may also be relieved with regular practice.

If you have retained your sexual fluid for four weeks or more, the exercise should start to take effect within three days after beginning practice. The testes feel warm, tend to "jump", and may itch somewhat. These indicate that the testes are receiving unusually high amounts of vital force. The tissues are already regenerating. These signs occur only if the exercise is done properly. A month or two of exercise will produce substantial increase in strength and well-being.

VENTING EXERCISE FOR HIGH BLOOD PRESSURE

After practicing scrotal compression for 2 to 6 weeks, some students with high blood pressure notice a large flow of chi energy to the head. They feel tension in the head because the blood has followed the upward flow of the vital power. This is not unlike a mild symptom of the "Kundalini Syndrome", in which freed energy races about the body out of control.

If you suffer from high blood pressure and haven't practiced meditation to open the microcosmic orbit (described in chapter 8) which distributes the energy evenly through the circuits of the body, you can meditate on two points to vent excess pressure. These are the Ming-Men, on the spine directly opposite the navel (between T-12 and T-13) and the Yuang Ch'uan (K-1 point), on the balls of your feet.

To locate the Ming-Men place a string around the waist like a belt. Make it perfectly horizontal and place it across the navel. The Ming-Men lies where the string meets the spine. If you have a big hanging belly, measure from where your navel was before it fell. When you bend over backwards from the waist, the point feels like a hole in the spine.

The other point, the Yuang Ch'uan, lies on the foot. When clenching the toes, it is the deepest central point on the ball of the foot.

Once you've found the point on both feet, tape onto them spiny little balls such as a prickly chestnut or plain tree seed pod. Place both hands at the back and press firmly on the spiny ball while concentrating on the Ming-Men point. This draws the chi and blood there.

After you feel the power flow to the Ming-Men, direct it down the spine and legs to the Yuang Ch'uan. Press down on the ball so that you feel the spines very distinctly. In severe cases it may take a month or two to get the power into the Ming-Men and bring it down to the Yuang-Ch'uan.

If blood flows too strongly to the head during or after scrotal compression, vent the power. Imbalanced force will flow out of the body through these two points. After practicing the scrotal exercises, many students open the microcosmic orbit so that their energy flows in a continuous circuit. This alone has often cured high blood pressure.

DIAGRAM 18

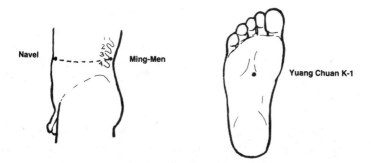

Navel   Ming-Men   Yuang Chuan K-1

THE POWER LOCK EXERCISE FOR SEALING THE SEMINAL FLUID

When you are well trained in this exercise you can use a variant of it during sexual intercourse, known as the Big Draw. The power locking method is done without a partner as a daily practice exercise. The method is the best for building power in the perineum to seal the seminal fluid. The sexual energy that we deal with here is different from the testicle breathing and scrotal compression and it's important to learn the subtle difference.

In the testicle breathing you move the cold sexual energy, the ching chi that lies in the scrotum in its yin state after production by the testicles, up to the head and then down into the body. With the scrotal compression exercise you force the chi energy that is produced in the organs—heart, lungs, spleen, etc.—down to mix with the cold ching chi resting in the sexual organs. Then you move the resulting warm energy upwards and circulate it.

In the Power Lock Exercise we arouse the sexual organ, turning the cold energy that lies in the seminal vascular duct into hot sexual energy. This heat is generated by the movement of millions of sperm cells. This yang energy is more explosive, harder to control, and always seeking the most direct path out to a cooler (yin) environment. In most men the path of least resistance is out the penis. In a Taoist master the easiest channel is up into the higher centers of the body. But it takes a lot of practice to control the anus muscle and the involuntary muscle around the seminal vascular duct to reverse the flow towards the penis and to help push up the sexual energy into the spine and upper body.

There are 4 levels of Power Lock practice:

1. Beginner: use muscles of the fist, jaw, neck, feet, perineum, buttocks, and abdomen to divert sexual tension and block the urge to ejaculate, and push upward the hot ching chi which created the aroused state.

2. Intermediate stage: less muscle use of the fist, jaw, feet, and increased reliance on the pelvic diaphragm, and sphincter, sacral, and cranial pump to help move up the sexual energy.

3. Advanced stage: less muscle in the perineum and more use of sacral and cranial pumps. Greater power of mind to move the ching to the crown center. By concentrating power at the upper part of the crown you draw the energy from the lower center to the higher center.

4. Most advanced stage: pure mind control only, no need to use the muscle, just use the mind power to command the penis, and command the ching energy to move up and down, to be erect or flaccid, as you will.

DIAGRAM 19

POWER LOCK EXERCISE

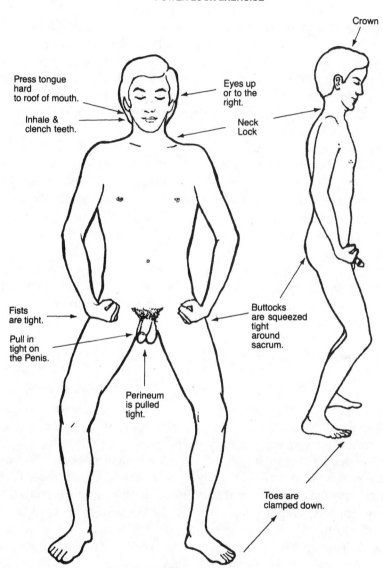

Crown

Press tongue
hard
to roof of mouth.

Eyes up
or to the
right.

Inhale &
clench teeth.

Neck
Lock

Fists
are tight.

Pull in
tight on
the Penis.

Buttocks
are squeezed
tight
around
sacrum.

Perineum
is pulled
tight.

Toes are
clamped down.

Ching Chi is stopped from escaping out the penis
& its energy is pulled up to the crown
until the penis erection subsides.

In this exercise, you need to arouse the penis about 90% of the way to orgasmic ejaculation. Do not go beyond the point of no return, or you will have no sperm chi to practice with for awhile. As you master the Power Lock you may fine tune how close you come to ejaculation and stop at 98% or 99%. Rub the glans of the penis until it is erect. When you have a feeling that orgasm is imminent, stop and do the Power Locking method 3 to 9 times or until the erection subsides. This counts as one exercise. Repeat this procedure—stimulate penis to erection and then do the locking until it subsides—as many as 3-9-18-36 times at a sitting.

Practice makes perfect. Once you gain control of your sexual organs totally in this practice, you will naturally have full control in sexual intercourse. I recommend practicing up to 10,000 times in order to gain advanced control, although some will naturally master it much more quickly if they have trained their mind through yoga, meditation, or other disciplines. If you are not involved in a program of daily physical discipline, I suggest you at least do some warmup exercises and stretching before practicing the Power Lock. This will tone up the energy in your organs and make it easier to feel your internal chi energies and thus hasten your command of your sexual energy.

POWER LOCK EXERCISE: STEP BY STEP

1. Sitting position is the same as in Testicle Breathing—feet flat on the floor, wear loose pants or naked from the waist down. Stimulate your penis to erection. Center your attention on your sexual organs and the expanding energy in the penis and scrotum.

2. Inhale deeply through your nose when near orgasm. Simultaneously clench both fists, claw your feet down, make them feel like vacuum pumps sucking at the floor. At the same time clench your jaw, tighten the cranial pump at the back of your neck and press your tongue firmly to the roof of your mouth. Inhale once more and draw up the entire genital-anus region, concentrating on the Hui-Yin (perineum), urogenital diaphragm, and especially the penis. Pull the energy from the penis to the perineum by squeezing as tightly as possible. Holding your breath, slowly count to 9 with all muscles fully flexed. When you are out of breath, exhale and release all muscles in the body. You may feel energy rush up and down, especially in the sexual region.

After exercising for a week or two, you may actually begin to feel the muscle contraction pull your penis up and in. The anus will feel like it's closed super-tight. Unless indicated otherwise, all breathing is to be done through the nose. Nasal breathing affords better control of the air inhaled. It filters and warms the air and supplies life-force of well balanced quality. The whole body must relax on the exhale. Allow all tension to flow out of you as if you were in meditation.

Inhale, clench, and pull up repeatedly on your sexual region, holding the energy at the perineum. The retention at the perineum is very important. If you release your attention the hot energy will drop down to the sexual organs or leak out to the penis. If you release the energy it will drop down and you'll have to start again. Do this for at least one week.

3. Start with arousing the penis. Clench fists, feet, neck, and jaw, on the inhale. Draw up the entire genital organs, diaphragm, anus, and especially the penis, pull the hot energy up the perineum and continue to draw it up to your coccyx. A little up from the bottom tip of your spine. Feel it enter the hiatus opening in the sacrum.

Activate your sacral pump by arching your lower back outward in order to straighten the spine. This makes it easier for the chi to rise. Hold the energy at the sacrum section, keep on inhaling and pulling, inhaling and pulling in the sexual energy from the sexual organs until you can feel the erection calm down. Sometimes it may need 3–9 inhalations with increasingly hard contraction. Squeezing the buttocks more tightly may help you force the ching into the sacrum. When you're out of breath, exhale. Then relax and let your sacrum and neck go back to their normal positions, this will help activate the two pumps.

If you practiced the Testicle Breathing (or already opened your microcosmic orbit), when you do the Power Lock it will be much easier to get the hot sexual ching to enter the sacrum. Otherwise this area is usually a little difficult to work through because sperm chi energy is denser than other types of chi and has to be pumped up. That's where the sacral pump comes in. Some people experience pain, tingling, or "pins and needles" pain. When the hot sexual energy enters the hiatus, don't be upset if it happens to you. You can help the ching get past the coccyx if you're having trouble with it by gently massaging the area with a silk cloth from time to time.

4. If you to go up to through your sacrum, spend the next week drawing the energy to T-11 on the spine, opposite your solar plexus. Repeat the same procedure—arousing, clenching , and inhaling. Pump up the energy up to the perineum, sacrum, then to the T-11, where you should retain it until it feels full of energy. It's really open when you feel the ching itself. Again, because sperm energy is denser than chi, you have to accommodate to it by bowing your spine outward to straighten it to increase the pumping action and allow for a freer passage of ching chi upward.

DIAGRAM 20

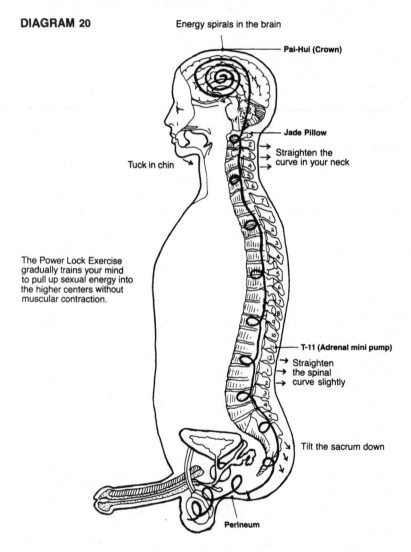

Energy spirals in the brain

Pai-Hui (Crown)

Jade Pillow

Tuck in chin

Straighten the curve in your neck

The Power Lock Exercise gradually trains your mind to pull up sexual energy into the higher centers without muscular contraction.

T-11 (Adrenal mini pump)

Straighten the spinal curve slightly

Tilt the sacrum down

Perineum

5. Your next stopping place is at your jade pillow. This is at the back of your head, between C-1 and the base of the skull. Do it in the same manner as described—keep drawing up the energy up to the perineum, sacrum, T-11, and the base of the skull. The cranial pump may fill with energy and pound furiously when the energy first moves through.

6. The next stopping point for the energy is the Pai Hui, at the crown of your head. Repeat the same process of arousing and deflating your erection by drawing the energy up. Make sure you tuck in your chin slightly and squeeze in the skull to further activate the upper cranial pump and keep the upper spine straight. Keep on pulling the energy to the top of your head until you get the erection to subside.

When the energy finally goes up into your head, you'll have the very distinct feeling of warmth and tingling sensations from the energy. The usual immediate response is that it feels good and amazingly refreshing. Some people claim they can think more clearly and are more creative; it's possible they are at a stage where they can easily convert the ching chi into expanded consciousness automatically. This sperm energy is later converted into the original chi, the pure life-force, in the spiritual levels of Taoist Yoga. When we get older we have used up so much of our brain energy that the fluids gradually begin to dry up, and leave a cavity in our head. The Power Lock helps to transport the sexual energy to fill the cavity; instead of storing it in the scrotum it is stored in the higher regions of the body/mind that can take immediate benefit from it. Taoists regard the sexual energy as a creative energy that can be transformed to any part of our vital organs, glands, or brain.

Practice the Power Lock until you can pull up the sexual energy from the penis to the head in one pipe. In the beginning you can just go from one station to another. Later the back channel (governor channel) will feel more open. Eventually you will be able to put your mind in the testicles and at the crown of the head and just bring the sexual energy from the testicles all the way up to the brain. Take time to really feel the sexual energy when you practice. Don't rush it, and always keep those pumps going after the exercise as you breath in and out. Gradually use more mind than physical pull when you do all this. Let the energy feeling be your guide.

7. When you feel the energy has filled the brain, concentrate on the mid-eyebrow and bring it down through the nose and the palate and down from the tongue to the throat center, heart center, solar plexus, and then down into the navel. This circulation is aided by the internal pressures created during the Power Lock. You press the lower trunk energy into and up the spine. At the same time, you press the energy in the upper body downward and hold the contraction as long as you can. When you exhale completely relax the whole body. The natural direction of the chi is to continue in a circle up the back of your body and down the front to the navel.

Continue cycling the sexual energy in this way until your erection subsides. In the beginning, and especially if your very aroused sexually, it may take 3 to 9 such cycles to accomplish. But after you've practiced for awhile, one such round is enough.

8. Perform 36 complete contractions in the morning and at night. Once you've got the hang of it, for the normal man 36 repetitions, morning and night, should not be unduly strenuous. If you are very aroused you will do fewer repetitions as each erection will take longer to subside. With such intensity of training, you will easily develop the muscle tone needed for effective seminal retention within a month or two. How quickly you progress is not important; what is essential is that you progress steadily. Rock bottom minimum should be one round per day just to keep the habit. If you happen to see a pretty woman or photograph that arouses you during the day, you can instantly perform the Power Lock and draw the energy up. Make sure your boss is not watching as he may think you're having a seizure.

The preferred times for these exercises are from eleven P.M. until one A.M. or 11 A.M. until one P.M. During these periods the tide of Yin Energy changes to Yang, and vice versa. The sun begins to rise around midnight and starts to set around noon. At these times the power flows very well. If you cannot practice during these hours, don't be discouraged: you will definitely advance so long as you exercise daily.

9. A final refinement to remember is that the lower contraction is not centered in the stomach or abdominal region. We concentrate on the front of the under trunk—the penis, perineum, and urogenital diaphragm. Our goal is to so train these muscles that they immovably dam up the seminal river. Then we will reverse the river's flow and flood the body with restorative energy.

Directing power from the upper and lower trunk toward the center of the body pours energy into the navel region. Since the seminal fluid (like the blood) tends to follow the chi energy, the navel, in effect, grips the seminal fluid and pulls it up into the body through the spine. So contract the urogenital diaphragm as if you were holding in a bladderful of urine. Lock the passage so tightly that no internal urge can burst through the sealing rings of muscle.

SAFETY POINTS FOR TESTICLE BREATHING, SCROTAL COMPRESSION, AND POWER LOCK

1. Never lie flat on the back during these exercises. The power may stick in the chest, causing considerable irritability and undue pressure on the heart.

2. Never lie on the left side when practicing. This also stresses the heart and overfills it with energy.

3. Never place any objects under your side while in the lying position. This will bend the channel of energy and may cause back pain.

If any of the problems mentioned in points 1 to 3 arise, release the energy safely by using the "Venting Exercise". Any pains or discomfort should disappear within one week of beginning to vent.

4. Practice on an empty stomach whenever possible. In any event, always wait one hour after eating.

5. Wear clothes or wrap yourself in a light blanket during this practice. You will perspire if the exercises are done properly and will suffer a chill if not covered. After practice change your clothes so that you are removed from the moisture of the fabric. There should be a gentle flow of clean air in the room. Avoid any drafts or wind. Wind tends to blow the chi power away. It might cause your energy to get cold easily.

6. Sweat should accumulate on the brow after five scrotal compressions. As you advance, beads of sweat should stand on your brow after three compressions. Rub this sweat into the skin: it has desirable properties which should be returned to the body.

7. Don't breathe through the mouth during these exercises. It is easier to control the flow of air when breathing through the nose. Inhalation through the nose charges the air with energy and invigorates the brain.

8. Do not be concerned if you feel little effect during the first days of practice. Students need varying amounts of time before heat flows from the testicles.

9. You must develop intense concentration. Keep the mind from wandering. Allow thoughts and images to leave without following them. Empty the vessel-of-the-mind of thoughts: powerful energy will stream into the void. Your power of concentration will develop greatly if you persist in this discipline. Learn the Microcosmic Orbit Meditation and do it immediately after practicing the Power Lock.

10. During practice close the eyes and follow the energy's path. The mind should not stray to thoughts or fantasies but strictly track the course of the power. This may sound very difficult. You will be amazed at how quickly you can become sensitive to your own energy. When you experience these energies within yourself, you will know exactly what we mean. Since the energy flows along natural courses, it guides your mind even as your mind guides the power.

11. Those who suffer from constipation should practice in the morning, the regular hour of bowel movement. These exercises will help greatly to remedy the problem.

12. For the method to be effective, you must not ejaculate for 30 days. After ejaculatory orgasm, the body must begin anew to accumulate enough chi pressure in the testes. If you have not learned to hold in the seed during intercourse, refrain from sex during this 30 day period. In this manner you will experience the full power of the method.

Of course, I am not opposed to your desire to have sex. I merely inform you that your progress will be retarded if you ejaculate. Begin learning now to sacrifice ejaculatory pleasure for greater pleasures to come. When you have accomplished these scrotal exercises with proficiency, you may more quickly master retention of the vital seed during love making. This is the main teaching of Sexual Kung Fu.

CLEANSING SIDE EFFECTS

1. It has been my experience that many students of this method soon begin to move their bowels with unaccustomed ease.

2. If you are infected with venereal disease, thoroughly cure yourself before engaging in this exercise. Otherwise the pain will be quite severe when you draw so much blood and power to the pubic region.

3. Some will pass an unusual amount of gas for a time and move the bowels two or three times per day. In this way the body uses its new resources to thoroughly cleanse and purify itself by completely natural means. The unusual number of evacuations and the gas cease within one or two months.

4. This purgative detoxification is followed by regular bowel movements and a deep sense of bodily purity and strength. The saliva becomes lighter and sweeter. Improvement in bowel function arises from the increased flow of vital energy into the entrails. This energizes the involuntary muscles and allows them to function with ease. There may also be a noticeable increase in burping, which is a healthy exhalation of impurities and noxious gas within the body. Burping also lessens after a time with the body much refreshed.

5. The Power Lock is excellent for curing hemorrhoids. Hemorrhoids are caused by sedentary life styles, accumulated heavy toxins, gravitational pooling of blood, stressful bowel movements, and depressed levels of chi energy in the Hui-Yin. In already existing hemorrhoids, the Power Lock may cause increased bleeding for two to four weeks. If the bleeding is not excessive, perform the exercise at ½ strength. You will gradually be cured. The exercise remedies specific causes of hemorrhoids. It evacuates stagnant blood from the anal blood vessels. While performing the Power Lock as a cure for hemorrhoids, you may use medication to speed the healing process. Horsetail Grass, Equisetum Narvensis, is an excellent remedy used as a tea and in Sitz baths. People who have serious hemorrhoid problems should consult your doctor first.

SUMMARY OF TESTICLE BREATHING

1. Choose your preferred position. Standing is well-suited to this form. Relax the whole body and concentrate on the testes.

2. Think the testes to rise in the scrotum as you inhale. Let them sink slowly as you exhale. Practice 36 to 108 breaths.

3. Relax: do not use muscular force. Keep the tongue on the palate, and feel the cool yin energy of the sexual fluids rise up your spine.

SUMMARY OF SCROTAL COMPRESSION

1. Choose your preferred position.

2. Breathe in very slowly through the nose, concentrating on the throat. Compress the air in the throat until you can inhale no further.

3. Swallow strongly to the solar plexus and hold the air there as if it were a ball.

4. Press the ball of air down to the navel region.

5. From the navel press the ball of air down to the pelvic region.

6. Press the ball strongly and continuously into the scrotum until you can hold your breath no longer. At the end of your breath capacity swallow the saliva strongly.

7. Rest by taking quick, shallow breaths through the nose.

8. Relax by rotating the waist several times.

9. Start with 5 repetitions and increase slowly to 36 at a sitting.

10. Keep the tongue up to the palate.

POWER LOCK IS THE BASIS FOR ALCHEMICAL SEX

Though they may appear elementary, the exercises in this chapter are highly refined techniques for increasing vital power. They represent the essential Taoist breathing technique. They are like sharp swords which must be used with care to perform their functions without harming oneself. If you follow my instructions closely, you will not suffer any distressing side-effects. Study the methods with seriousness, assimilate every line of the text. Persist until you have succeeded.

These methods are received from many Taoist masters. The breathing exercises in this chapter, for example, synthesize the teaching of four Masters. Each believed his Method the supreme secret and had notable results with his breathing technique alone.

Nothing will come of nothing. You must spend time in practice to reap the benefits. An ounce of practice is worth a ton of theory. Modern life affords little time for anything but getting and spending. You must be willing to surrender a part of time to speedily advance. The practice must become part of your daily routine. You will make some progress if you do the exercise more often than not. But if you practice as regularly as jumping from bed in the morning, progress will be swift, and chi will begin to build in your upper body which you should collect at your navel.

To make full use of the ching gathered at the navel requires study of the Taoist methods of meditation. Slightly below the navel is the lower "tan tien" center, the lower field of energy in the body within which the Taoists store chi before refining it back upward. The chi moves in circles between the lower, middle, and upper tan tiens, and each time it spirals past it is refined into higher quality of chi. The process of refinement and balancing of the energy is taught in the Microcosmic Orbit, the Fusion of Five Elements, and the Lesser Enlightenment of Kan and Li courses.

It's not unlike taking crude honey mixed with wax and dirt and dead bees and methodically refining it into the sweetest of nectars. The Taoists treat sperm like raw honey. The Power Lock is the step of preventing the raw honey from leaking out of an old bucket and storing it an a new and well-sealed jar. This jar was placed at the level of the navel about two-thirds the way back towards the spine, and was called by the ancient masters the "cauldron". In this cauldron they mixed and cooked the different chi energies of the body in a process they called "alchemy"—the precursor of modern chemistry.

The secret alchemical agent they used was nothing more than ordinary sexual "essence", your ching. But without it, none of the higher levels of alchemical meditation work. So these simple Sexual Kung Fu exercises—Testicle Breathing, Scrotal Compression, and Power Lock—may seem simple and too rudimentary to effect spiritual development, but their proper mastery is essential before you can move on to loving a woman with full command of your sexual and spiritual powers. Your sexual essence is an elixir of life and the fountain of your youth, and is worth training vigorously to safeguard.

Scrotal Compression, and Power Lock—may seem simple and too rudimentary to affect spiritual development, but their proper mastery is essential before you can move on to loving a woman with full command of your sexual and spiritual powers. Your sexual essence is an elixir of life and the fountain of your youth, and is worth training vigorously to safeguard.

---

*If a woman performs any of the exercises in this book, substituting her ovaries as the source of energy, she should keep her panties on to prevent any chi from draining out.

CHAPTER 7

POLARITY IS THE KEY TO TRANSFORMING SEX ENERGY

"Sexual interaction is comparable to water and fire. Water and fire can kill man or help him, depending on how they are used.
—*Pao, the plain master*

To be a Taoist is to experience life as a harmonious flow of life energy. In the traditional Taoist terms, this flow in humans is from "chi", to "ching", to "shien"—from breath to sex essence to spirit. It flows both visibly and invisibly, in a never ending cycle, as it circulates within you, between you and the world, and between Heaven and Earth with man in the middle. It is the blood that flows between heart and kidney, the love (and hate) that passes between man and woman, the storms and sunshine that circulates between sky and earth.

Many people drown in this flow of life; they are simply overwhelmed by it. Some can't "get" enough flow and feel cheated or bitter. Others drift aimlessly without purpose, alienated and unaware there is a flow. Regardless of your attitude toward life, nearly everyone seeks at some point, to anchor themselves in a love relationship. Such is the power of the flow of ching chi, of sexual essence between man and woman. This much is obvious. What is also obvious but is almost always overlooked is the polarity between male and female, and the subtle flow between their two magnetic poles.

This polar exchange is overlooked because the flow is invisible to the physical eye, and because its workings are often too subtle for the uncultivated mind to perceive. That is why Taoists study the workings of chi, ching chi, and shien. These energies, also called the three treasures of life, are the subtle language of life, and to speak in them properly takes years of practice and refinement. At first approach it may seem like learning a foreign language. But after a few lessons you quickly realize you were born speaking this language and merely forgot the subtle grammar of chi energy while being intensively schooled by parents and teachers in more mental subjects.

This flow of energy between opposite poles of male and female is the key to harmonizing the flow of energy in one's life. It is the simplest and most basic secret, not only of the Taoist masters but of every esoteric tradition. It is the key to mastering the Taoist secrets of love. It's simple because its based on the natural law of the universe—that positive and negative forces attract and bond with each other. Its as true for a simple pair of magnets locking together as it is of the protons and electrons locked into the dance of subatomic particles that form the atom. The Taoists called this polarity yin and yang, terms that have become popular today in the field of holistic health, but are not well understood in terms of their functioning in sexuality.

One way the Taoists describe it is with the simple metaphor of cooking. Yang is fire and yin is water. Man is the fire, and woman is the water. When man makes love with a woman, he cooks the woman's water (in her womb) with his fire (penis). The woman is almost always sexually stronger, for her water puts out the male fire; his erection loses its flame. Yin, the soft and yielding, always conquers yang, the hard. In the same way water (rivers are yin, or female) triumphs over solid rock. Thus a stream slowly wears away a giant mountain and carves the Grand Canyon a mile deep.

YIN AND YANG: BATTLE OF THE SEXES

This battle between yin and yang is seemingly endless, just like the never ending battle between the sexes. In fact, the Taoist sages also used the metaphor of combat to elucidate the act of sexual love. For some men love is a passionate struggle for domination and surrender; to the Taoists it was more a lawful play of opposites. Ideally you enter the battle of the sexes with a spirit of gamesmanship. You approach not with the intention of defeating your lover, but in the hope of matching her grace and receptive energy with the exact complementary male skill and force.

Unfortunately, few men today seem to proceed with such tact in love-making; as a result, most are beaten soundly within minutes by the woman. This failure is due to tactical ignorance of both the male sex organs and the nature of sexual energy. Misunderstanding of love's strategic laws is so widespread that a myth has developed that the average man cannot fully satisfy a passionate woman.

In fact, the average man can unfailingly satisfy his mate when he learns to discipline his forces. Untutored man's nature is to attack: he possesses the offensive weapon. Woman's is to defend: she protects without exhausting herself. When man assaults furiously and discharges the sperm, he crumbles. Yet the woman may remain most eager to continue, even if she kindly denies it and thus "spares" her opponent.

To pursue the martial metaphor of the Chinese. . . . The woman's shield and short sword is her vagina and clitoris. Man is armed with a long spear alone, his penis. If man attacks too violently with his love weapon, woman easily fends off his thrusts and does him in when he exhausts his seed. But if man remains beyond woman's striking range, she drops the shield from fatigue. The contest will be over before man has lost his vehicle of higher vitality.

The point is this: Man must stop throwing away his sexual energies. When he stops the sperm loss, woman is no longer in a position of superiority. She meets her match and no longer suffers disappointment. Man doesn't exhaust himself and retreat in humiliation, yet feels he has met a good match. Woman reaches the limits of her erotic capacities and is ready to make real peace with her opponent.

The sages thus advise you to use your tactical weapons first. Hold the strategic one in reserve. In other words, use the finger, tongue and other parts of the body before using the penis. Through tender and skillful use of your other limbs in foreplay, you may bring your partner to a state of very high receptivity as the first step in gaining equality with a superior opponent.

Her breasts will rise, respiration and glandular secretion will increase. You should wait till fluid rolls to the vaginal lips before using your chief arm. Give your lover time to fully enter the condition of love before you enter her.

The battle between man and woman is over when both recognize that neither can "win" by either dominating or submitting. At that moment, both become free to surrender to each other and exchange their deepest love—their vulnerabilities have been matched and their fear of losing is neutralized.

HIGHER ORGASM IS A DELICATE BALANCE
OF POLAR ENERGIES

But how to reach that point of tenderness, where both lovers joyously yield and receive life from one another? It sounds great on paper, but what happens to tense energies left over from a tough day at work and an argument with your wife about whether she should go back to work? How do you keep daily politics out of the bedroom? This chapter will offer some practical ways to approach love-making with the goal of balancing the flow of yin and yang power. But first understand the principle of polarity is dominant in this sexual practice.

The single most important point to remember about polarity is that yin and yang energies are not separate energies: they are one and the same energy, but with two different charges. They never exist apart from one another, but are always in fluid motion, like a pendulum swinging back and forth, passing from hot to cold, and gradually moving to stillness at the perfect moderate temperature. Another metaphor is to see man and women as two sides of the same coin. During love, the coin spins rapidly, fusing the two sides into one.

That is how man and woman can become "one": they simply realize the flow of sexual energy between them is continuous and belongs to them both. Each lover is at opposite ends of the polar flow. When the exchange of ching chi reaches a certain intensity and balance the solid bodies of the two lovers begin pulsating as if charged with electricity. The feeling of having solid flesh disappears. You are suddenly a pillar of vibrating energy held in exquisite balance by your lover's field of energy. This is a total orgasm of body and soul. The battling ego shrinks to its true size, a tiny grain of sand, and reluctantly begins humming in chorus with the ocean of the subtle universe that rhythmically washes over it.

Many men may have a glimpse of this, but few are able to sustain the experience because they discharge the energy from their half of the polar field by ejaculating. This is not true orgasm; it is merely releasing the discomfort, the exquisite "itch" of too much excited energy that has nowhere to move but out.

A true orgasm occurs when both man and woman continue to pulsate together. Their sexual energy completes a full circuit between their two magnetic poles, charging each of them more fully than before. This circle is the Tao, the black and white teardrop symbols of yin and yang flowing into each other in perfect circular harmony.

The flow of sex energy alone cannot complete this circle; love must be present. The mind must participate in sex with a totally attentive feeling. This circle of energy cannot connect if a man only joins his penis with a woman's vagina without loving her with his heart. That is like holding the ends of two horse shoe magnets close and then only touching one arm from each magnet. The other arm also wants to connect, to seal the magnetic attraction. Only when both positive and negative poles of both the man and the woman are locked in place can the energy flow with any power and stable balance. That is why sex alone, without love makes you unhappy— you're only connecting one half of yourself to the woman, and your lower half at that. The flow of chi in the Tao's circle is broken, and without that total flow between yin and yang no amount of sex will satisfy your deeper desire for wholeness.

The ejaculatory orgasm to which most men are so deeply attached restricts their life force to the genitals. During sex the penis literally bursts with life, as it is too small to contain the expanding sexual force. The penis was not designed to hold your life-force anymore than it was designed to be your brain and central nervous system. The real function of your penis is to conduct life into and out of the body. The sex organs are only doors through which life enters and issues forth.

When the upper poles of men and women are connected—at the heart and mouth—as well as the genitals, then the magnet can become an electro-magnetic dynamo. Then the chi can nourish the ching chi in the lower half of the body, and combine together to be transformed into spirit in the upper half. If both man and woman cultivate their chi upward, and refine it to a high level through meditation and love, they can develop a polarity which creates a super magnet and conducts even higher spiritual energies through their human form. Such experiences break through the bounds of individual pleasure and sensation, and go beyond the satisfaction of their personal egos to attain an entirely different state of being.

Perhaps you know a couple who is radiantly happy and deeply loving and do not practice any esoteric method of love-making and who you assume ejaculate and have orgasm to their heart's content. You are right to ask—why bother learning these seemingly

DIAGRAM 21

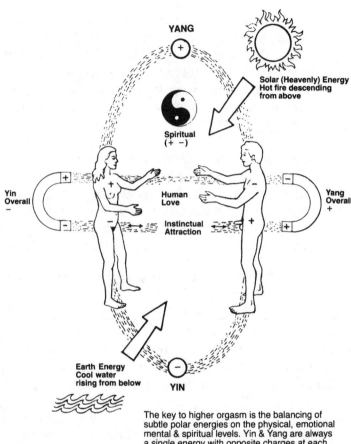

The key to higher orgasm is the balancing of subtle polar energies on the physical, emotional mental & spiritual levels. Yin & Yang are always a single energy with opposite charges at each pole.

complicated and time-consuming Taoists exercises and methods of sex energy transformation? Why not just love your woman the way you know now, and let nature take its own course? Why meddle with the one pleasure that above all others should be free of schooling?

The simplest answer is that Taoists are trying to help nature take its course within humans, not to alter its basic processes. The radiant and loving couple you know could be doubly radiant and live 10 or 20 years longer in good health to enjoy their love if they conserved their ching chi and practiced the transformation of the sex energy. Perhaps their radiant happiness is more dependant on

external circumstances than you are aware—a good job, preoc-
cupation with children, etc. Will they appear so radiant in old age?
Is it progressing to more subtle levels? The Taoist love techniques
serve to speed up, intensify and stabilize your natural evolution.
There is no limit to the scale of good health and profoundity of love
possible. At the higher levels there are always new spiritual chal-
lenges to be met. The balance of polarity moves beyond the poles
of man and woman and you become aware of the play of opposites
between Heaven and Earth.

The Taoists know this high level of harmony is a tangible
experience that can be permanently known to man, they call it
Immortality. They prepare for it by conserving their sex energy
and harmonising their spirit with their lover. In this way love-
making becomes, in western terms, a way to draw nearer to God. It
can become the worship of divinity in the temple of your lover's
body and soul.

PREPARE THE YIN ESSENCE WITH GENTLENESS

As the man, it is your responsibility to see that your lover's organs
are literally first warmed. This is the Taoist way of harmonizing the
yin essence, of increasing her receptive power to love-making. Her
vital organs—kidney, liver, heart, lungs, spleen/pancreas—actually produce and refine the chi needed for love-making. If her inner
organs are weak or feeling sick, the music of your love-making will
be discordant or heavy no matter how good you are feeling. To
hear the music of the celestial spheres you must learn to orches-
trate her feelings and sensations with your own. Generally, it takes
longer for her organs to warm up and get into fine tune than it does
a man.

To return to the simple Chinese metaphor, think of woman as
water and man as fire. A man can light his fire quickly but if he
burns up his wood too soon the pot of water won't have time to
boil. The water will warm more slowly than the fire. So the man
should conserve his firewood while slowly warming up the
woman's water. Observe the basic rule of cooking: don't put your
carrots and peas (your penis and testicles) in the pot before the
water is already about to boil. A lot of men don't know this, since
they have little experience in cooking. If you toss the carrot and
peas in a pot while the water is cold, the carrots absorb cooking

heat and it takes the pot of water much longer to heat. The carrots also don't cook as well this way, and may turn out soggy and not as tasty.

So its best to wait until the water in the woman's womb is about to boil before beginning intercourse. The traditional Taoist texts mention nine things to look for in a woman as a sign she is truly ready for the man: A woman's energy goes through nine stages as her organs begin to warm and release their harmonious chi. It was described by the Mysterious Lady, a sex consultant to the Yellow Emperor of China nearly two thousand years ago:

1. Her chi is in her lungs when she begins to breathe rapidly.
2. The energy has moved to her heart when she kisses the man.
3. She hugs the man: chi is in the spleen.
4. Her vagina grows moist: chi is in the kidneys and genitals.
5. She moves her pelvis and bites gently: chi has penetrated the bones.
6. Her legs grab tight around the man: chi is in the muscles.
7. She caresses the penis: chi is in the blood.
8. She kisses with deep passion: chi has arrived in her skin and flesh.
9. She surrenders herself and moans in ecstasy: chi has entered the liver and released her spirit. She is truly ready to receive the man and exchange her yin essence with his yang essence.

The purpose of waiting until the woman is fully ready will become clear when you practice the semen retention technique taught in the next chapter. The man and woman begin to "steam up" the sexual essence, the ching chi, but if the pot is not properly prepared and the temperature is wrong, it will be difficult to successfully transform the sex essence into spirit. If the man lets his fire go out (by ejaculating his seminal fluids) before the woman is ready to begin the steaming process, then it will be impossible to refine the male and female essence together into a single nectar.

THE ART OF PASSION: TIMING AND FREQUENCY

The number of times of intercourse bears little relation to the satisfaction and happiness of lovers. A woman may be very well pleased with one round or totally uninspired with fifteen. The point is to love her with irresistible tenderness from the start.

Try to enter neither too early nor too late. If you are too early, you may tire before she has reached the peak of her desire. If you are too late, you will miss the heights of her pleasure. Enter at the proper moment and satisfy her the first time.

Just as you should not eat until you're stuffed, so you should not make love until you're exhausted. You should slightly desire food after a meal, and you should still desire your lover after you've lain with her. A Taoist master of love strives for harmony by curbing excessive greed. Sometimes less is more. Don't satiate your sexual desire, or it will turn into distaste. Extreme yang (expansion) gives birth to yin (retreat). Unless your lover is very highly-sexed, once a day seven days per week will be too much for her if you are a Seminal Kung Fu Man. If she doesn't consciously inhibit her orgasm, her appetite for daily loving will decline. The macho myth of "giving it to her umpteen times" is an attempt to cover futility in a haze of supposedly impressive numbers. There are very few partners who will not be richly pleased by one beautiful act of intercourse. Many will experience several orgasms in one long loving.

SEX POSITION AFFECTS THE FLOW OF ENERGY

I say little about sexual position because there are many other works available on this subject. The most thorough text with lavish illustrations is Sexual Secrets by Nik Douglas and Penny Slinger (Inner Traditions, New York). This text shows over 30 classic Taoist positions for making love and also includes the special postures for healing various illnesses. The essential key to choice of posture is governed by the hidden laws of energy flow. Remember these two points and you can create any energy you desire:

1. To relax and harmonize, place like to like: belly to belly, hand to hand, mouth to mouth, open eyes to open eyes, etc.

2. To stimulate and excite, place together unlikes: mouth to genitals, genitals to anus, open eyes to closed eyes, etc. The art of love is to interweave stimulating and harmonizing positions into a sublime dance.

THE COLD WATER SKINNY DIP FOR PREMATURE EJACULATION

Once you have fully aroused the woman, you will be ready to enter her. You will be quite hard and prepared to leap in. Should you enter her with your penis at maximum size? Maybe. If you are an accomplished Taoist lover, you may enter when you please. You will have developed a degree of self-mastery that gives you perfect freedom in love. But if you are just beginning to control your passions, you may prefer to cool down somewhat.

One extraordinary procedure for those who are too quick on the trigger requires a bowl of cold water. The technique is simply to dip you penis into the cold water until erection has diminished about 50%. This should take only a few moments. Then count slowly to 30, thinking of nothing but counting itself. During this time continue to caress the woman.

After your brief swim you may please her greatly by stirring the penis around the outside of the vagina. While whirling, you may again count to 30. Slowly breath deeply while stirring. Your partner's entire body will ache to receive you. When you finally introduce yourself, she feels as if the world flowed into her.

Unlike the stereotypical macho brute, you have not coughed forth your vitality shortly after entry. When others are dead, you are just being born inside of her. Your partner has already been mounting for quite some time. You are beginning to climb. The goal is not to climb just one peak together, but an entire series of mountains, each higher and with a more spectacular view than the previous peak. An ambitious journey requires some disciplined training—but it will be fun to train with your lover in bed.

THE CENTURY COUNT: BUILD YOUR STAYING POWER

This useful mind control technique is a breath exercise. Slowly count from one to one hundred. Let no extraneous thought enter your mind. Coordinate deep, harmonious breathing into your lower abdomen with the counting. Count a complete inhalation and exhalation as one.

This is not nearly so easy as it may sound. Most people have difficulty counting from one to ten without wandering. When the mind strays, begin the count over till reaching 100 with no random thought.

This method of calming the agitated spirit will greatly help you develop the self-control to pull back from ejaculation. If you've not practised relaxing, you will have difficulty resisting the urge to release the seed.

Practice the 100 breaths twice daily. After a period of serious practice you should be able to clear the mind and calm most violent agitation with few breaths from the depths of the pelvic diaphragm.

The Cold Water Skinny Dip may be used by those readers who have difficulty exercising any degree of self-control at all. It is a simple mechanical technique to help you begin to exercise self-restraint.

The Century Count will help you actually learn to command the penis to cool off when too hot. To retain the semen you must be able to withdraw excess heat from the genital region at will. With regular practice you will prevent ejaculation far more easily than seemed possible but a short time before. It is an important step toward the higher forms of esoteric love. Esoteric knowledge alone is useless or worse, for it may engender a complacency that precludes doubt, or experimentation with real people and events. Knowledge with living application through practice is the goal of this work. The Taoist approach is fundamentally practical.

Most books claiming to improve the art of loving literally bury the reader under a bewildering variety of second-rate methods. It is better to learn a few excellent methods in greater detail. I am familiar with many other techniques, but my experience has shown a student fails in this practice if his mind is overloaded with information. A boxer who knows 20 different punches usually falls before one who knows two or three punches that he has honed to perfection. First master the fundamental principles, by "getting" the energy inside your body using these techniques, then improvise as you will in bed.

The finger, tongue, penis each has its own unique character. The penis may give supreme union, but it is dangerous for the beginner to overuse. Until you've gained a degree of self-control, reserve it for strategic interludes. When woman is well-prepared, a mere touch of the penis is more satisfying than many passionate strokes of intercourse without proper foreplay.

Ripeness is all. There is more taste and nourishment in one

ripe apple than in ten green ones. Only the woman ripened for reception of the penis can adore your male yang essence with her every cell.

THE FOUR ATTAINMENTS OF THE JADE STALK

In order to harmonize fully with a woman who is going through the nine stages of arousal, the man will naturally pass different phases of arousal before entering her. The Yellow Emperor is said to have asked: "If I wish to make love but fail to gain erection, is it wise to force intercourse?"

The Mysterious Lady replied, "No, it is not wise. The Jade Stalk (penis) should first pass the Four Attainments before intercourse will be proper." Naturally the Emperor asked, "What are the Four Attainments?"

"If the Jade Stalk is not able to erect", she replied, "the yin and yang energy is not in harmony. Firmness is the first attainment. If the Jade Stalk erects, but is not swollen, the chi is insufficient in the blood. Swelling is the second attainment. If the man's Jade Stalk is swollen, but not hard, his chi has not penetrated to his bones. Hardness is the third attainment. Finally, if the Jade Stalk is hard but not hot, the vital energy has not reached the man's spirit. Heat is the fourth attainment.

It is far more important to have a small but hard penis than it is for a man to have a large but semi-soft penis. That is why no man has any true biological advantage over another in sex. Anyone can cultivate his internal energy to a high level of intensity regardless of the outer appearance of his body. Other practices like Iron Shirt Chi Kung, Tai Chi Chi Kung, and meditation all help develop a high level of chi cultivation where energy can be passed or exchanged with a woman without using a penis as the channel of transmission. A light touch of your hand, a glance, or a thought will suffice to send the energy. But even this would not make the penis obsolete, as there are always more refined levels of love-making to be enjoyed.

You can observe your own penis to know the level of your arousal. What if you have not reached the highest level of having a rock hard penis radiating tremendous heat, but the woman is ready to receive you? I suggest you enter her and pass the other attainments of the Jade Stalk while making love. You can do this

safely—without ejaculating—while inside her by using the Power
Locking or Big Draw. However, it is very tempting to release your
seed when your penis reaches this degree of arousal, so in the
beginning you may need to lock your seed in before reaching the
fourth attainment.

THE NINE SHALLOW/ONE DEEP THRUSTING METHOD

There are a great number of thrusting methods. The Kama Sutra
alone offers many different ones. We suggest a powerful method,
which we consider among the "cream of the crop." Our method is
based on the number, NINE, a figure of great importance in Taoist
practice considered a powerful yang energy.

The essence of this thrusting technique is to go nine shallow
and one deep. The one deep thrust, besides varying sensory stimulation, forces the air out of the vagina. This allows you to create a
vacuum inside her with the nine shallow thrusts which follow. You
never withdraw completely: this would break the vacuum seal.
Rather, you hover at those outermost inches of the vagina which
are covered with a dense net of nerves.

The nine shallow, one deep rhythm delights your partner. The
vacuum has tremendous effect: she feels empty then full, empty
then full. This pause pleases because you constantly refresh her
senses with change. When we eat our fill, we want no more. But
one delicious taste (the deep thrust) increases desire. We satisfy
then stimulate desire. We create desire than renew satisfaction.

The other reason that shallow thrusts satisfy is that the
woman's most sensitive area is about one inch inside her vagina on
the upper wall. This point connects a vast network of nerves in the
sexual organs with the rest of her body. This is known as the G-
spot, after Graffenberg, the scientist who discovered it, and is also
the site from which females ejaculate a fluid when highly aroused.
The Taoists consider this fluid also to be highly charged with her
essence that is absorbed directly into the head of the penis glans.

Continue going nine shallow, one deep until accomplishing
nine full sets. The number of short thrusts thus totals 81, another
potent number. At first you may go 3, then 6 cycles before building
up to the 9. This potency will be increased if you swallow her saliva
every time you pause for a deep thrust. This fluid is highly charged
with her yin essence and will balance your expanding yang energy.

DIAGRAM 22

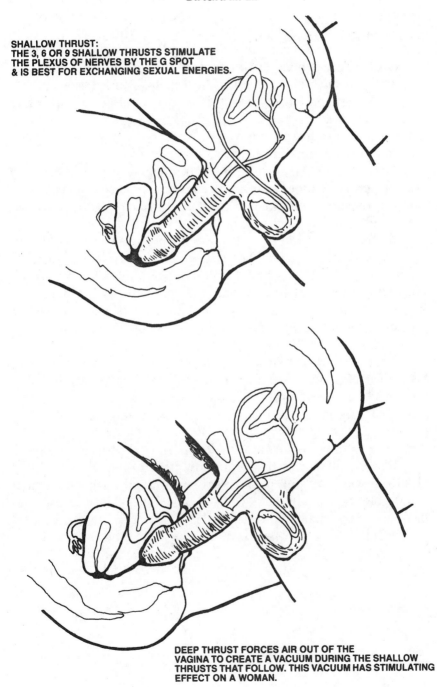

SHALLOW THRUST:
THE 3, 6 OR 9 SHALLOW THRUSTS STIMULATE
THE PLEXUS OF NERVES BY THE G SPOT
& IS BEST FOR EXCHANGING SEXUAL ENERGIES.

DEEP THRUST FORCES AIR OUT OF THE
VAGINA TO CREATE A VACUUM DURING THE SHALLOW
THRUSTS THAT FOLLOW. THIS VACUUM HAS STIMULATING
EFFECT ON A WOMAN.

On reaching this goal, you may rest or use the more sophisticated techniques found in Chapter 8, The Secret of Semen Retention.

Once you have relaxed and removed surplus electricity from the testes, recommence active thrusting. You are in an extremely pleasurable state, calm yet able to keep the seminal fluid and erectile power through another series of thrusts. Then rest again.

You may prefer to thrust in slowly and to depart more quickly. This way is well adapted to woman's deep-seated nature. Enter slowly because she grows aroused more slowly than man. Untaught man is quick to begin and quick to finish.*

Since she must make life, she naturally begins and ends over a greater period of time. Man must consciously accommodate himself to woman's primoridial rhythm. With reverence light the sacred candles in her thighs.

If she is taken too abruptly, the flush of pleasure has insufficient time to spread over her entire nervous system, Sensation remains fixed in the genitals. Think of it this way: when you pinch yourself for a second or two, only the spot actually between your fingers feels the sensation. But if you hold on for a long time, the sensation spreads over a wider area, eventually flowing to remote limbs. As with pain, so with pleasure.

Therefore, thrust slowly: each thrust is itself an act of love. Woman wakes according to her own mysterious cycles. To defy the laws of creation is to suffer sure disappointment.

You may prefer to thrust out somewhat more quickly. You have already stimulated her: she needs some particularly poignant sensation to fling her toward greater heights. Extra thrill may be provided by quicker retreat after slow penetration. Do not thrust all of the way out: pull back to a 1" or 2" depth. This movement away from the woman flicks your up-bowed penis into strong contact with the woman's clitoris. This is a seat of her erotic sensitivity. Suffuse her with pleasure, then sting with a hot surge.

---

*She needs less instruction than you: Man is God's secret, Power is man's secret, Sex is woman's secret.

CHAPTER 8

THE SECRETS OF SEMEN RETENTION

"Reject all reasoning about sex; practice special exercises. To be able to make love and not emit is the secret of returning the semen. Increasing and aiding the semen is the way of the life-force."
—*Plain Woman's advice to the Yellow Emperor 2nd century B.C.*

In the centuries past, the Emperor of China invariably called in the court sages, usually Taoist, to get advice on his sex life. Before accepting the advice of any sage, so the story goes, the Emperor required any prospective master to prove his sexual control. He did this by offering the would-be advisor a full glass of wine and demanding the sage insert his penis into it. If he was truly a master, he could absorb the wine into his penis, and then release it back into the wine glass. This was taken as absolute proof that the sage could also absorb a woman's sexual fluids, her yin essence, and therefore knew the secrets of Immortality.

This practice of absorbing fluid into the penis is quite real, and can still be seen on the streets of India today. One enterprising yogi in Bombay sucks up oil into his penis in private and then publicly lights it on fire as he urinates it out, claiming it is divine fire. Amusing, but not very inspiring as a model for the transformation of sex energy. This yogic suction technique is one that many people confuse with the true practice of semen retention.

Drawing any fluid into the urethra of the penis is accomplished by creating a vacuum in the bladder through certain physical exercises. It is a dangerous practice because it is easy for the male prostate or bladder to become infected by the inhaled fluid, especially female sexual fluids drawn during love-making from the highly bacterial culture of the vagina. Some yogis have become ill from this practice, and thus all methods of semen retention have gained a reputation in some circles as being unhealthy and leading to impotence and prostate problems.

I warn my students never to suck in a woman's fluids. The Taoist method of semen retention I teach is directed towards a single goal—the transformation of sex energy, or ching, into higher levels in the body, mind, and spirit. The sperm seed is held only so its essence is not lost outside the body. The method is useless unless the ching is withdrawn from the seed and pulled up and circulated throughout the body. There is no need to draw in a woman's sexual fluids inside your body; the head of the penis glans is specially designed to absorb the woman's powerful essence directly through the skin.

But by far the most powerful exchange with this Taoist method occurs on a level of subtle energy. That is why I teach all my students to circulate their chi in the microcosmic orbit as the prerequisite to understanding the cultivation of ching from the raw physical level of sperm to the refined subtle energy of a shien, or spiritual being. When they have opened their microcosmic orbit, it is already a minor enlightenment. The mind has begun to realize it has control over its own subtle energy. Ultimately you learn that all mind is the movement of subtle energy.

LEARN TO CIRCULATE YOUR "CHI" IN THE MICROCOSMIC ORBIT

The methods of chi cultivation explained in detail in this book—from Testicle Breathing to the Big Draw method to the valley orgasm—all involve drawing sexual energy stored in the testicles up the spinal column and into the brain. When full, this energy will come down the front into the throat, heart, and navel. The brain and pituitary gland will aid in distributing this powerful energy to wherever it is needed, whether for fighting off illness, answering a child's question, painting, or making love. This is a unique attribute of sexual ching over other types of chi with special functions, such as liver chi. Sex energy is extraordinarily versatile, and can be transformed into many different functions. This is one reason it is so nourishing to our spiritual being. It can easily digest it, almost as if it were baby food.

It is much easier to cultivate your energy if you first understand the major paths of energy circulation in the body. The nervous system in humans is very complex and is capable of directing energy wherever it is needed. But the ancient Taoist masters discovered there are two energy channels that carry an especially strong current.

One channel is called the "Functional," or "Yin" Channel. It begins at the base of the trunk midway between the testicles and the anus at a point called the perineum. It goes up the front of the body past the penis, stomach organs, heart, and throat up and ends at the tip of the tongue. The second channel, called the "Governor," or "yang" channel, starts in the same place. It flows from the perineum upwards into the tailbone and then up through the spine into the brain and back down to the roof of the mouth.

The tongue is like a switch that connects these two currents—when it is touched to the roof of the mouth just behind the front teeth, the energy can flow in a circle up the spine and back down the front. The two channels form a single circuit that the energy loops around. This vital current circulates past the major organs and nervous systems of the body, giving cells the juice they need to grow, heal, and function. This circulating energy, known as the microcosmic orbit, forms the basis of acupuncture, Western medical research has already acknowledged acupuncture as being clinically effective, although scientists admit they cannot fully explain why the system works. The Taoist, on the other hand, have been studying the subtle energy points in the body for thousands of years and have verified in detail the importance of each channel.

It is this loop of energy about the body which also carries the sexual current from the testicles and spreads the vitality to other parts of the body. This has a profound effect on your health, as it triggers the glands to release the sex stimulating hormones that regulate body chemistry and ultimately affect your ability to do any thing. It has an especially strong influence on the quality of your love-making, as on the biological level sex is largely a question of hormonal balance.

DIAGRAM 23

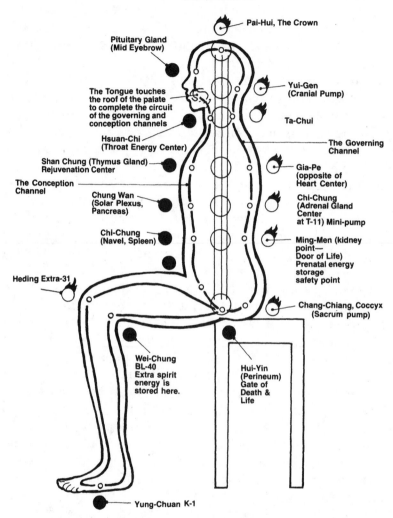

Pai-Hui, The Crown

Pituitary Gland
(Mid Eyebrow)

Yui-Gen
(Cranial Pump)

The Tongue touches
the roof of the palate
to complete the circuit
of the governing and
conception channels

Ta-Chui

Hsuan-Chi
(Throat Energy Center)

The Governing
Channel

Shan Chung (Thymus Gland)
Rejuvenation Center

Gia-Pe
(opposite of
Heart Center)

The Conception
Channel

Chung Wan
(Solar Plexus,
Pancreas)

Chi-Chung
(Adrenal Gland
Center
at T-11) Mini-pump

Chi-Chung
(Navel, Spleen)

Ming-Men (kidney
point—
Door of Life)
Prenatal energy
storage
safety point

Heding Extra-31

Chang-Chiang, Coccyx
(Sacrum pump)

Wei-Chung
BL-40
Extra spirit
energy is
stored here.

Hui-Yin
(Perineum)
Gate of
Death &
Life

Yung-Chuan K-1

Learn to circulate your Chi in the Microcosmic
Orbit to assist mastery of semen retention
& transformation of sexual energy.

The sexual energy that moves in the microcosmic is a primordial energy. Human life begins with the piercing of an egg by a sperm cell. This is the original act of Kung Fu in the battle of yin and yang. Sexual Kung Fu is the recreation of that act within the male body. Only instead of forming a foetus from a fertilized egg growing inside the woman's womb, the sperm energy penetrates to higher energy centers inside the male body and gives birth to man on a spiritual level. It is drawn upward by the microcosmic channel where it literally gives a man a rebirth, a "new life"—the confidence of controlling a powerful flow of creative energy and the satisfaction of a deep sense of harmony. Whenever you are "in love" with a woman or with life at large, energy is flowing into your microcosmic orbit. It is the feeling of intense connectedness, of being centered in the warm flowing current of life.

THE IMPORTANCE OF THE MICROCOSMIC ORBIT

By opening this microcosmic channel up and keeping it clear of physical or mental blockages it is possible to pump greater amount of sexual energy up the spine. If this channel is blocked by tension, then during the sexual excitement of love-making the hot sperm energy will seek the quickest alternate escape route and go out the penis. The sexual power is then lost until the body goes through the long and physically taxing process of manufacturing more sperm. Some of man's power of magnetic sexual attraction is temporarily lost by this discharge of sperm. There are some methods of kundalini and tantric yoga that devise a very powerful flow of energy up the spine to the head, using mantra, breathing techniques, yogic postures and locks to channel the sperm power upwards. Leaving to circulate the microcosmic orbit is an important step to sealing this energy within the body so it will circulate and revitalize all parts of the mind and body. Otherwise when intense pressure builds in the head much of it escapes out the eyes, ears, nose and mouth and is lost. This is like trying to heat a room with your body heat while all the windows open—you're going to have a very high fuel bill. You'll spend a lot of sperm energy that isn't recoverable for immediate practical use, such as sharing it with your lover.

The easiest way to open the microcosmic energy channel is by simply sitting in meditation a few minutes each morning and relaxing. Allow your energy to automatically complete the loop by letting your mind flow along with it. Start in the eyes, and mentally circulate with the energy as it goes down the front through your tongue, throat, chest and navel and then up the tailbone and spine to the head.

At first it will feel like nothing is happening, but eventually the current will begin to feel warm in some places as it loops around. The key is just to relax and try to bring your mind directly into the part of the loop being focused on. This is different from visualizing an image inside your head of what that part of the body looks like or is feeling. Do not use your mind as if it were a T.V. picture. Experience the actual chi flow. Relax and let your mind flow with the chi in the physical body along a natural circuit to any desired point e.g. your navel, perineum, etc.

Those interested in fully mastering this method of relaxation and opening the microcosmic orbit can refer to my first book "AWAKEN HEALING ENERGY THROUGH THE TAO." The best lover is a fully relaxed man who understands what is going on inside him. The man who masters this easy flow of energy inside the body's microcosmic orbit will find tapping into his sexual powers a simple and natural step.

Experience has shown that the Sexual Kung Fu practices taught in this chapter were quickly and effortlessly mastered by students who first studied the microcosmic orbit and opened its two channels of energy flow. So study of the microcosmic orbit is highly recommended to all students of Sexual Kung Fu who seek to truly master the techniques taught here. Progress to the higher levels of transforming sexual energy without first learning the microcosmic is very difficult. Many people may already be "open" in these channels and simply need to be told where the energy flows in order to do it. Others get it simply by being very relaxed and living close to nature. The benefits of the microcosmic orbit extend beyond facilitating the flow of sexual energy, and include prevention of aging and the healing of many illnesses ranging from high blood pressure, insomnia and headaches to arthritis.

Mastering the microcosmic current also prepares the serious student for utilizing other energy-conserving techniques that complement Sexual Kung Fu such as "Iron Shirt Chi Kung I, II, III," a method of packing and storing chi energy into vital organs. Another powerful technique is Tai Chi Chi Kung, a condensed form of Tai Chi Chuan that circulates chi energy between body, mind, and spirit and strengthens muscles, tendons and bones. (Both of these techniques will be available in publication at a later date.)

Let's move into the first technique of semen retention during love-making. Even if you don't sit daily and circulate the microcosmic current, just being aware that it exists in your body and functions automatically during these practices should help you more quickly master the methods of Taoist loving. You may even learn it through your love-making; all it takes is attention. The less "automatic" and the more conscious you become of the functioning of subtle chi energy in your body, mind, and spirit, the greater your freedom to creatively love and be yourself.

DIAGRAM 24

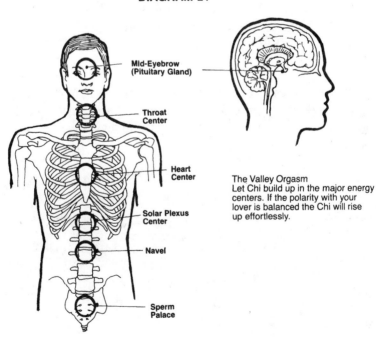

The Valley Orgasm
Let Chi build up in the major energy centers. If the polarity with your lover is balanced the Chi will rise up effortlessly.

EXTERNAL LOCKING: THE THREE FINGERS METHOD

Three Fingers Method of seminal retention has been practiced in China for more than five thousand years. It is so easy and simple that anyone can learn it quickly and with considerable effectiveness. The method seals in the vital fluid from the outside with fingertip pressure. It requires slightly more coordination than stepping on a garden hose to stop the flow of water.

The Three Fingers Method involves essentially this: Several seconds before the moment of ejaculation, press the mid-point between the anus and the scrotum with the three longest fingers of the right hand. This seals in the fluids and much energy.

THE PRACTICE:

1. Locate The Point: Apply the pressure at the mid-point between the anus and scrotum. This point, which lies at the very bottom of the trunk, is a "door" through which energy enters and leaves the body.

2. Apply pressure: Apply pressure neither too hard or too light. The proper amount of force must be found with experience. Generally speaking, the stronger the finger tips, the less pressure needs to be applied to halt the fluid.

DIAGRAM 25

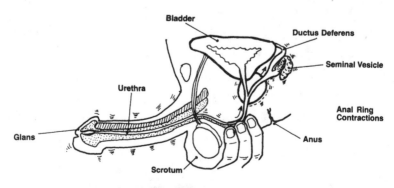

External Locking Method:
Several seconds before the moment of ejaculation press the mid-point between the anus and scrotum with the three longest fingers of the right hand.

3. Use Three Fingers: The passage through which the semen travels tends to slide away from one's fingers. Two fingers cannot hold the tube and block it at the same time. We use the second and fourth fingers to press both sides of the urethra and anchor it in place. Then the middle finger presses directly on the urethra itself, which doesn't slip away because it is pinned on both sides by the other two fingers. The fingers should be curved slightly. The middle finger is a little more bowed than the other two in order to provide a solid, even wall through which the fluid cannot pass.

4. Timing: As soon as you feel the inevitability of ejaculation, apply the fingers for External Locking. If you wait too long, no force can stop the flow. When you know that ejaculation is imminent, apply the fingers. The locking should be applied before, during and after the contractions. Lock until you are certain that the pumping has ceased completely.

The net result of locking in the semen is that much fluid flows back to the reservoirs from which it came. There is no harm whatever done to the bodily organs, for the tissues in this region are highly elastic and accept the fluid which returns when you reverse the flow.

It might seem that the seminal reservoir cannot hold fluid beyond a maximum level. This would be true if the male reproductive system were a simple hose and tank. This it is not. When the fluid reaches a high level, several things happen.

First, production of sperm automatically declines. This saves the energy and materials needed to produce the nutritionally-rich sperm. Second, there is a natural tendency for the body to reabsorb these fluids spontaneously. Third, the Taoists have perfected a system for "steaming" the seminal power up to the higher vital centers, thereby reducing pressure in the lower sperm ducts and prostate gland. This involves transmuting the liquid sperm to a higher energy state. It is somewhat like boiled water becoming a gas, a property which allows moisture to travel upward to the sky while still retaining the essence of water. The liquid ching is likewise transmuted into a different and more mobile energy form that retains the creative essence of ching.

Remember that the force of the seed is more than mere chemical analysis can explain. Any scientist can stew together the ingredients of the sperm. But inspiring them with the power to reproduce life is a much more difficult task. It is the life in the seed which we seek to conserve and transform.

The main use of this method is for beginning and intermediate practitioners of Sexual Kung Fu who have not yet mastered the Big Draw method of retaining semen yet want to continue love making without losing their seed. In short, it is an external crutch that should be thrown away when you have thoroughly learned the more internal practices. You may experience a little discomfort after the first few times after you try this method. This is normal and no more cause for alarm than stiffness in long-unused muscles after a good workout.

TIMING AND SAFETY POINTS

1. Don't overdo it at first. For the first few weeks, use this powerful practice no more than once every two or three days. The elderly and sick should use the method not more than twice per week at the beginning of practice.

2. After using the method, the vital heat may so increase that you will feel quite thirsty. Simply drink more water.

3. After practicing External Locking for one to three months, and in some cases sooner, the sexual drive will be appreciably heightened. Erections will be more frequent. Increase your sexual activities at a moderate pace. Don't abuse your newfound power.

4. The practice requires strong fingertip pressure. If you are too weak to do it do several fingertip pushups every day. Use five, then four, then three fingers and increase the number of pushups as your strength develops.

5. Since a small amount of seed will remain in the urethra, some semen may leak out when erection is lost. Thus, to use this practice for birth control, you must withdraw from the vagina before erection falls. For contraceptive purposes urinate before entering the woman for a second act of intercourse. To be 100% safe use this method in conjunction with a spermicidal foam or other contraceptive of your choice.

6. At first you may experience light fatigue after sexual activity. However, the body's vital reserves will rapidly increase so that all fatigue will disappear despite a minor loss of power.

7. Some vital energy is lost in this method. Loss is avoided with the more perfect Internal Locking Method described later in this chapter. The energy loss of External Locking is usually 40 to 60% of the power of the seed. Nevertheless, this is greatly preferable to indiscriminate ejaculation of the fluid. The External Locking very appreciably improves strength and virility. It is an excellent beginner's method and prelude to the Internal Locking.

MASSAGE THE PERINEUM AFTERWARDS

After using the External Locking, you must massage two key acupuncture points of the body. The first of these points is called the Hui-Yin or perineum. It is the midpoint between the anus and scrotum. You pressed this point to lock in the seed. The other point is the Chang-Chiang, midway between the coccyx and the anus.

DIAGRAM 26

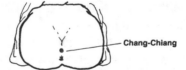

The Chang-Chiang point lies between
the coccyx tip & the anus.

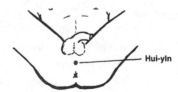

The perineum lies midway between
the anus & the scrotum.

Gently massage the perineum & coccyx
areas to facilitate reabsorption of the
seminal fluid & to prevent congestion
of energy in the prostate gland.

Hui-Yin: This is the starting point of the energy path running up the front of the trunk. It is the bottom of the trunk. The Hui-Yin links the highest point, the "Crown" of the head of Pai-Hui, with the lowest point on the sole of the foot, the Yung Ch'uan.

From the Pai-Hui (the crown of the head) the power of the heavens is drawn into the body. From the Yung-Ch'uan (sole of the foot) the power of the earth is absorbed into the body's web of etheric energy. The Hui-Yin (perineum) is thus the central point between the crown and the sole. It is a crucial midway juncture of energy transmission.

Through the Hui-Yin (perineum) the Yin energy, the energy of the earth, enters the trunk. The energy of the testes also enters and leaves the body through this door. In other words, when the door of the Hui-Yin is closed, it retains the life energy. But when ejaculation opens the Hui-Yin, vital power can spill out with dire consequences. Slowly flowing blood settles and stagnates in the Hui-Yin. When the blood lingers there due to weak flow of the chi and gravitational influence, many health problems arise. Hemorrhoids may develop. The veins bloat with blood when chi constantly leaks out through the lower body energy door.

Chang-Chiang: The point lies between the coccyx tip and the anus. Through this point the power flows up to the head. From the head energy will radiate forth to the entire body.

At the Chang-Chiang many major nerves terminate. It is never the beginning of the second main route of electrical energy in the body known as the Governor Meridian. This route runs from the Chang-Chiang to the Pai-Hui to the palate of the mouth roof.

Massage the Hui-Yin and Chang-Chiang vigorously with 27 to 81 circular rotations on the point with two thicknesses of folded silk cloth. Massage with the middle three fingers. The use of silk cloth helps prevent irritation in these sensitive areas. It also increases the flow of power by generating electricity.

The massage helps release muscular tension and facilitates reabsorption of the seminal fluid. It is essential in preventing any prostrate problems. Most importantly, it stimulates the power flow up to the Pai-Hui Crown of the head.

BE AWARE OF THE MAGNITUDE OF POWER GENERATED

The power which you have begun to generate with retention of the seed is enormous. It has the force to crack massive bone. For this reason the sutures atop the skull of advanced adepts often loosen. The power can drill through the plates of the skull, increasing cranial capacity and opening direct access to higher energies.

The practices advocated herein may allow one to regain part of the prodigious learning and regenerative powers of the child. The only humans with loose skull sutures are the evolved adept and the infant. The meditational practices taught in the books and courses at the Taoist Esoteric Yoga Centers allow one to replicate another aspect of the child's life processes. They allow one to direct energy along the passages of electrical respiration used by the foetus in the womb. The foetus uses energy far more efficiently than the human being at any other stage in his/her existence.

The vastness of this accomplishment in the womb makes other works of human creation seem comparatively insignificant. The meditational process acts to renew the fountains of creative energy that flowed when we were in metamorphosis from a single microscopic dot to a quadrillion-celled human being.

After one to three months of practice the beginner at seminal retention may experience a certain feeling of pressure in the head. For some this feeling will be very unpleasant; for others, it will be not only tolerable but rather pleasurable. This feeling of pressure is the vital power rising to the top of the head with unaccustomed intensity. It is a sign of progress: the body has far exceeded its usual capacity of life force.

Those born for the practice of esoteric loving enjoy this life intensity. This feeling is an early sign of the development of a super-chemistry of the body. It has been popularized by Hindu-based yoga teachings in the west as the Kundalini force. With this chemistry energy normally lost is retained and transformed into higher states of health and consciousness. A gradual heightening of this vital force poses no danger to your health. However, if the power surges too strongly or grows very uncomfortable, it may be released or vented to other parts of the body. Physical labor, massaging the feet, and a heavy grain or meat diet will also help to ground this energy.

If you don't wish to perform the venting exercise (see chapter six) or to advance further on this path at this time you may simply ejaculate once or twice to release the excess power. Then once again carefully harbor the seed for superior health and pleasure until the pressure builds to too great a point. Again, you ejaculate if you wish. Even this practice of ejaculating once or twice every one to three months will result in a substantial economizing of energies lost in the ordinary way of life. You can enjoy tremendous advantages if you hold on to the seed regularly in this way without advancing to higher levels in the practice.

ROTATE SEX ENERGY TO THE HEAD AFTERWARDS

Rotation of the sexual energy upward is a most important practice after External Locking. The three finger method keeps much of the power from escaping but it does not, by itself, drive the energy upward. Thus a special technique has been evolved for this important removal of the power.

This method removes sex power from the lower centers to the reservoirs of power in the head. When the head is charged to capacity with energy, high quality energy overflows to the entire frame. The method is similar to Testicle Breathing (chapter 5), with the difference that there is a reservoir of ching chi amassed during love-making and held inside the lower trunk of the body. Because the energy is already removed from the testicles and is warmed (but in the process of cooling) after love-making, this rotation of energy to the head is far more potent than Testicle Breathing.

Basic Technique: After intercourse using the External Locking, wash and massage the Hui-Yin and Chang-Chiang points with a silken cloth, or your fingers if none is available. Then assume a lying position on the right side. Draw power from the penis, testes and Hui-Yin up to the head. The tongue must be pressed against the palate, as in all exercises where the energy is circulated.

Draw up the power from sexual organs as in the testicle breathing. Don't use too much force as you inhale the air. Upon exhalation, fix the power at the highest point to which it has flowed. Do not let the power fall from its highest point when you exhale. Then draw up the power anew from the three lower centers on the next inhalation.

To understand this process, you need only think of filling a very long straw with water. The bottom of the straw is at your penis/testicle and the top of the straw is the crown of your head. The straw is too long to fill with one breath, so you must inhale and then stop the end while exhaling. Otherwise, the fluid will run out, and you will have to start all over again. Fix the power at the level to which it has been drawn, then exhale; then inhale the fluid still higher. You will feel a cool energy (or warm if still sexually aroused) leave your groin and pass up your spine.

Keep driving the power higher and higher up the spine into the skull and Pai-Hui. It may take one or two months for the power to pass the coccyx, but once it passes this difficult bridgehead, it will leap up to the middle of the back. Then it will jump to the nape of the neck and from there up to the Pai-Hui.

After some weeks or months of practice (depending on the individual's body and frequency of practice) the head reservoir will fill and the power will run down the front of the body with relative ease. It travels through the point between the brows, then down through the roof of the mouth to the tongue tip. It continues through the throat, chest, and navel. Collect the energy at your navel, when the chi is full in the navel (cauldron) it will overflow to the sex center and rejuvenate the sex organs, and complete the circuit at the Hui-Yin.

This technique will not be realized overnight. While you feel the lukewarm (the retained sperm) in the lower body within days or weeks, it may take a few months to bring it completely up the back and into the head. Don't be discouraged: if you persist the power will definitely flow. You will open a critically important route for the passage of vitality to all parts of the body.

When you have completed this circuit, you will feel a flow of cool energy, the Yin Energy, circulating the entire length of the route. This is a very important accomplishment and marks the completion of a cardinal step in your increasing power and health.

SUMMARY OF THE EXTERNAL LOCKING METHOD

A. During love-making
1. When you feel ejaculation is imminent, use the three fingers to stop the flow of the seminal fluid.
B. After love-making
1. Wash and gently massage the Hui-Yin (perineum) and Chang-Chiang (coccyx) with a folded silk cloth.

2. Lying on the right side, draw the power up to the head from the penis, testes and Hui-Yin. When full let it flow down to the palate,

throat, heart center, solar plexus and collect the energy in the navel. Finally recirculate the sexual energy back to strengthen the sexual organs.

INTERNAL LOCKING: DRAW NECTAR UP TO THE GOLDEN FLOWER

More than any other part of the book this method requires close study. It explains in detail the essential practice of semen retention, transformation, and exchange of male and female energies. You will do well at first to adhere closely to the technique as I describe it. When you attain a fundamental mastery, you may experiment and make suitable changes. You will find certain techniques consistently effective. Everybody is different, so use what works best. Remember that seminal retention is a means to an end and not itself the ultimate goal. We save seed to gather energy so that we may more deeply delight in love and life.

True esoteric methods are not complicated. If only a genius can do it, it is probably no great practice. The simplicity of esoteric love is itself the real secret. I explain everything in fine detail so there will be no lingering questions or risk of misguiding you. But once you get it, its simple. For brevity's sake I will refer to the practice of "Draw Nectar Up to the Golden Flower" as simply "The Big Draw." This is the abbreviated term my English speaking students use in place of the more ancient Chinese name, and describes the process most succinctly.

For the sake of clarity I have broken down the Big Draw method into its component parts. When practiced properly it is a single action performed by your unified body, mind, and soul. If you feel these three aspects of your person are not well integrated, work on mastering the Big Draw on the physical level and meditate everyday on the microcosmic orbit to aid in evenly distributing your energy. You may go through a rough period if you have a lot of blocks or impurities that your newly heightened chi is attempting to clean out. With continued practice you will feel the chi of your physical body become more integrated with the subtle sexual essence and spirit of your person. You will know this by the way your life begins to flow more smoothly and lovingly.

THE SECRET STEPS TO BLOCK EJACULATION
IN THE BIG DRAW

To resist the urge to ejaculate you must block the nerve impulse that causes ejaculation. The basic technique for interrupting the impulse is strong, rapid clenching of the under trunk muscles, teeth and fists. You do this nerve-blocking after you have finished the first round of thrusting.

Step 1: Stop Thrusting, Squeeze Tightly and Retreat.
    As a thrusting technique for the beginner I suggested three slow, shallow thrusts followed by one deep thrust to the bottom of the vagina. The most sensitive part of the vagina lies at the outermost two inches. This region is thickly covered with nerves and corresponds to the first two inches of a man's penis. Deeper inside, the web of nerves grows less dense.

DIAGRAM 27

THE BIG DRAW

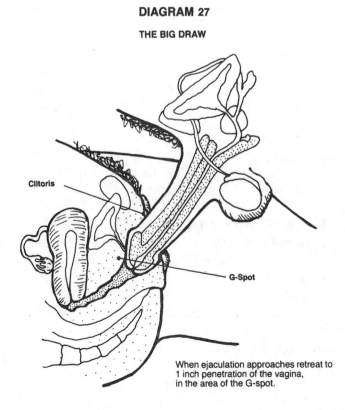

Clitoris

G-Spot

When ejaculation approaches retreat to
1 inch penetration of the vagina,
in the area of the G-spot.

As you dive deeper she grows tighter. Consequently, seminal retention becomes more difficult. In terms of our "battle of the sexes" metaphor, plunging deeply too often is like repeatedly entering too far into enemy territory. There the encircling enemy overcomes you. Retreat from deep penetration is treacherous. To do it successfully requires great discipline and little movement.

With practice you build up first to six shallow, and later nine shallow, alternated with one deep thrust. If you are a novice at seminal retention, or if you encounter a new or exciting partner, you may find it difficult to go 81 shallow (and 9 deep) strokes before resting.

When you first sense ejaculation approaching, no matter what the number of strokes, stop thrusting and tightly close the urogenital diaphragm. When you stop thrusting do not pull out altogether. Retreat to about one inch of penetration in the vagina. Remain there until you've regained control. Thrusting itself generates a great deal of electricity. Still more electromagnetic energy is produced during the sex act because the hundreds of millions of sperm swim more quickly than usual. As energy accumulates in the genital system, local nerves shoot stimulation up the spinal column to the brain, which gives the order to fire. In this sense even genital orgasm really occurs in your mind. You are just training your mind to have a higher, more mentally and spiritually integrated orgasm.

If your partner tries to wrap her body around you and pull you in deeply, retreat to the point where she can no longer follow you. When she lowers her arched back, follow her down, staying near the mouth of her vagina. Teach the woman to rest when you need to recover your composure: never forget that she is your supreme ally when you gain her loving cooperation.

Step 2: Do 9 Rapid Hard Contractions While Holding The Breath.
After inhaling through the nose, quickly perform 9 very hard contractions of the entire undertrunk musculature, teeth and fists. This is a variation of the form you have been practicing as the Power Lock exercise in 36 repetitions. In that exercise you did one long muscle contraction for each deep breath. For the Big Draw you do 9 rapid muscular contractions for each breath. These contractions are very hard and absorb so much power that little energy remains in the nerves to trigger ejaculation. Do up to six sets of 9 contractions, until the urge to ejaculate leaves you.

With this method your excited sex energy tends to leave the nerves and lodge in the contracting muscles. The breath taken after 9 contractions must be drawn in quickly so that the nerve impulse is cut as frequently as possible. Repeating the 9 contractions 6 times should definitely reduce the urge to ejaculate. You may do less than the 6 sets of 9 contractions if fewer sets allow you to regain self-control. Because you are lying in the arms of a woman with your penis inside her vagina, your seed will be far more volatile, like a young bucking bronco with a spur under its saddle. The added nine contractions of the Big Draw are necessary at first to rein the seed under your control. In time you are able to remove the irritating bucking caused by the spur and enjoy a smooth and powerful ride.

Your genital glands expand in preparation for shooting forth the fluid. The Big Draw contractions reduce their size, literally squeezing the energy out of them and lessening sexual-electrical tension. The shorter the time interval between contractions, the greater the power of the muscles to grip the seed. If much time elapses between clenchings, the muscles get poor traction. Inhalation also must be too swift to allow energy to slip back into the genital region. Holding the breath through all 9 contractions weakens the nerve impulse to ejaculate.

Your goal is to change the direction of the seminal fluid. Physically speaking, the speed of your sperm energy must be accelerated up the spine. Acceleration takes place only at the moment of muscle contraction itself and not while holding onto the contraction. Thus, it takes many separate contractions to drive the fluid deep into the body and defeat the urge to spend your seed.

Step 3: Clench Buttocks Tightly.

Tightly clench your buttocks. The importance of this cannot be overemphasized. The driving power of the largest muscle in the body must be turned to advantage. Bring the two cheeks together with such force that you actually lift up the whole body.

Maintaining good tone of the buttocks is crucially important for overall health. When this muscle is flaccid, power continuously drains out of the body. When it is firm one of the two main lower body energy leaks is plugged. The other lower body energy leak is through the penis in ejaculation.

One can tolerate pain more easily when clenching the muscles very tightly. Just as the nervous impulse called "pain" is weakened by hard muscular contraction, so is the nervous impulse to ejaculate weakened. In both cases the muscles absorb energy: this interferes with the nervous message. Contraction of certain key muscle groups withdraws energy from the genital area. Clenching the buttocks is especially helpful in breaking the nerve circuit between the brain and genitals at the base of the spine. Squeeze the buttocks until they are rock hard; the message to ejaculate is in effect intercepted and never delivered.

Step 4: Clench Teeth Tightly.

Clench your teeth and push your tongue hard to the roof of your mouth. Clenching the teeth tightly interrupts nervous flow at the head and neck. It also helps tighten the buttocks. These two muscle contractions must be simultaneous, so that they reinforce each other and secure complete locking. As you clench, press the semen deeper and deeper into the body. Greatest retraction of fluid occurs toward the end of the count: during the 7th, 8th and 9th clenchings you drive the fluid most deeply inward. Be irresistibly determined to force back the fluid. The contractions from 1 to 9 should grow harder and stronger.

As you prolong the act of intercourse, your pleasure will grow more intense. When you reach a high level of pleasure, you should keep the urogenital diaphragm constantly closed. This helps prevent the sperm from sneaking halfway out the door. Stop the fluid behind the dam. When it has spilled over, attempts to stop it or to harness its power are futile. You must stop the ejaculation before the sperm has begun to move within the body.

Step 5: Pull The Wave Of Energy From Genitals to Head

The Big Draw may be conceived as an internal wave beginning with contraction at the penis tip, moving through the perineum and buttocks up the spine to the head. In this way the energy, traveling along the crest of voluntary muscular contraction, will be forced up to the crown.

If you have difficulty drawing power to the head, you may draw it first to the navel. After it accumulates there for a while, again direct the power down to the hui-yin and up the spine to the head. It should help it flow more easily, particularly if you have carefully harbored the seed.

DIAGRAM 28

THE BIG DRAW

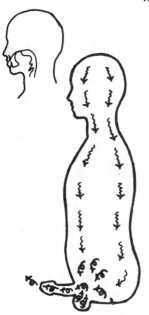

Inhale & pull orgasmic energy to the head. If you have difficulty drawing power to the head, first draw it to the navel, accumulate it there & direct the power down to the Hui-Yin & up the spine to the head.

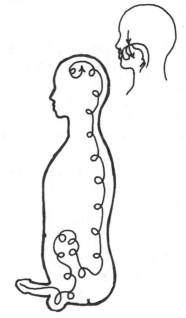

Exhale & release yang energy and all tension by relaxing the head, throat, chest, adbomen & pelvis. Let the relaxation spread from the top to the bottom of the body in a wave. Allow the energy to flow into your partner.

Relaxation after the Big Draw dilates the contracted blood vessels in the penis. It is actually at this point, where no effort at all is exerted, that you absorb the greatest amount of yin energy. During the Big Draw the woman's power enters the man's lower body. During relaxation the power shoots up to the higher centers. This effect is particularly noticeable when you have practiced the Power Lock Exercise.

At first the repeated exertion of the Big Draw may seem very difficult, and ruinous to love-making, but with practice it will become easier to perform. Hold back the mutinous seed that would crash through the lower body door and disperse your powers. Your will power to control semen loss will grow stronger each time you use it. The stronger your will power to prevent loss of your sexual essence grows the greater your will power becomes in all of your life. In work, play, family relationships, your will to love and spiritually grow unfolds with a renewed vigor that daily will surprise you.

Step 6: If Erection Is Lost, Begin Thrusting and Use Gentle Sucking.

After the first round of thrusting and Hard Contractions, you may occasionally contract the penis head inside the woman while you are thrusting. The penis head is like a baby gently sucking milk at his mother's breast. You begin to lightly draw the Yin in this manner. The Big Draw has greater effect when the penis is already filled with Yin energy from Gentle Sucking.

Keep clear in your mind the difference between the Gentle Sucking and the Big Draw. Gentle Sucking accompanies regular thrusting. Only the penis head, testes and uro-genital diaphragm are contracted: the rest of the muscles remain relaxed and do not draw in power. In this technique we do not drive the energy far. We prevent our own energy from inching forward and leaping out into the woman. We also fill the penis itself with energy which we will transfer to the head with the Big Draw.

BIG DRAW FOR WOMEN

The woman should also perform the Big Draw, using the vagina to suck in the Yang power from the man's penis. The detailed explanation for women will be found in the next book, Ovarian Kung Fu. Until the detailed explanation appears, she may simply adapt the principles of Seminal Kung Fu and perform the Big Draw on her ovaries. Women often have a good intuitive understanding of the process; hence their sexual superiority. But higher levels of love always exist. I strongly suggest that women train to suppress her genital orgasm. This will appreciably reduce her loss of energy in the act of love. She too can gradually achieve a "higher" orgasm as a "mysterious portal" to the Tao. Man and woman can attain the Tao together by this way of "dual cultivation."

THE BIG DRAW AND MASTURBATION

The Big Draw method works well for single men who either cannot find a woman partner or who have chosen to remain celibate. Men with lovers may also choose in the beginning to train themselves alone. In fact, I recommend this for most men, as it is much easier to block the urge to ejaculate when you are not being stimulated by the heat and touch of a woman. The Big Draw for single men is performed exactly the same way as described for couples, only instead of thrusting into a woman's vagina the single man stimulates his penis glans by caressing and massaging it.

This is different from masturbation which ends in ejaculation. You must break the urge to ejaculate before the semen escapes, using the rapid hard contractions and clenching of the Big Draw. This may be done in any position—standing, sitting, or lying—but standing may be preferable at first as it firmly roots your feet on the ground and connects you with its cooling yin energy.

A good reason for practicing the Big Draw alone is that you can clearly observe if you have mastered the first level of the method, physical control over ejaculation.

When you arouse your penis, massage it until you sense the first glimmering of the urge to ejaculate, and then do the Big Draw before the sperm begins to move. You should do the contractions and raw repeatedly until you see your penis become flaccid. The stiffness of your penis becomes the barometer of your ability to do the Big Draw. The more quickly you can soften the erection, the closer you are to mastering the method. Eventually you will be able to command it down with your mind by merely drawing the energy out of your penis and bringing it to your head without any muscular clenching.

This method can be extremely useful to any man who feels sexually frustrated. You simply make love internally, between the yin and yang poles within your body, imagining you are pulling the ching chi up to make love to your highest center, the crown. However, if you lose your seed while masturbating it will go for nothing, and thus masturbation is far worse than losing your seed to a woman, who at least gains from it and gives her sweet yin essence in exchange. Even if you retain your seed, masturbation offers only a very dry, yang energy that can be very fiery and intense but imbalanced, unless you know the higher level meditation to de-

velop the male yin energy pole. That is why masturbation should
be used for training purposes only; it is not advisable to develop a
strong attachment to it that might prevent you from maturing. This
training stage for some men might last as long as a year or two. It
will depend on how frequently you practice the Big Draw and other
pelvic exercises and on the availability of a suitable partner.

MORNING ERECTION HAS POTENT CHI

The other occasion in which all men can use the Big draw alone is
at night or in the early morning in bed when they wake up with a
powerful erection. This is very powerful and pure ching chi produced after your body and mind have been charged with sleep.
Some Taoists think this is the most potent chi available to a man. It
is undiluted by any psychic toxins from another, and your own
mind is so relaxed and free of outside tension that it can absorb the
energy more easily than at other times.

   You can do the Big Draw lying in bed on your right side until
the erection disappears. It may take more contractions because of
the amount of sexual energy pooled in the sperm palace. If this
produces too much energy in the head, be sure to bring it down to
your navel by focusing your mind there and spiralling it a small
circle 3" in diameter. Do this first clockwise (imagine a clock at
your navel facing outward) and then counter-clockwise. This will
balance and center the excess energy. If this is insufficient, do the
venting exercise as well.

INTENSE ENERGY IN THE HEAD MUST BE VENTED

During the Hard Contractions power is drawn in forced up from the
lower trunk. Power is simultaneously forced down from the head.
Thus tremendous pressure builds in the mid-trunk. This high pressure energy must be vented: it cannot go out the penis or anus for
you have locked these shut.

   It shoots up to the ear and eye and escapes slightly from these
apertures. As the power passes through these organs it invigorates
them. If the eyes are kept open at this point and moved somewhat
in their sockets, more restorative energy will flow to them

   The power which you have begun to generate with retention
of the seed is enormous. It has the force to crack massive bone.

For this reason the sutures atop the skull of advanced adepts often loosen. The power can drill through the plates of the skull, increasing cranial capacity and oepning direct access to higher energies.

The practices advocated herein may allow one to regain part of the prodigious learning and regenerative powers of the child. The only humans with loose skull sutures are the evolved adept and the infant.

After one to three months of practice the beginner at seminal retention may experience a certain feeling of pressure in the head. For some this feeling will be very unpleasant; for others, it will be not only tolerable but rather pleasurable. This feeling of pressure is the vital power rising to the top of the head with unaccustomed intensity. It is a sign of progress: the body has far exceeded its usual capacity of life force.

Those born for the practice of esoteric loving will enjoy this life intensity. This feeling is an early sign of the development of a super-chemistry of the body. With this chemistry energy normally lost is retained and transformed into higher states of health and consciousness. Such heightening of vital force poses no danger to your health. However, if the power grows very uncomfortable, it may be released, vented to other parts of the body, used to im-power meditation or spent creatively in other areas of your life and work.

AUTOMATIC MIND CONTROL OF EJACULATION

According to Taoist tradition, in the beginning of mankind our ancestors had the ability to control sex instinctively. They could control emotions, ejaculation, and sex as they wished. But gradually our ancestors were drained off of this ability. Through over-sex, overpleasure, overdrinking, and over thinking by overspend-ing themselves, they gradually lost this ability. This ability can be restored to the mind by training it to automatically stop the leakage of sexual energy. The key is repeated practice of the big draw until you do it instinctively. Then the nectar of your sexual essence will flow continuously up to the crown of your head, the golden flower. In Automatic mind control the pineal gland is the most important key to link the sex organ to the brain.

The greatest goal for this locking is that after 6 to 21 months, or 10,000 Big Draws, you will be able to use the mind alone to draw it up anytime or anywhere, whether standing, sitting or talking. If you can draw up and shut the leaking door continuously for a week, that means you are beginning to assume control. At that point, put your concentration on the crown (pineal gland) and try to just think the power up without using any big force, and eventually the door will close automatically and for as along as you want. When you put your mind at the crown, its pulls the power up to the head.

Some people may pull too often, or do it the wrong way thus feeling the power stuck in the heart. To release it drink honey in tea or use the hand to brush it down the front of the body towards the navel where it is safer to store. If energy remains stuck in the heart, just do normal breathing and use the mind to cure. Start circulating your chi from the perineum. Breathe in and think from the Hui-Yin (the Gate of Death and Life) up to the top of the head (pineal) and down to the third eye (Yin-Tang) between the eyebrows. Stop for awhile. Then breathe down and when it passes through the heart, try to think of it as flowing down like a waterfall and entering the navel 9 to 36 times will gradually take the power stuck in the heart out.

You will eventually reach the state where you can control your sexual urge anytime you want. Even at night when erect, you can just pull the power up and the erection will drop and the mind and the sex organs will be at one. You can control sex like a voluntary muscle of the arm. The understanding it takes to reach this stage depends on the person. Some get it quicker and some more slowly. Practice is the key. After trying for a while you will eventually have more confidence and can command the sex organs or command the door of immortals (Gate of Death and Life) to open and close at will.

Points to remember:

1. After you've really succeeded in using the mind to control the urge of ejaculation, the second or third day you may feel some pain in Hui-Yin or penis. This is a normal thing to happen. The mind orders the muscles to contract and push the fluid back which uses a lot of muscle power to hold that flow. Naturally, you will have the soreness of muscles in that area. Just rub the Hui-Yin in that area and try to relax the muscle. After a few more times you will not feel anything any more.

2. Some people, if they have been collecting a lot of power this way, might feel very hot and some might have an irritating feeling to vomit or headache because the sexual energy is stuck in the head of chest and the power is too great. This is a mild case of the "Kundalini syndrome". The method mentioned of eating honey or brushing the chest alone cannot solve the problem. You may have to use running to burn the energy away, or other extensive exercises. The energy should be disposed of in a non degenerate way. Completing the Microcosmic Orbit is the most important safety valve to help distribute the sexual energy evenly.

3. In the final stages of automatic mind control of sexual energy, there is no need to clench the teeth, anus and buttocks. The whole body stays relaxed and you contract not the buttocks but the front urogenital diaphragm and the perineum only.

4. To more easily achieve the goal of automatic internal locking, bear in mind you can do internal locking any time you want, driving the car, sitting down, coffee or doing work. Practice contracting the urogenital diaphragm, the contraction in front, not the buttocks. Do this until you can fully control an erection or an urge to ejaculate with a flicker of your mind.

PART III

**TRANSFORMING SEXUAL ENERGY INTO
SPIRITUAL LOVE**

CHAPTER 9

THE YIN AND YANG EXCHANGE: CULTIVATING THE VALLEY ORGASM

"Yang can function only with the cooperation of Yin, Yin can grow only in the presence of Yang"
—*Yellow Emperor's Female Consultant on Sex.*

Our universe changes perpetually because of the eternal flow of yin and yang energies. The very essence of yin-yang exchange is the cyclical alternation of day and night. Due to this alternating energy flow, this respiration of the heavens, living things can grow. Were there only day and no night, all would be burnt; or if there were only night and no day, nothing would have strength to grow. As living things, humans are also subject to the law of yin and yang exchange.

The human being can live happily only if he/she is in harmony with the principles of life. If one violates the law of the yin and yang interchange, by forbidding the sexual communion of yin and yang energy, energy will not flow in the body. The life force will slowly stagnate and leach out. Life will become a long slide into depression interspersed by spasms of enslavement to the passions.

If you have learned to block the urge to ejaculate, or even decided that you have the will to learn the Tao of love, you are on the threshold of a new experience. That experience will alter your perceptions of your own body and mind. It will change the way you see your lover, and change your understanding of sex and love.

Drawing Nectar up to the Golden Flower is incomplete without the Exchange of Yin and Yang energy. The Golden Flower is the light at the crown of the head. The Big Draw conserves your nectar, the sexual essence. It is exchanging your ching with your lover that transforms it, and in the process gives you an experience of sex which is deeply shared as love. Your orgasm will be totally unlike that known to simple ejaculators. As you make love over periods of time, the pleasure spreads over and fills the entire body. This orgasm of the whole body is unknown to quick-ejaculating males whose thrill is confined primarily to the genital area. Most important you will gain a new sense of inner equilibrium that will be stored in your body long after your pleasure has become a flitting memory.

This method prolongs penetration to one-half hour, one hour, two hours, or more. You can enjoy this form of sexual love indefinitely without paying for your pleasure with your life force. The difference is in the type of orgasm. The ordinary one may be called the Peak Orgasm: one fleeting moment of intense, even excruciating pleasure, then nothing.

Taoists advocate the Valley Orgasm: continual rolling expansion of the orgasm throughout the whole body. The Valley Orgasm provides more gradual, but ultimately greatly heightened ecstasy. Carlos Suares used an image similar to the Taoist Valley Orgasm to distinguish true loving in sex from ejaculation: "Erotically, the man is more like a valley watered by innumerable streams than like a deep gorge where an overwhelming torrent rushes along."

During the Valley Orgasm, lovers can relax and have all the time in the world to share their tenderness. There is no frenzied explosion, only wave after wave of higher subtle energies bathing the entwined man and woman. The Valley Orgasm is not a technique, but rather a certain kind of experience that the lovers allow to happen to themselves. But it can be encouraged by following this time-tested process:

1. **Timing:** after thrusting, relax and exchange energy.

Following the Hard Contractions of the Big Draw return to thrusting. After another round of 81 shallow (and 9 deep) thrusts, you may again be drawing near ejaculation. Meanwhile, the woman has been highly stimulated by your passion. She, too, may be approaching orgasm.

When she becomes very excited, the vaginal lubricant flows

DIAGRAM 29

ORDINARY ORGASM

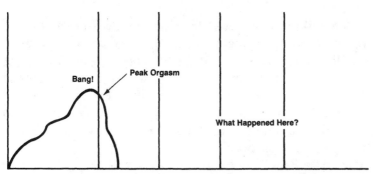

Bang! Peak Orgasm

What Happened Here?

Genital orgasm with ejaculation is intense but cuts short love-making.

VALLEY ORGASM

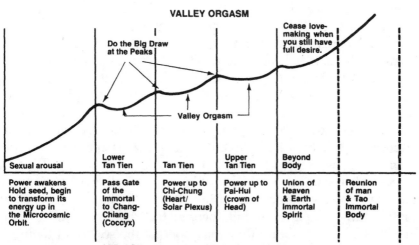

Do the Big Draw at the Peaks

Cease love-making when you still have full desire.

Valley Orgasm

Sexual arousal	Lower Tan Tien	Tan Tien	Upper Tan Tien	Beyond Body	Reunion
Power awakens Hold seed, begin to transform its energy up in the Microcosmic Orbit.	Pass Gate of the Immortal to Chang-Chiang (Coccyx)	Power up to Chi-Chung (Heart/ Solar Plexus)	Power up to Pai-Hui (crown of Head)	Union of Heaven & Earth Immortal Spirit	Reunion of man & Tao Immortal Body

Valley Orgasms are spontaneous openings for lovers, to higher levels of Taoist Chi cultivation.

more freely. In this fluid there are large amounts of Yin energy. Following the second series of thrusts you need to perform the Big Draw a second time to prevent ejaculation. Or if the woman is about to have an orgasm, cease rubbing while she performs the Big Draw. In either case, the momentum of your sexual energies should be established and moving up toward your higher centers.

At this point cease thrusting and begin to exchange the restorative energies with her. You will gently release the hot, male Yang energy into her. She will release the cool, female Yin into you. Remember you cannot take in her power without giving freely of your own. The exchange heals both. Man needs the soft receptive energies a woman produces to achieve perfect balance. And woman needs the expanding male energies to attain her own higher harmony. This is the underlying reason for the attraction of the sexes to begin with.

2. Position: When you cease from active thrusting and begin your embrace in any pleasing position. If the man is heavy, the woman should usually be on top. If the woman is stronger than the man, she should usually be on the bottom so that he can draw the power more easily. If the woman is weaker she may be on top where she can draw more readily. In any case, make sure it is a position you can rest in for a long while. You should keep two extra pillows handy for this purpose.

3. Coordinate Breathing With Your Lover.

"Chi" means "breath" in Chinese. Life is breath. All living activity has the quality of inhalation, exhalation, or some combination of the two. This is why Chinese philosophy classifies everything as Yin (exhalation) or Yang (inhalation) to a greater or lesser degree. The act of love is essentially an act of respiration. You breathe your ching into your lover's body and soul. You inhale this life energy by drawing it up to the head and exhale it into your partner.

So after you have stopped thrusting and embraced your lover, coordinate the breathing. Each partner places his ear near the lover's nose with chest to chest. In this position you can easily feel the other's breathing. In the act of love the breath cycles stimulate and harmonize all processes of life. Physically breathing together unifies the two partners and focuses the rhythm of all of their energies so that together they may contact the source of their life current. You should become so sensitive to the presence of her breath that you feel yourself inside her breath as deeply and strongly as if you were pushing your penis into the bottom of her vagina.

4. Inhale Power Up Spine To The Head, Exhale Out The Penis.

After you breathe together for a time, gradually draw the power up to the crown of the head. On the inhale the man thinks the yin power from the vagina into the penis and the woman thinks the yang power from the penis into the vagina. Both draw it back to the Hui-Yin, (the perineum) the Chang-Chiang (the coccyx) and up the back in steps to the Pai-Hui (crown). From there it goes through the tongue which is, during the whole exercise, raised to the top of the mouth.

The goal is not to use muscular force to help (as in the Big Draw), but simply to use the power of thought to direct the sexual energy. Think it up. This instruction may sound baffling on first reading, but those who have begun to do sexual kung fu will start to feel the power and will understand intuitively what I mean. The power will rise to the head eventually as your mind learns how to direct its own chi energy connecting the mind and body.

In the beginning, you can accelerate the exchange of yin/yang power with a long, deep muscular contraction. When the vaginal fluid seethes inside the woman, inhale slowly and deeply through the nostrils. While you inhale contract the penis, Hui-Yin, anus, buttocks, jaws and fists, in that order. As you tighten this contraction, think the power into the penis, past the Hui-Yin, into the Chang-Chiang and up the spine into the crown of the head. When you have finished the inhalation, hold the breath and contraction for as long as you can. Keep drawing the power up to the head until you can hold the breath no longer.

DIAGRAM 30

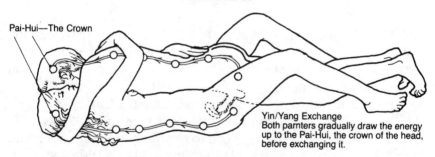

Pai-Hui—The Crown

Yin/Yang Exchange
Both parnters gradually draw the energy up to the Pai-Hui, the crown of the head, before exchanging it.

When you release the breath, consciously give your excess Yang energy and heat to the woman. To successfully bestow the power upon her, you must exhale deeply. Release all tension by relaxing the head, throat, chest, abdomen and pelvis. Let the relaxation spread from the top to the bottom of the body in a wave. When the gentle wave reaches the pelvic region, send the Yang warmth energy not seed!—into the woman through the penis. The contraction and relaxation should be done gently, creating a feeling of pulsation travelling between your body and hers.

Lovingly offer her your essential energy. This surrender shall carry with it all emotions of love and devotion. This is not mean sentimentality. It will inspire her to surrender her nourishing yin essence and to totally embrace the yang within yin. This is the nature of her fulfillment. If you attempt to withhold your energy, she will sense—consciously or unconsciously—your sense of separateness, your stubborn ego, which is in one sense nothing more than energy stuck in one place (usually the head in the male). So allow her to absorb the Yang energy she needs while you surrender the excess which might have forced you to ejaculate. As the urge to ejaculate fades with relaxation, the Yin energy will flood your entire body while the Yang floods into her.

If you are just beginning to practice, you may be so overwhelmed by the sensations of sexual love that it will seem impossible to distinguish her yin energy from your yang. Everything may seem hot and explosive and a single energy. As you build up your nervous system to handle higher charges of energy without ejaculating, the exchange of yin and yang energy will gradually come into awareness. If you build energy at successive points in the body, greater powers of exchange will open to you and your lover. You can start by drawing the power to the Hui-Yin and meditating there.

If the man has more power than the woman he may help the woman to open her centers by sending his power to her unopened centers: both concentrate their attention on these points. Chi will flow wherever the mind is focused. After the power flows into the Hui-Yin (perineum) send it back up to the Chang-Chiang (coccyx). While meditating there, you will feel a little pain and tickling on the scrotum as the center opens. Then to the Ming-Men, door of life in the back opposite the navel, T11 the adrenal glands. When you feel the power's warmth there send it up to the Gia-Pe point between the shoulder blades.

After it flows there it will feel very warm and will spread to the lung. Next direct it to the "emerald pillow" Yui-Gen, at the top vertebrae on the back of your head. There will be a feeling of heaviness when the center opens. From there bring it up to the crown of the head, on a line drawn between the ear and the nose. The head may feel very heavy or as if there were something drilling up from inside the head. Then transfer it to the point between the mid eyebrows.

Remember that you can't open all of the points in one sexual embrace. To open one point may take many exchanges of yin and yang. If you ejaculate, the power is very hard to exchange, for man loses much power and there remains little to be transferred up. When the energy is full in the upper region then it will come down from the tongue. Bring it down to the navel, and collect it in the navel.

5. The Plateau Phase: Circulate Your Microcosmic Into Your Lover's Orbit

Depending on the level of vital energy and the spiritual development of the individual lovers, a couple over time will experience new "openings" that occur during their love-making. This means you will suddenly find you have made a quantum leap in your feelings and awareness. This usually happens during the plateau phase of the yin/yang exchange. The period of love-making when you are not thrusting passionately is referred to as the "plateau" phase. The "peaks" are the moments prior to the orgasm averted by doing the Big Draw. The "plateau" is the physically passive exchange of energy that occurs between the peaks.

DIAGRAM 31

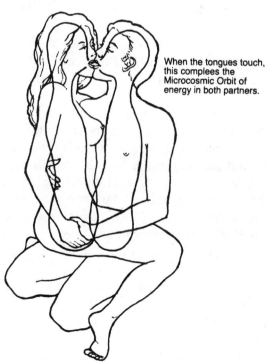

When the tongues touch, this complees the Microcosmic Orbit of energy in both partners.

The subtle energies within your resting bodies are not passive at all, but are moving dynamically between partners, building to a new level of sexual-electromagnetic tension. It is an internal wave of energy building up, an ocean wave that gathers momentum and crashes, only to be replaced by the next wave. After the sexual energy has been raised to a high intensity by thrusting and drawn up the spine on the route of the "Microcosmic Orbit" with the Big Draw, the yin/yang exchange can begin to happen in many different ways.

In the beginning the energy exchange between lovers may seem to be chaotic and happening between any two points of bodily contact. As you grow more accustomed to the energy gained by stopping your ejaculation you will begin to discriminate the clearly defined channels of the microcosmic orbit rising up the spine and descending down the front of the body. During the plateau phase of love making you may feel a warm flowing current passing between her vagina and your penis and between your lips/breasts.

These are the two individual microcosmic orbits joined into one larger flow circling your two bodies. This will greatly enhance the balance of energy in both lovers and deepen the bond of loving in their life. The chi flow is increased in amplitude: you may even feel like a warm electric current is passing between you. This effect often occurs quickly in lovers in good health practicing the Big Draw ranging from only a few love making sessions to several weeks or months.

The two microcosmic circuits, that of the man and the woman, can be joined in a number of different ways. The most common is the intersection of their two circular orbits at the mouths and genitals of the two lovers forming a figure eight. The figure eight can cross as the Microcosmic energy drawn up by the man up his spine is passed into the woman through his tongue, which acts like a kind of electrical switch. The male energy then enters her Microcosmic orbit and goes down her front (functional) channel and down through her vagina, into the penis and back up his spine. The woman circulates her orbit in a parallel fashion, up her back channel and down his front channel before it re-enters her body at the vagina and goes back to her perineum and spine. This is the simplest way to consciously direct this level of exchange of yin and yang energy.

Each couple can play with different figure eight patterns of exchange. At first you may verbally tell your lover what you're concentrating on. Later, as you become more sensitive to your own and your lovers energy, the chi exchange itself will become a silent language, punctuated by the pleasure of sending a tingling warm current into your lover. The figure eight may cross at your mouths only, or at your genitals only if you are not kissing but still lie within her. It may snake around your governor channels—up your spine and down hers, or vice versa.

At this level many couples experience spontaneous openings of some of the 8 special psychic channels taught as the "Fusion of the Five Elements" meditation in the Taoist yoga system. (see chap. 18) These channels include the positive and negative arm and leg routes, the belt routes spiralling around the body, and the thrusting route up the center of the body. Don't be alarmed if your energy goes wild and begins moving in ways to which you are not accustomed. Many lovers experience a column of energy rising on a line midway between their bodies; if it happens to you, just relax and enjoy the play of the subtle energies. Some couples report the chi shooting up to the top of their heads and showering down in a fountain of nectar. Others feel like they are wrapped in a cocoon with their lover, with lines of invisible energy being spun around them.

When you've opened all your psychic channels and you know what is possible in terms of energy exchanges, you will then be free to choose the path of expressing your love at will. It is interesting that lovers who know nothing of these esoteric methods sometimes have similar experiences during sex. They can't do it at will but they do know it first hand from spontaneous opening of subtle energy channels. The Taoist secrets of love are designed to focus your awareness on the infinite possibilities that lie within you. This concentrated awareness is what spontaneously sparks these experiences of divine energy exchange. In this sense love is universally the path to greatest freedom—the more you share with your lover, the more choices open to you.

6. Cultivate A "Valley Orgasm" In The Three Tan Tiens.

When both lovers have shared their chi in the Microcosmic Orbit or other psychic channels, their energy is both intensified and balanced. This sets the stage for a true fusion of their being in the valley orgasm.

The "valley orgasm" is an even higher experience of yin/yang

exchange that goes beyond the Microcosmic. It may occur spontaneously in any couple dedicated to expanding their love and spiritual awareness. No technique can guarantee it will happen, but the
methods taught here vastly increase the probability of a couple
enjoying regular valley orgasms during lovemaking. It is a state of
prolonged orgasm that generally occurs during the plateau phase
when the yin and yang energies come into an exquisitely delicate
balance. It is a fusion of opposites, a meltdown. However, do not
be disappointed if you learn to block ejaculation and master the Big
Draw but do not have a valley orgasm. That happens frequently
and should be expected, especially in a stressful urban setting
where there are so many distracting forces working against the
sustained balance of subtle energies.

DIAGRAM 32

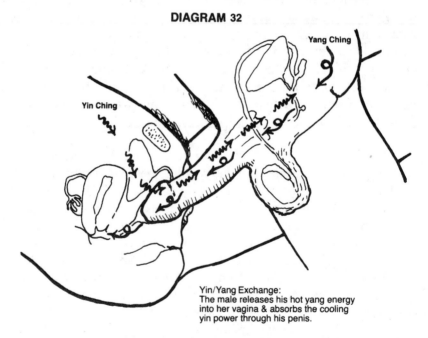

Yin/Yang Exchange:
The male releases his hot yang energy
into her vagina & absorbs the cooling
yin power through his penis.

The lovers simultaneously experience an ''opening'' of an
energy center during a valley orgasm. This releases a tremendous
energy that is truly thrilling as it radiates out to fill every cell of
your body and joins it together with your lover. The Hindus call
these centers ''chakras''. The Taoists refer to them as lower, middle and upper Tan Tien, and locate them in the abdomen, heart,
and head.

In truth, the entire body is one Tan Tien, or field of energy, but in practice it is easier to learn with smaller vortexes of energy until you can handle the greater power. The sequence of opening them is generally starting with the lower and moving up. If higher centers open before the lower ones the energy may be unstable and short lived. In that case the lovers should direct their higher energy into the lower centers to create a more grounded polarity. Filling the lower body with higher energies will lend greater fullness to the feeling of intimacy and create a greater foundation for future exploration of the spiritual world of the two lovers.

The opening of these energy centers is the actual process of transforming your sex essence into spirit. The valley orgasm actually is a fusion of ching, chi, and shien in the two lovers. All three are normally present in everyone, but in a divided and weakened state. The two lovers can supply energies missing in their partner and bring out recessive energies with the simple presence of the opposite subtle polar energy. When you open a new energy center your mind makes a leap in awareness by fusing these three in a spontaneous alchemical process. Your own spirit is purified and is one step closer to becoming centered in your body.

It's important to know that these centers cannot be "forced" open, any more than a child can suddenly be forced to grow up. There are natural stages. That is why you must relax to entice the Tan Tiens to open; then you will experience a valley orgasm as a spontaneous gift, a sparkling jewel bestowed upon you by the Tao. It has been described as a state of profound clarity and serenity, but even these phrases are insufficient to convey its deep beauty and truth.

The more deeply you learn to relax during the yin/yang exchange, the more deeply you can surrender yourself to your lover, the more likely you are to reach the balance of polar forces needed to open each center. This process happens in a split second but can take months or years of subtle fine tuning of energy between lovers. That is why a committment is usually needed to get to the higher levels of dual cultivation—it requires a great deal of time to understand the play of subtle forces and to refine your more gross physical and emotional energies.

Your nervous system must also be strong enough to handle the increased flow of chi experienced during a valley orgasm. That is one of the reasons I teach strengthening exercises like the Power

Lock in chapter 6. Any Tai Chi, Yoga, Chi Kung or other purifying
meditative work is invaluable in this respect as it speeds up and
clarifies the process. Sensitive couples that want to have valley
orgasms without any formal physical discipline could use the sexual cultivation practices taught in this book if their health is good
and they do the Microcosmic and fusion meditations.

DIAGRAM 33

When lovers are in close embrace subtle
yin & yang energies concentrate into
vortexes from the genitals to the head.

The Valley Orgasm can happen when both lovers have harmonized their will power and their breathing during the yin/yang exchange. The energy is flowing between the man and woman and
they collectively focus their attention on each center. It helps to
mentally spiral the energy in a three inch diameter circle (male
clockwise, female counter clockwise) at a point about three inches
inside the body near its center. You should experiment with the
location of the point you focus on, as some people find the energy
is more powerful a little closer to the spine.

The chi energy likes to move in a spiralling motion, so by mentally spiralling at key points you may trigger the release of a far more powerful vortex of energy, the valley orgasm. This spiralling movement of the chi itself is caused by the interaction of male and female energies. This can be seen geometrically in the symbol of the female—the circle, and that of the male—a straight line with an arrowhead. The fusion of these two signs is a spiral which is a circular energy containing a linear energy moving towards the center of the circle. When a man and a woman make love the same thing happens—the yang chi enters the circle of the yin chi. The chi fuses, the circle of energy expands, and spirals upward through both their bodies.

The energy will naturally travel in this sequence, spiralling through:

1. The navel center, or lower Tan Tien is the joining of the many routes of the body. When the navel is opened, all routes in the body will be joined. You will regain something of the terrifying vitality of the new-born baby, for its energy has been fed to it by the mother through the navel,

2. Move the power to the solar plexus, which controls the digestive system, stomach, spleen and liver. This will greatly strengthen your health and will. At the solar plexus center the power is much stronger and purer and widespread. But you must open the navel first for the power to flow up.

3. Move the power into the heart center, which is so important to strengthen the heart and lungs and to amplify your power of love and sympathy. This is the center of the middle Tan Tien, and extends into the areas immediately above and below it,

4. Next move it up to the throat. The throat energy center is the thyroid gland and is the door of the energy between man and Heaven. As it controls speech, it is also known as the creative center.

5. From the throat send the power to the Yin-Tang (or third eye) between the brows which controls the nervous system and soul. Its development calms one and lessens the influence of stress and fear. The head is the upper "field of energy" or tan tien.

6. Finally direct the power to the Pai-Hui, the crown, the center of spiritual knowledge and the doorway to higher spiritual evolution.

VALLEY ORGASM SUMMARY

1. First make love actively, using 3 or 6 shallow strokes for each deep one, or 9 shallow and 1 deep.

2. Stop thrusting when you feel near orgasm. Use the Big Draw to bring power up to the Pai-Hui.

3. Embrace and synchronize the breathing. Get in a comfortable position with no undue stress on the limbs.

4. Open the Microcosmic Orbit by directing your chi around the circuit with the power of thought.

5. Exchange power by circulating your energy in and around your entwined bodies using meditation. Focus your attention on the polar balance of energy in your lower Tan Tien. When the power builds move it upward in a wave towards your middle and upper tan tien.

6. When your energy has been transformed up, or you feel the loss of 50% of your erection, start to thrust again if you wish and build up more energy, keeping the urogenital diaphragm closed, and stopping before ejaculation.

7. Exchange power several times. Each time try to bring the energy up to increasingly higher centers, meditating on each Tan Tien for as long as you feel comfortable.

8. Women should also perform the Big Draw during the act of love. It will help her to tighten the vagina, stimulate hormonal production, and it offers the same benefits of longevity and spiritual development, just as the man's practice does. Remember the Big Draw is a muscular and mental practice; whereas the exchanging practice is a mental and spiritual operation. The higher energy in women is different from men. This study merits a complete work of its own which is projected for a later volume.

In the true Taoist dual cultivation both man and woman are regenerated in the practice, and neither is harmed. It is highly important the practice is not used for selfish interests. I recommend that neither partner have genital orgasm in the higher stages of the practice, although it may not be as great a loss for a woman and might even stimulate her to higher levels sometimes. When one partner approaches too near the orgasmic abyss, the overheating partner must signal the other to stop motion. Either may lessen the urge of orgasm by immediately doing the Big Draw to vent the power away from the genitals.

In the Taoist practice of "single cultivation", a man alone can also induce a kind of inner valley orgasm by learning to balance the exchange of yin/yang energies between his different Tan Tiens. There is a method of "self-intercourse" induced by reversing the polarity between certain organs which is quite wonderful. This is meditation experienced as lovemaking and is a higher practice that ultimately the individual lovers in a couple should learn to master. This is part of the "Lesser Enlightenment of Kan and Li" described in chapter 19.

THE BIG DRAW AS A CONTRACEPTIVE METHOD

Taoist cultivation of sexual energy can aid you in creating the healthiest and most organic contraceptive ever devised. I personally did not ejaculate for ten years using this method, and never had any unwanted pregnancy. When my wife and I decided to have a child, I ejaculated twice. The first ejaculation was solo, to clear any weakened sperm cells out of my body, cells that were weakened because I had drawn their chi up to my higher centers during meditation. Then my body responded by vigorously producing new sperm cells to replace those lost in the first ejaculation, and I focused my intention and energy on making them as powerful and healthy as possible.

I ejaculated only once in my wife in order to get her pregnant. Of course, we were careful to choose the beginning of her ovulation, so my sperm had several days to swim around chasing after her egg. Our child, Max, is the result, and as any of my students can testify he is a living dynamo. I believe we gave him the best start in life possible by guarding my seed and cultivating it to maximum health by cultivating the health of my body, which produced the seed.

However, there is a warning in all this. Because your seed becomes stronger as a result of these practices, it is much easier to impregnate a woman should you slip and lose it. Even though you are one hundred percent confident of your mastery of your seed I would recommend using a backup artificial contraceptive. Don't meddle with the body; avoid vasectomy or sterilization. Condoms prevent absorption of female yin fluids and may slow or weaken your sensitivity to the passage of chi energy through the penis.

To be safe, use a backup contraceptive even if you can prevent orgasmic ejaculation of your seed. You can still leak some of the clear "water" or semen which lubricates the passageway for the sperm out of the penis during the plateau phase of exchanging energy. This watery seminal fluid may carry a few invisible sperm eager to meet some lonely egg. This is also a caution against sleeping with women whom you do not love—an unwanted child will cost everyone far more dearly than the momentary sexual pleasure is worth. Remember that you are not only cultivating your sexual energy, you are cultivating the Tao in everything you do and think. Try to do it wisely—avoid big problems by taking the correct small measures.

A WOMAN'S VIEW OF DUAL CULTIVATION

Michael Winn conducted this interview with a 35 year old dancer, teacher, psychotherapist, housewife, and mother of one child.

MW: Did you find it difficult to learn the female half of dual cultivation, Ovarian Kung Fu?

Student: I've been practicing it for about 2 years. The concept was simple, the physical part was fairly simple, but it has taken me time to find my own needs and balances in sex. It was more difficult to help my partner to not have orgasms than to turn my own orgasm back. The question of whether or not to have an orgasm, whether or not it gives me energy or depletes me of energy seems to change. It depends on a couple of things. It depends on the type of orgasm, the type of energy between myself and my partner and where my energy is during that sexual encounter during that day or time or emotion.

MW: So, if your energy is at a low place, does your orgasm take you to a high place? Or if you're at a high place, does the orgasm drain you?

Student: I think if I'm in a low place, stirring up the sexual energy will increase my energy. But going all the way and having an ordinary orgasm will deplete me. If my energy is high, stirring up the sexual energy will make it higher and clearer and having an orgasm won't deplete me. It sometimes can give me more energy. When my partner gets more energy from my orgasm he's learned how to transfer it back to me so I don't lose energy from an orgasm, unless I'm depleted to start with. Then I tend to want to really conserve and do the Big Draw.

MW: Do you think this has radically changed sex for you?

Student: Definitely. Without a doubt. It's very special. I would say the ability to tune in to each other is really heightened. The harmony is far beyond what sex I had before. It's turned the sexual act into a really high art form of communication. Sex was great for me before, but this is much deeper. It has to do with the ability to communicate physically and psychically which I have gotten to at other times in my life, but this is a consistent path of getting there.

MW: So, let's break this down, is it just more physically intense?

Student: It's more intense, it's warmer, it's longer. And I think longer is a big part of it. I can have a whole body orgasm, and sexual excitement all over my body. I had that before a few times, but it happens much more often now. I can sustain the orgasm a long time. They last longer, a couple of minutes sometimes. Before it was only a few seconds. I'm really tuned into different types of orgasms now which I hadn't been before.

MW: What are the different types of orgasms?

Student: Each one is different. There are real gentle, mellow ones, there are intense ones, there are really driving forceful ones. They can happen in different parts and happen in the brain. It can happen in the genitals. I have used it for healing and it works. A couple of times I had an orgasm I've directed it to the weak organ to be healed, but I find it more useful to hold back on the orgasm and send the energy there. I have found one trick that really seems to intensify and lengthen an orgasm and that's to go into it about ½ way and then begin to hold back on it.

MW: So when you are already into an orgasm you can do the ovarian kung fu.

Student: Yes. It's as if you would withdraw from it but since you are already into it, it continues it and lengthens it and makes it last for a real long time. What it does is instead of turning off the orgasm if I'm already into it, it makes it last for a real long time. I send the energy up my spine. I'm not actually doing the Big Draw clenching contractions. I'm just tightening the vagina muscles and tilting the pelvis back. It's a slight arching of the spine out so the back is rounded.

MW: And that prolongs your orgasm.

Student: Yes, tremendously.

MW: Is it because the spine is aligned that the energy can travel up easily?

Student: Probably. I'm not sure how it's pulling energy up, I found out about it trying to keep an orgasm from happening in my partner. When I start to have an orgasm it will trigger him to orgasm and I don't want that to happen. So if I start to have an orgasm and I feel his orgasm coming on, I'll pull back. I pull his penis out of my vagina and start to send my energy up. And what I found often happens is that just prolongs the orgasm in me.

MW: So you'll have an orgasm withdrawn from him; you'll have the orgasm more privately.

Student: Yes, I'm trying not to pull him into it. At other times we stay together if he's feeling totally in control, and that's wonderful.

MW: What's the response amongst other women doing Ovarian Kung Fu?

Student: Generally it's good, they like doing it. Most women I talk to tend to think they had it all together before.

MW: I've heard that a lot also. Is that a common reaction?

Student: To tell you the truth, there are only a few women that I think who have really been practicing with partners. Some of the women are doing the exercises, but I know only one other woman who has been doing it with a partner. It's pretty much my own isolated experience, there just aren't enough women doing it.

MW: Have you ever felt, in terms of the quality of your sex, the quality of the energy, a high vibrational level?

Student: Yes. Sometimes I have a sense that I'm under water after an orgasm is over. I see things differently, and there is a buzzing in my ear. I've also had this happen after an intense meditation.

MW: How has Ovarian Kung Fu practice affected your daily life?

Student: It's made me more sensitive to my partner and more sensitive to my own energy. There is a deeper level of tenderness and I think from this there is the impetus to conserve one's energy. To hold and cultivate it is precious. I think when you do that you create a certain type of presence in the world, and other people respond to you in a like manner.

MW: In terms of your energy and sharing it with your lover, what's the difference between energy and love? Is just having more energy in physical intensity the same as having more love?

Student: It's not just physical; it feels psychic. You're creating a loving relationship. The sex is a vehicle in creating harmony. The Taoist methods put more power into your emotions, into everything. There have been times in the middle of love making that we've both just cried, it is so powerful. That quality of tenderness, that connection. So it's definitely more than physical.

MW: On any level, do you feel you can distinguish between yin and yang energies?

Student: I don't think of it as yin and yang, but I do feel his heat going up my spine, and it transforms me. I feel more like a woman. But I couldn't define it as feelings. I would just define it more as a special energy. It's like fanning the fire inside yourself and then allowing yourself to melt into it.

MW: So what's the difference between this chi exchange and love?

Student: It's one way of exchanging love. It's one way of sharing energy. It creates more polarity. I feel fed, it's like a food. I get yang energy, and hot yang energy allows me to then create more yin. I become more balanced. I'd felt it before but I couldn't always get to it. And it wasn't as intense.

MW: Has this increased your appetite for making love?

Student: Yes. It's increased my appetite but I'm okay without it. I feel so satisfied so that it's not an absolute requirement. And also the Ovarian Kung Fu allows me to transform my sexual energy up so I don't get crazy if I'm horny and he's not. But when the opportunity is there I like to take advantage of it.

MW: Did you ever feel that your partner was more concerned with conserving his energy than in actually making love? Did you ever feel it got in the way of love making?

Student: No, never. It has only enhanced it. Sometimes it is frustrating when it doesn't work. But I look forward to getting better and better at it.

CHAPTER 10

THE SEVEN SPIRITUAL STAGES OF CULTIVATING SEXUAL ENERGY

In the practice of exchanging sexual power with one's partner or absorbing one's own seminal power there are many ways of proceeding. Each individual must develop himself using his current stage of evolution as the starting point. There are higher, more purely spiritual levels of transforming human consciousness than the beginning techniques of sexual cultivation taught in this book. But it is impossible to fully comprehend them and attain lasting benfit from them until a man is able to exert positive control over his sexual drive.

Many yogis, gurus and masters from the East have arrived in America thinking themselves fully enlightened, but soon discovered they had not achieved control over their sexuality. They had merely repressed their sexual desires while developing their higher spiritual centers. Some may have been genuinely accomplished but were trapped by their religious or cultural taboos against sex. This imbalance is made possible by the strong local taboos against free sex in the orient.

The Eastern culture is still tightly controlled by religious or family pressures that greatly reduce the temptation to have extramarital sex. The penalty for being discovered is too great and would ruin the "career" of an aspiring yogi or other spiritual teacher who is assumed to have transcended the sexual urge. In the climate of unbridled sexual freedom that exists in America, their

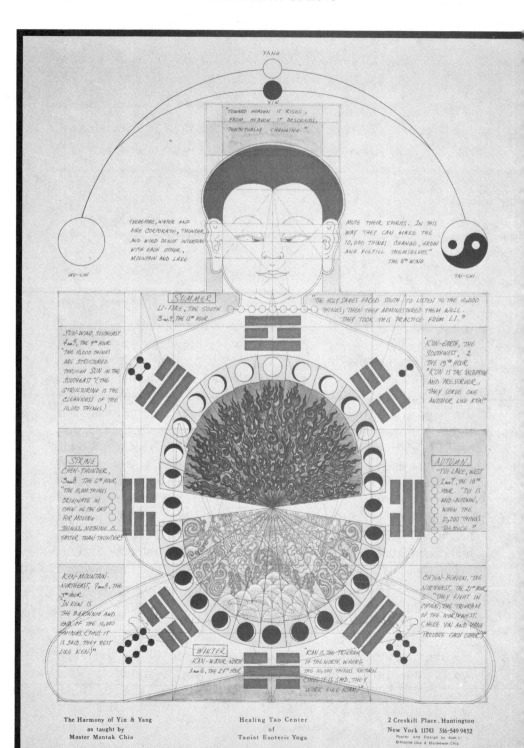

The Harmony of Yin & Yang
as taught by
Master Mantak Chia

Healing Tao Center
of
Taoist Esoteric Yoga

2 Creskill Place, Huntington
New York 11743 516-549 9452
Poster and Design by Juan Li
© Mantak Chia & Maneewan Chia

sexual urges re-emerged forcefully and became stumbling blocks in their spiritual development. Many slept with their followers, who later became disillusioned with their guru as he proved himself too human and attached to sex for the pleasure of it.

Some spiritual leaders are very critical of "lower" attempts to transform sexual energy using physical techniques as described in the beginning methods of Taoist dual cultivation of chi energy. They ignore that man is human and will make mistakes even while pursuing a spiritual path. Because sex and eating habits are deeply engraved in the nature of a man, you can't change these habits overnight. But if a man gradually changes inside, his habitual way of thinking and behaving will alter to conform to his innermost spiritual nature. This is the essence of the process of chi cultivation. The likeness is to a young tree beside an old tree: the first may bend easily but the old will not be bent so suddenly. Sexual essence, or ching chi, is our own internal fountain of youth, the sap flowing in the young tree. When you conserve and circulate it, it has a rejuvenating effect. Your mind, body, and spirit become more supple and pliant, then spiritual development can happen gracefully without great struggle. When the sap has run dry and you are crooked and arthritic, the path is painful and difficult.

IS DUAL CULTIVATION A LEFT HAND PATH?

Certain people involved in spiritual practices will recoil from Taoist cultivation of sexual energy and accuse its practitioners of using the "Left-Hand Path." By Left-Hand they mean that it involves the use of man and woman meditating together while sexually coupled. For this reason the practice appears to them suspect, tainted, or somehow less pure than a meditative practice or prayer which does not consciously involve sexual energy. In the Right-Hand path one takes a vow of celibacy.

Sex is not by itself spiritually undesirable. Without it no holy man would ever be born. The purity of the practitioner's intent in dual cultivation is critically important, as it is in every spiritual practice. If the intent is to control another person, then the practice can become "black". The crucial distinction is whether there is an attempt to interfere with the will of another, for his/her "good" or ill. Any manipulation or interference charged with subtle energy is a form of black magic, unless the other person freely asks for help or love and willingly expresses the desire to receive it.

Otherwise, there's nothing to fear from sex—it's part of you, you're born and die with it, it gives warmth and power to human love and is charged with the same polar forces as the rest of the universe. In fact this path of cultivation is called "White Magic" by some Taoists, as it teaches people how to reach a pure polarity by balancing their yin and yang. Even my master's name, "White Cloud", taken from this sacred mountain in China where he lived reflects this teaching. There are other powerful paths that focus more strongly on the yang or yin energy, but I find them more risky. Some people criticize the use of sex as a "red" yoga, but they are confusing this color with the fire energy of passion. In dual cultivation you mix equally the white and the red, his seed and her blood, mind and passion, the primal man and woman, the yang and the yin. From that you alchemically distill a neutral essence, a precious elixir that is without color, with the power to transform your soul into an immortal spirit and body. This elixir is made of refined chi and ching and spirit and takes years to prepare properly.

No saint or guru or king is born without reproductive organs. So everyone born man has to go through the male stage of sexual development. How fast and what kind of method he uses to pass through it differs, but he will experience sexual arousement, erection and ejaculation. If he can pass this worldly stage quickly, perhaps he can become a monk, a saint, Master or Guru. Or perhaps he will choose to remain an "ordinary" person in the world.

Many of the high Taoist masters keep a low profile and do their work silently. If you met them you would not think them extraordinary unless you were aware enough to sense the serenity about them. Their energy is like a gentle breeze waving across the room, touching everyone in a special way. In Taoist cultivation the man and woman meditate together. They use the natural human sexual urge as a bridge to higher consciousness. Taoism provides techniques to help a man to master his sexual impulse, so that he is free to choose the way of life he prefers. The alternate is to be a slave to animal instincts or sexual frustration. No matter how deeply these may be buried, they will find a way to surface if left unattended.

LEFT HAND PATH

Even among the Taoists who were ambivalent about the practice of dual cultivation and maintained strict celibacy, it was not because women or sex energy were considered dirty, impure, or evil. The yin essence of a woman was always acknowledged in China for its power and harmonizing influence. The doubts about the practice of exchanging energy during sex mostly centered on whether the adept—male or female—practicing the technique would continue to progress beyond the sensual and emotional pleasures of sex to achieve the highest spiritual awareness.

There is real danger of confusing your emotional attachment to your lover with attunement to the higher subtle union of yin and yang. I would say it is a phase that for most men cannot be avoided, but that in time and with continued cultivation of your energy through meditation, Tai Chi, and related practices you will naturally pass beyond it. This does not mean living without emotions; it means keeping them in balance and using the emotions that do arise to lend positive power to your chi cultivation process. It is more dangerous to force yourself into celibacy before you are really ready for it, as you will never know if you have really mastered your sexual desires and emotions or just avoided or otherwise suppressed them.

Celibacy can also be very distracting if you enter into it prematurely. You can easily build up more sexual power than you are able to balance in your meditation. You may have the inner will to resist sexual involvement with women, but if your soul keeps wandering back to them in dreams or thoughts you will lose energy and it will divide your attention. For this reason men need women; whatever the difficulty in coming into balance with them, their very presence affords a certain primal peace of mind.

In this sense, dual cultivation is the safest path, as it leaves no stone unturned. You have someone to accompany you on this long journey through life, and that makes it fun if you enjoy your path you stay on it more surely than someone who forces himself into an austere program of self denial. A woman's heart filled with yin essence is beautiful, accept it. You can both use the relationship as a microcosm of the universe. It will act as a mirror and reflect back to you a certain spiritual truth. This feedback from a partner is valuable and is one of the reasons the Taoists often worked in pairs, and not just lovers. There is valuable support and feedback in every relationship.

In Right Hand Cultivation, you use your own mind and body as a microcosm of the universe. Celibacy makes your life simpler, less messy, and the borders of one's individual conciousness are more sharply defined. This saves energy and can make for rapid progress in meditation. But it can also lead to a certain sterility, if you're not careful, the illusion of perfection in an inner world that negates the reality of the material world.

It's like being inside a crystal ball and looking out at the world but not actually experiencing the world and coming into harmony with it. You may find yourself avoiding your real life obligations, or falsely believing that you are separate from the world by virtue of your spiritual energy attainment. If you believe this you may have fallen into the common trap of putting too much energy in your head, and broken true contact with your body, and the five primal elements.

There is nothing to fear in the world if you keep your integrity, your balance of body, mind, and spirit. In the case of dual cultivation, you needn't be afraid of a woman. Her yin energy may seem different or discomforting at times, but the challenge a man takes on is to absorb that energy and use it to increase himself and balance her by increasing her yang. Spiritual men who are afraid of women, who avoid them for fear they will get attached or contaminated, are trying to protect a self-contained male spiritual ego. Many are afraid they will not be able to match the woman's power over them. This is blocking the flow of the Tao. It's as irrational as being afraid of water. You could drown in water if you fell off a boat in the middle of the ocean. But you wouldn't refuse to drink water because of it. It's a question of balance, of harmony between the five subtle elements. You can control this balance more easily once you've learned to control your seed. Then if you add her water essence and your seed energy to the soil everyday, a healthy garden will bloom that you can both share.

CULTIVATING THE RIGHT HAND PATH

One method of the Right Hand path that students of the Tao may wish to try is the following. After retiring to bed early, awaken in the early hours of the morning, somewhere between midnight and

6:30 AM. Often an erection spontaneously occurs at this time; if not, one can easily be induced. When erection is attained, assume to the proper lying position.

Perform the Big Draw 9, 18 or 36 times depending how soon erection drops down. Each time shift the power up to the head. When the head fills, the power is allowed to descend to the heart, solar plexus, and navel respectively. Then it will proceed down to the Hui-Yin and rise back up to the head, completing a full circuit. This meditating form is very strengthening and may be engaged in every night if the student so desires, with increasingly beneficial effects.

I have found this exercise to relieve many difficulties men may experience with the prostate gland. It involves a literal pulling away of any undue tension tending to swell and irritate the gland. It also serves to open the routes of electrical energy in the body which will increase your permeability to your partner's energy, as well as to all other sources of life.

Some Masters regard the powers that are connected with sexual intercourse as dirty or unrighteous power, somehow not pure. If you are concerned by this, you should know the hour of 12 P.M. is considered the purest one, for yang changes to yin at this moment. But remember, the power gained is like the money that people earn. Some people earn it in the high and easy position, some earn it from hard physical work like sanitation men, truck drivers, window cleaners. The money they earn is the same. Can you judge which one is the righteous man? It's not the money you earn that counts; it's how you spend it. The Taoist spends his energy cultivating himself and others to the highest level possible, using his left hand, right hand, and no-hands.

NO HAND PATH OF THE TAO

In my meditation classes I go beyond, into things that cannot be taught in a book. I expand on the Taoist approach to increasing man's freedom absolutely. This is the Taoist teaching of the three levels of enlightenment, and beyond that, Immortality. We Taoists have many secret ways of reaching our pure being. In Iron Shirt Chi Kung, I teach a technique for weightlifting on the male reproductive organ which literally pumps great quantities of the sperm power up into the head and body. In China or India, you might wait a lifetime at the feet of a master before he taught you this secret. I have no secrets, only the desire to teach others what I have learned. The problem is to find students with the patience and self-discipline to practice it.

Remember that the seminal power we use in Sexual Kung Fu is more than the nutritional value of the substance, however high that be. Here we are tapping into a nearly infinite source of electo-magnetic energy from the sperm. They are moving constantly and creating, by elementary principles of electro-magnetics, human electricity. We have stopped the disastrous waste of energy from frequent ejaculation, and have begun to elevate it's power more completely to the heart and head.

DIAGRAM 34

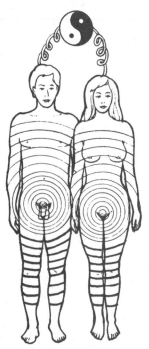

The No Hand Path of Tao
Yin & Yang energies are balanced.

In the Iron Shirt Chi Kung practice, we increase the stability of our life energy by rooting it more firmly in the earth and packing the chi energy into the fascia, bones and hollow cavities of our

body. In the Taoist Esoteric Yoga technique of "Lesser Enlightenment", or Kan and Li, I teach the esoteric formulae for increasing
the yin and yang powers within the body and "steaming" the
stored chi and ching up into the heart and head in a more refined
form. In the "Greater Enlightenment" you learn to absorb yin and
yang energy from sources outside your body—the earth, sun, and
moon—and "steam" those up in an alchemical process of refining.
But unless you can first master your own creative sexual energy,
you shouldn't even dream of mastering the subtle realms rest of the
universe. You will spend your life chasing illusory powers or a
false sense of oneness that will wither away in old age or on your
death bed, when you realize you can't carry your dreams with you
into afterlife.

According to Taoist tradition the basic process of transformation in stages of bodily energy is this: the sperm energy is channeled into the warm current or Microcosmic Orbit. The warm current is transmuted into mental power and this power or "soul" is
finally transmuted into the highest manifestation, which is pure
spirit. When this spirit is embodied in an Immortal Body, it gains
freedom to work in different spiritual planes at will. This is a step
beyond the awareness of cosmic oneness.

The man who practices Taoist cultivation inevitably becomes
more aware that all living things are one. He knows that power
flows into him from others and back to them again. Whenever there
is life the power flows. He understands this truth by experiencing it
in his body. After these experiences selfish motives gradually dissolve. To take from another is to take from oneself, for one is the
other. To dirty another's stream is to dirty ones own: there is one
stream in all creation, and that is the stream of life.

So I offer the reader a sequence of methods to choose from so
that you may spontaneously advance without any strain or forcing
on your part. It is advisable to proceed from one step to the other;
most spiritual people began with lower forms and gradually step-
ped up.

It is wrong to think the use of human sexual energy on the
physical plane is from an impure left-hand path, because it is the
path everyone must travel. If you start with the left hand, you will
eventually progress to the right hand, and ultimately attain the no
hand path. But you can't get to the highest attainment without first
ascending the lower ladder step by step, with both hands firmly

grasping the rungs. As you climb, the right hand and the left hand alternate in stabilizing your balance. You don't let go until you have reached the top of whatever the ladder is leaning against. Then you can stand on firm ground and kick the ladder away and stand with "no-hands"—empty hands free to do whatever you choose next, be it to climb another ladder or stay where you are.

Those who are not really involved in a daily Taoist practice such as Sexual Kung Fu may criticize the use of sexual energy to evolve. But if they studied and came to know the complete system, they would understand there is no left-hand and no right-hand path, only yin and yang mixed harmoniously in an infinite multitude of forms.

Everything leads to it's opposite: sex leads to no-sex; oneness leads to twoness (twoness of yin and yang) twoness leads to three-ness and everythingness leads to nothingness (Wu Chi). This is true cultivation of the Tao—the No-Hand Path. With No Hands life becomes effortless.

There is a stage in Tai Chi Chuan sometimes referred to as "wonderful hands". A beginner learning Tai Chi may use 90% yang energy to move his body. An intermediate student may use 60% yang and 40% yin. A master of Wonderful Hand Tai Chi uses 50% yin and 50% yang. A Taoist master creates this same balance at every moment in his life. This is the No Hand Path of the Tao. It is wonderful because it is so graceful and effortless, the way the whole human being should live.

THE SEVEN SPIRITUAL STAGES OF
TAOIST SEXUAL ENERGY CULTIVATION

First Stage: PHYSICAL CONTROL OF SEED LOSS. This control is exerted within the "human plane" of consciousness, as are the first five stages of Taoist Cultivation. The finger is used to stop the flow of semen during love making or masturbation. This slows the loss of vital fluids and helps to redistribute it to the needy parts of the body. Using the finger may block ejaculation of the seed but it will not redirect the ching chi upwards. You will have a normal orgasm and lose 60 to 70 percent of the seminal power (electromagnetic power produced from the motion of the 200–500 million sperm), but keep most of the seed in the body. The seed will gradually decay and the hormones will be absorbed back into the body.

But the body will conserve some energy by producing less sperm. It cuts back production automatically when it senses that it is already contained inside. After practicing this "external locking" method the penis will drop down and you may feel quite tired. After a certain time it will improve body health, strength, and result in a deep increase in sexual life. It will also build up power, but this takes a longer time because most of the yang power is lost during the ejaculation.

Second Stage: PHYSICAL AND MENTAL CONTROL OF SEXUAL ORGASM. This stage uses a combination of external finger pressure and the internal locking method of "Drawing the Nectar Up to the Golden Flower", or the Big Draw.

Before ejaculation, you use your finger to press on the Hui Yin and at the same time use the Big Draw to draw some energy up, before it can leak out the penis. In this way you lose less than in the first stage, but the penis will drop down and you will still have a normal orgasm centered in the genitals.

The opening of the Microcosmic Orbit is the key to allowing the flow of energy to move upward instead of being forced to move out the penis. Once you can get the energy into the coccyx it will begin flowing easily up the spine for most people. When you can feel the pressure of the chi in your head you must begin circulating it down to the navel.

Third Stage: MIND CONTROL OF SEXUAL DESIRE AND ORGASM. After more practice with the Big Draw, you will eventually control ejaculation with your mind only. You will be able to do the Big Draw without physical force and will gain the ability to play with your orgasm. This will occasionally result in releasing sperm, but gradually you will develop the power to stop physical ejaculation and enjoy the experience of a different but more highly pleasurable kind of orgasm, the "valley" orgasm.

If you can stop before going too far by ejaculating, you can draw and exchange the power from the woman. In that way you lose one but gain one. You lose mainly yang energy and receive the thing you need, yin energy. It's almost a barter; you have too much yang and woman has too much yin, so you exchange energies, each one receiving the proportion of what he or she needs. This method involves a higher consciousness, higher self-control and getting away from erotic thinking and imagining the act of love. Think of the energy you have given to your lover as a conscious sacrifice made at the altar of higher consciousness.

This third stage is higher than the second stage, for your mind has entered into a new relationship with the ching chi. Your mind has begun to integrate your sex essence with your general chi energy into a single unified being. There is a big difference in the experience of people who have practiced using only the mind and those who use the finger and Big Draw combination. It is far superior to simple coitus interruptus. Big Draw shifts the excess power in the reproductive region upward to the higher centers of the body which can store the power for greater uses. Your sexual essence becomes food to nourish your higher spirit.

In this stage, if people use the Big Draw, they can increase the power they have each time. When they use this method in making love they will not feel tired. They can have as much sex as they want although they frequently have it less often because the quality is so deeply satisfying they feel stronger and are able to control themselves and overcome other worldly desires that have a controlling influence on their lives.

However, at this level you should be aware you are drawing this extra energy from another imperfect human being. For this reason, you must be able to overcome the failings of this person within yourself. In this third stage, both partners must be very understanding and be highly involved in this practice. If one partner is not involved, it is very hard to work together exchanging the power. If your partner has troubles, or is upset, you can absorb this psychic distress into yourself. If the method will not work, sometimes it is because one partner is having personal trouble. That is the very first thing to check out, and correct with meditation or other therapy. Otherwise you will absorb these troubles into your system, where they will act as psychic toxins.

The method might seem to be unfair if your partner is very sad but you are cheerful and energetic. She will receive life-force happiness and energy from you, but you will absorb her sadness and her burdens into yourself. Only if you are highly committed can you purify her and help her tremendously by guiding her onto a higher path that will free her from her inner toils. For this reason you must be very selective of your partner, for you will be literally drinking of the life essence of the person. A vulgar, vain or jealous person is what you will tend to become if your partner has these qualities in abundance—or at least, you will have to use your greater power of love and benediction to consume these lower impulses.

Fourth Stage: EXCHANGE ENERGY WITHOUT HAVING SEXUAL INTERCOURSE. For the male this practice is easier with a youthful female partner who has not borne children and still has great vitality, or with any woman who has cultivated her chi to powerful levels through meditation. It is a method of self-healing that can be used by young people, but is more likely to be employed by older people who have less interest in an active sex life yet seek the rejuvenating powers of sexual energy. The most famous practitioner of this level is undoubtedly Mahatma Gandhi, who insisted his 18 year-old niece sleep chastely beside him at night. The spiritual fires burning brightly within Gandhi needed the nourishing and cooling balance of a female's ching, yet cultural and religious standards forbade sexual contact as a Hindu holy man.

During the Middle Ages the knights sworn to the code of chivalry were under similar pressure to sublimate their sexual drive into a kind of sublime spiritual romance. A chaste kiss from a damsel or a nonsexual embrace with loving eye contact were idealized in legends such as the Holy Grail myth (a clear symbol of the quest for pure female energy within each male knight) and in the songs of troubadors.

Today the practice is useful in situations where two friends wish to deepen their spiritual contact or heal each other, but because of marriage ties or other competing relationships do not want the disharmony that might arise from a sexual affair. Taoist philosophy has high respect for the stability of harmonious relationships, but it also recognizes the need for the spiritual freedom to balance and nourish one's personal elements. This method allows a greater range of freedom in relationships beyond the limiting categories of lover/not-lover, and encourages the blossoming of spiritual friendships in which the exchange of sexually polarized energy is acknowledged gracefully and without shame. It is a delicate and wonderful way for two people to cultivate their energy together. Married couples may find it another way to deepen the sharing of their love.

This level can only be practiced by a man who has already mastered the first three stages and has attained a certain level of spiritual self knowledge. He has learned that what he's seeking is not to be found in the external woman, in her sensuality. His chi is moving not outward to his senses but inward to his center. He seeks the inner woman within himself and finds it easier to tap his own yin power when stimulated by the presence of strong female energy.

Method: Lie or sit facing your partner. Having physical contact is optional—such as holding hands or embracing—but you should feel aroused by the presence of your partner. Focus your attention on the subtle energy field of your partner; you must "feel" his/her aura. In the beginning absorb his/her energy into your lower Tan-Tien. Draw the power to your head, gradually opening the passage to allow greater flow of energy. At higher levels of this practice energy can be absorbed directly into the heart or into the head, but it must be well distributed to avoid imbalances from developing. If you do this every day you will get tremendous power; much of which comes from your own body, a yin power of the seminal fluid which is much purer than the first and second steps. By cultivating this new sensitivity within yourself you can greatly hasten your own and your partner's growth.

Fifth Stage: BEYOND SEX. This is a stage that highly disciplined Taoist Yogis aspire to. You are still on the human plane, but your energy is much higher than the level your energy attains when you sleep at night, which is already quite pure. This stage involves no sexual stimulation at all. In Taoism, this method is known as the "Life Hour" meditation or the "hour of tsu", as it is employed between 11 PM and 1 AM. The Tao masters have learned that the power that you absorb from your own body can stay in your body forever. The power which is absorbed from another person will not stay as long or become readily a part of your own. It's just like blood transfers, in which the cells will stay for 24 days and then die off. The goal of esoteric sex is to learn the secret power of balancing subtle yin and yang energies. But sex is man's habit. You have to move up and gradually change your routine. You would not expect to change a lion from eating meat to eating grass over night. When you get higher and higher in the practice you will change your habits easily without anyone forcing you or telling you what to do.

It is common after sleeping to awaken and feel an erection. This is because sleep has filled the body with sexual essence and chi life force. Your penis is erect with power. At this time it is very important to draw the power up so you can enjoy its intense and pure strength. If you don't draw it up it will go out. Many people are tempted to have sex or to masturbate and they lose much power by doing so. This stage is higher than the first four stages, for without a human partner, there is a total absence of erotic thinking and hence closer proximity to the original emptiness of the Tao. The penis is erected by virtue of its own power. In Taoism this technique is considered highly secret.

Sixth Stage: TRANSFORMING SPIRITUAL ENERGIES BEYOND THE MIND/BODY. This stage is for people who have a higher spiritual education in advanced yoga, meditation or Taoist Chi Cultivation. Many who approach this level believe they are following a righteous or saintly path by detaching themselves from worldly things. This often results in aspiring yogis trying to keep down sexual feelings. But in fact all must deal with sexual desire before mastering this stage.

This high spiritual stage solves the human need for sexuality, the quest for primordial creative energy, by teaching the human to absorb energy directly from the universal, all-pervading life force. You must first spend years gradually absorbing power on the human plane until the energy of your mind, body, and spirit—chi, ching, and shien—are full to the point of overflowing (stages 1–5). Then you can work on larger fields of yin and yang energies beyond your body, and project your chi where it does the most good.

Many people try to skip impatiently up to the divine aspects of their nature without fully understanding the human and animal components. As one spiritual sage put it, "It is easy to know God, but hard to be a human being." This is why Taoists cultivate themselves from the foundation, and emphasize rooting in the earth as a prerequisite to invoking power from the Heaven.

The power of sexual energy is insignificant compared to the totality of cosmic energy, the Tao. But for humans sex is extraordinarily powerful and a bridge to the vast powers of the universe and the spiritual realms of the consciousness. Failure to cultivate this energy properly is one of the most common obstacles among men to sustaining consciousness in the sixth stage. Many men obtain a temporary glimpse into this realm through meditation or vision, but few can sustain living in it.

The vital chi energy which formerly was used to create generative (sperm) power, is now diverted in the body and channelled directly to higher centers of energy. The Taoists refer to the stages of this process as Lesser Enlightenment. When perfected, the body becomes permeable to heavenly energies directly without any intermediary stage whatsoever and ceases producing sperm cells.

On this higher plane, the Pai-Hui (crown) and Yin-Tang (third eye) are the two points which can absorb the universal power and Yung-Ch'uen (ball of foot) the point that can absorb the power from the earth. In this state you can practice with morning and noonday sun, and with the moon. You absorb the earth power by the Yung Ch'uen through the feet and get heavenly power and sun energy by the Pai-hui. This offers the pure super conscious power from the universe, balanced with the moon energy entering through the Yin-Tang, or third eye.

Using the Greater Enlightenment formula the universal energy is transformed and mixed with your own energy so it can become useful on the human plane. This universal energy is so raw that our body needs to transform it and adapt it to our bodily needs. When you get to this stage, you gradually do away with human power resources. This is the stage at which some Taoists cease eating food and become breatharians; they retire to the purity of secluded mountains and dine on the subtle energies of nature. My master reached this stage but was forced to leave his mountain retreat because of Japanese bombings in WWII.

Seventh Stage: UNION OF MAN AND TAO. This stage is what the Taoists call Immortality. I can't yet describe it from personal experience, but it is well documented in the thousand volume Taoist canon, including the names of many individuals who reached this state. You can believe it or not, or dismiss immortality as metaphor for some kind of cosmic awareness. But the Taoist teachings are clear this is meant literally and not symbolically. The highest creation for man is to create oneself consciously. Union with the Tao suggests the total act of self-creation from the original chi or the Wu chi. See chapter 19 for a fuller description of the seven higher meditation formulas of the Tao that lead to this state of divintiy.

All seven steps will gradually guide you up to higher spiritual attainment, but it is up to you to choose how far you wish to pursue your own evolution. I cannot recommend any one step for you to go on as being better than another. No one can tell you how to live your life. Many people historically use the first and second steps to live beyond a hundred years. Tradition holds others have used the third and fourth steps to live a happy energetic life for several hundred years in some cases.

The second, third or fourth steps might be better for you when young and you desire several partners. Then when you are more mature you may want only one wife. The young often desire a very beautiful wife, but after you are married for years, beauty is not the main quality in a wife. A plain girl with lovely character may be the best for achieving spiritual serenity. It depends on your spiritual will and her level of cultivation and maturity.

Likewise the seven steps. I don't know what step you will pursue. I only offer some guidelines. Some men may not be ready for many more lifetimes to change stages. After you read this book you may abandon the Sexual Kung Fu practice altogether and go on happily ejaculating like Niagara Falls.

But if you want to get involved in cultivating your energy you will spontaneously evolve and move toward higher spiritual levels. Your goal will be realized most quickly if you apply yourself with singleminded devotion to your spiritual evolution. Eventually it will become effortless as you stop struggling against your nature, which is the same in essence as the Tao. Your awareness of the universal subtle energies will grow naturally and you will move up by yourself, not according to any religion or philosophy, but from an inner guidance.

The great Chinese physician Sun S'su-mo, (581 to 682 A.D.) famous for inventing the small pox innoculation and who lived to be 101 years, astutely noted the problem of progress in his Recipe for Making Priceless Gold:

"In youth, man does not understand the Tao.

At middle age he hears much about the Tao but does not practice what he hears.

When he is old he sees the truth of Tao, but is too weak to act on it."

CHAPTER 11

ORGASM AND WU WEI
by Michael Winn

"Man is aroused by the chi of woman, and his Jade Stalk is called to action. Woman is aroused by the chi of man, causing the waters within her Secret Gate to flow. These movements are the natural outcome of the universal yin and yang. They cannot be duplicated by human will alone."
—*Taoist Canon*

There is some historical debate about whether the female has an infinite amount of yin essence and thus is capable of endless multiple orgasms. This is the point of view of the Taoist medical texts from the 8th century, which suggest that men should stimulate women to have as many orgasms as possible, thus releasing the maximum yin essence.

Women's energy is lunar, following a monthly cycle. She loses her energy each month through menstruation. But she is also renewed by the earth energy every month, which does give her tremendous orgasmic potential. But multiple orgasms can be very draining, depending on the type of orgasm and the woman's level of energy. Because a woman's sex organs are inside her body it is far easier for her to transmute the orgasmic energy up to higher centers than it is for a man. That is why many uncultivated women are more spiritual than similarly unaware men. These men instinctively toss their seed outward and lose its spiritual benefit.

But when a man begins to cultivate his seed, he can do it day and night if he has the discipline. His body will speed up production of its seed. This permits a man to cultivate his chi more rapidly than the woman, who is bound to a slower monthly cycle. This is why many of the gurus and masters are male. The other reason is that women by nature are yin, and thus closer to Emptiness. They simply don't feel as strong a compulsion to pursue such a yang, expansive goal of teaching outwardly. Women have a different journey.

But this is also the very heart of man's fascination with woman and with her orgasm, which is a kind of inward teaching for the male adept subtle enough to learn from her. The female orgasm is an inward explosion—or implosion—of her yin essence. In the valley orgasm man can experience this imploding yin energy in his different Tan Tiens as a fusion, a kind of meltdown. Yin represents earth energy, or physical matter. What happens during her orgasm is that the very structure of her body is vibrating and imploding, and by harmonising your energy with hers you are opened up to a new and polar opposite experience of your body. The woman's wisdom is that if you go deep into the earth, your body, it will lift you into heaven. It's an initiation into an inner mystery of being that women are empowered to give men, but can't bestow without an infusion of male energy as a catalyst.

Lovers who have no esoteric model to guide their path sometimes gain glimpses of this meltdown state when they languish in a kind of sweet trance after love-making and their energies fuse in a spontaneous valley orgasm. Their bodies may feel transparent, or they may feel like they are floating; sounds arrive with a tinkling crystal clarity, and colors in the room seem brighter, as if freshly washed. This is an altered state of consciousness in which they are perceiving with purity and directness the primal unity of the natural world.

The goal of Taoist cultivation is to sustain and intensify that state, in which the separateness we ordinarily feel is dissolved and integrated into a higher reality. A higher orgasm of our mind and body magically moves us closer to the original chi which exists everywhere. The pure fusion of the yin and yang subtle energies in the microcosm of our body reminds us that the same is happening in the macrocosm—that the sun and the moon and earth and the Milky Way literally make love with one another. The planets attract each other with vast electro-magnetic and gravitational fields. The stars and quasars shoot out hot yang streams of light and radiation to be received by the cold yin vacuum of empty space. We witness this cosmic love-making from afar, reflected in the eerie light that reaches us on earth by way of the moon or shooting stars that streak across the sky. Perhaps all this light energy ends up being sucked back into the womb of the universe, the black holes, beyond which is true nothingness, what the Taoists call "Wu Chi."

In a parallel sense the male's seed is his solar or nuclear energy. He cultivates or stockpiles it so it can be exploded in a controlled manner in his tan tiens. It is then emitted out into his personal space as radiant heat. A woman can absorb it and give it back in material form as a cooling mystic heat which heals. The Taoists call the balance of mind within which this alchemical process of transformation effortlessly occurs "Wu Wei". This is translated as "non-action", and sometimes taken to mean that the Taoists are passive mystical observers of nature who never get involved for fear of upsetting the delicate balance of yin/yang. What it really implies is a neutrality, or state of receptivity, so that anything can spontaneously happen. It's a passive state in the sense that the entire universe is pure potential, but it is active in that it exists in total harmony with the universe that is dynamically manifesting itself every moment. You are eternally free to act or not-act, depending on what the situation demands.

On a practical level, women might be seen as living closer to the state of "Wu Wei" than men, for it is their nature as yin to empty themselves and receive the universe to realize fullness. This yin essence is what makes a woman's energy so spontaneous and attractive to a man. The less effort she makes, the more natural and easy and accessible she appears to a man. A woman can just lie there and get pregnant; she makes the very act of creation seem simple. Men, on the other hand, are yang, with an expanding energy that seems to imply great effort to sustain itself. How can men effortlessly get bigger or stronger or create anything without work and more work?

Perhaps men can find an answer in their experience of the valley orgasm. This orgasm of the total mind, body, and spirit is entered into effortlessly. When you are in the valley, strolling through the lovely scenery that includes only you, your lover, and the subtle cosmos, you remember how easy and natural this higher harmony is, that you've been there before, but forgot it while you were busy struggling out in the world to earn money, raise a family, etc. You don't have to work to create this sense of loving peace. To the contrary, this state of "Wu Wei" is achieved not by exerting yourself, but by lying in relaxed intercourse with your lover and simply being with her. Wu Wei is nothing more than being balanced in the field of pure subtle energies generated by your bodies and by the pre-existing fields of yin/yang energy in the universe. Your love-making is practice for staying in that relaxed state, so eventually you'll be able to constantly feel that deep serenity within yourself after you return to the world of chores.

I have found the spontaneous effortlessness of the valley orgasm reaches to the very heart of the Taoist teachings. Some men may get trapped by their fascination with the techniques of chi cultivation—by the mechanics of the Big Draw method. They may get a lot of chi from it, but if they are trying too hard they may never experience the valley orgasm or the wu wei process, which is a delicate balance of non-striving yin energy and very directed yang energy. When the two are balanced in a valley orgasm you experience the full paradox of standing still (yin) and moving at the same time (yang).

That is why the great Taoist poets write of the paradoxical nature of the Tao. Wu Wei is doing nothing, but everything happens. My first experience of the valley orgasm took me and my lover by surprise, probably because we expected the Taoist esoteric methods of love making to be like the deep solo meditative experiences both of us had experienced for a number of years before we became lovers. During the valley orgasm I felt like I was in two places at once. My body was imploding and fusing inwardly, while my awareness was expanding outwards into larger energy fields and subtle realms of being impossible to describe.

I found it amazing the way my body seemed to take its cues from my lover's body. My entire body started to vibrate rapidly at the same speed as hers and stayed attuned for some minutes. Despite the orgasmic intensity, my body temperature was neither hot nor cold, but even and pleasant. It was very different from my previous meditative practice which stimulated the kundalini energy to rise in a column of hot electric yang energy and led to explosive opening of my crown or third eye centers. It would sometimes put me into a trance where I forgot I even had a body. My conscious mind would shut down while my body raced to absorb the high dose of subtle yang energy.

The point I'm trying to make in describing such a subtle and subjective personal experience is that Taoist cultivation teaches balanced meditation in all the body's tan tiens (or chakras). This is considered the most stable marriage of yin and yang—the cooler grounding lower centers receiving the heat from the expanding higher centers, the classical mixture of fire and water. This is the middle path of the Tao—staying grounded in your body while on a lifetime journey though the subtle energy realms.

The spiritual direction of Taoist dual cultivation is not Sudden Enlightenment, or astral travel, dissolution in bliss, or fantastic visions. These might occur as temporary side effects of the practice. But the main intention of the Taoists aspiring to immortality was simply to maintain a dynamic balance of energy during the 10,000 ordinary moments of the day. The Taoists are suspicious of any transcendental path that claims to be very high and very quick or that leaves the human body uncared for in the rush to become divine. Their wisdom is that what counts is an evolution that lasts, and that such growth usually comes slowly and steadily. The 10,000 daily moments when stretched over 25 years adds up to a 125 million moments, so you have plenty of opportunities to practice cultivating the your chi over a lifetime. Fortunately, these millions of moments occur one by one, making the task simpler, and a bit less imposing.

Many people in the west want 60-second Enlightenment, and they may well get what they project—Enlightenment that lasts 60 seconds. The Taoist process may seem slow to some with its insistence on circulating higher energies into the lower centers. It seems much easier to open a third eye and go to the spiritual worlds directly, without bothering with a clumsy and heavy physical body. This is the value of the Taoist practice of dual cultivation of sexual energy. It leads to the acceptance of the ordinary moment, of human desire, of the never ending sexual impulse, as a valuable in-the-body way of understanding the Tao.

This emphasis on the ordinary in daily life being an essential part of the wholeness of the Tao is why the ancient sages did not live for peak spiritual experiences, or seek an explosive peak orgasm in sex. This seeking after bliss is like trying to be all yang. It is an extreme state. The valley orgasm is not just a code name for bliss. It balances the yin energy of our earthly body (and the Karma, or suffering, it creates) and the bliss of transcending it with heavenly yang energy. When this bodily suffering and heavenly bliss are balanced, they cancel each other out. Emptiness is the result. This is true serenity, remaining empty even as you acknowledge both poles of experience as possibilities. Neither pole controls you, so you are truly free to choose. The desires for bodily pleasure and spiritual transcendence are born and destroyed every moment. You remain both empty and full, and life becomes a tai chi dance. When you experience this, you have tasted enlightenment. When you can stay that way, you are immortal.

PRESERVING POLARITY:
WHAT DOES IT MEAN TO BE YANG?
By Michael Winn

"A Sage will practice the Tao. A fool will only admire it."
Ancient Taoist proverb.

I interviewed several dozen of Master Chia's students in the course of writing this book with him, and was deeply struck by the differences in attitude to sexual cultivation between men and women. In couples that were practicing the methods taught here, the men were more fascinated by the energy generated or the states of mind that might be reached. The women were more concerned to know that their man loved them; whether or not he succeeded at his spiritual technique was secondary.

Some women were worried initially that all the time their man spent doing Taoist exercises and meditations meant less time for his relationship with her. A few complained that a sense of technique invaded their love-making. Most admitted that this negative aspect seemed to disappear as the Taoist semen retention methods began to work. The love-making grew longer, and the added time allowed for more tenderness to develop in the relationship.

Other men began doing the Taoist practices and encountered resistance from their lover over the holding back of ejaculation. Their women felt that when the man ejaculated, it was a more total surrender of himself to her and thus more loving. These women were also concerned that by missing his ejaculation the woman might somehow be at fault for not bringing him to full conventional orgasm. Most of this resistance is due to lack of spiritual education, or may be an unconscious attempt to maintain sexual power over a man. As one woman explained it to me, "some women get a feeling that they can possess their man only when he has surrendered by ejaculating. She isn't consciously aware of the energy equation, but it may be the way she alleviates her insecurity about his love for her."

In this kind of relationship the man's ejaculation has become a kind of football on the sexual playing field. The pattern is one where after the man surrenders his seed, he unconsciously holds back from her in other ways to conserve his energy and identity. She unconsciously senses this, and thinking she is strengthening their relationship encourages him to ejaculate. When he learns the Taoist method of retaining his seed and moving the energy up within himself, she resists because she is losing the tangible symbol of his surrender to her, his semen. Her motives are loving on one level, but unfortunately they are possessive.

The only remedy for this situation is for the man to share his experience of increased energy and love with her. Taoist lovemaking is impossible to master if the relationship is poisoned by jealousy and possessiveness over the exchange of lower sexual energy. The essence of the process of esoteric love is to transform the energy up to the heart and spiritual centers before exchanging it with your lover. This highlights the importance of the man returning to the woman the energy he has received from her during sex. If he tries to keep it for his own personal ends or projects it out his third eye into some fantastic vision, he disperses the chi and breaks the cycle of exchange with her. This is why the Taoists believe it is better to repay the immediate source of your energy—your lover— as she can use the higher transformed energy you give her to balance herself and you.

The energy of the two partners in the relationship begins to move in an upward spiral, and becomes more exquisitely refined with each spiral. It eventually expands to embrace friends and family members in the dynamic. This spiral relationship is actually expressed in the Taoist symbol of yin/yang circling endlessly around in a circle. The male energy is directed, like an arrow moving in a straight line. The female energy is rounded and embracing, like an empty circle. When they intersect, the circle embraces the straight line and bends it in a spiral. Taoist love-making is a spiritual ecology system for recycling lower energies into higher ones, with Enlightenment and Immortality being phases of the spiralling process when the energies get very pure.

However, most of us, myself included, are still very mortal and struggling with our ego. Once I leave the small and private world of sexual intimacy or meditation, my public ego adamantly refuses to adopt a stance of spontaneous non-action, of Wu Wei, and keeps insisting I plan ahead for my own self-interest. To ameliorate this selfish tendency, I try to focus on serving the ever-changing balance of subtle energy around me instead of my ego. My ego is very good at lying to itself and is always getting me into trouble with its own projections, rationalizations, and hidden agendas. Seeing things in terms of their energy encourages a certain neutrality—I stop struggling to get money or position and look at what kind of energy the things I want really represent.

While it is easy to misinterpret the quality of chi I feel in myself or sense in a person or situation, I feel that ultimately the energy doesn't lie because it is the very glue connecting me with other beings, both human and spiritual. In this sense Taoist chi cultivation is a method of refining one's power of intuition, of knowing beyond one's rational mind. Most western men find it easy to accept this in theory. But the balancing of yin and yang energy can seem very abstract and impractical. I read Taoist poetry and the *I Ching* for years and liked it, but never got a deep "gut" feeling of what was really happening with yin and yang.

Only when I began doing Taoist yoga and practicing testicle breathing, the big draw, the microcosmic and fusion meditations did I experience in my body the distinct subtle energies of hot and cold, and the energies in the five major organs, heart, kidney, etc. I had to get trained by Master Chia on what to look for. When I saw it right inside my body I felt ecstatic, like Christopher Columbus confirming the world was not flat. There was a cool, yin energy inside me, a new dimension of my being to explore. I set sail on the Taoist path with the faith that the world was round and I would return to my starting point a bit wiser. I find that spirit has enlivened my love-making as well. Dual cultivation has become an adventurous journey into a new part of myself and my lover.

Yin and yang are not just concepts. They represent real qualities of chi energy that can be stored in your body and used in your ordinary life. A purely intellectual approach to Taoism is one of the toughest obstacles a highly educated western student has to overcome. Westerners consider the intellect to be the mind, while Taoists see intellect as just one tool of the whole mind-body-spirit. When Taoists cultivate their chi and refine the union of body, mind, and spirit with their spiritual exercises and alchemical meditations, they are training the mind to live in a world filled with dynamic fields of energy.

This means to be a Taoist you stop living in a disembodied world of words and concepts constructed by your intellect. You don't stop thinking, but you may need to learn how to think-feel with your whole being. To do this you will develop faculties you forgot you had and which are right now sitting dormant in the 90% unused portion of your brain and body capacity. That is why sex is so healthy for western men; it is the only time many of them escape from the conceptual prisons of their intellect and ego, and gain an experience of being wholly in the body.

If you are just beginning to cultivate your chi, don't worry if you have trouble distinguishing between yin and yang energy. Just do your exercises and meditations daily. When you begin to sense any vibration, warmth, tingling, or altered sense perceptions it is a sign your body is waking up to its subtle energy. In time you will realize this play of ying/yang energy is not an abstract metaphysical game, but your personal destiny. By knowing it you can slowly come to grips with the source of the subtle forces working through your psyche. These are the polarized energies that find their way into your hormones, your health, your behavior, your male personality, your perceptions of who you are and what the world is all about.

Some men get the confused idea that becoming spiritual means dropping their assertive masculine qualities and becoming passive, meditative, wearing soft flowing clothes, and acting motherly and nurturing after the yin female model. According to Taoist teachings, this is a mistake; if a man becomes too yin he is in danger of losing his polar attractiveness to women and the very qualities that satisfy them both sexually and spiritually.

Instead of becoming spiritual, you may become a sissy—soft, yielding, and spineless. Balancing the yin/yang polarity within your psyche does not mean you should weaken your yang energy and shed your masculine qualities. The goal of Taoist cultivation is not androgeny, to make life colorless and sexless. It's not to prove that there is really no difference between men and women, since both are "one", in a bland soup called the Tao.

The difference between the polarity of masculine and feminine is what creates energy. The dynamic tension between yin and yang is what gives life to a relationship between a man and a woman. Every man and woman has both yang and yin poles within themselves, and will express a wide mixture of masculine and feminine qualities in their personality. But a man's primary subtle energy charge will be yang, and it is only in relation to this that he inwardly cultivates the yin pole of his yang energy. This may outwardly change the quality of his masculine energy, softening his rough edges or leading him to direct his male energy for more wholesome and loving purposes. But he will and should remain male in his orientation with the outer world, because that is his true nature. Women love strong men; the point of cultivating your chi is to become more sensitive and feeling within that strength. Likewise, you must help your lover to develop her strengths as well.

On the psychological level, I will risk the generalization that one of the major difficulties men have in practicing dual cultivation, is in harmonizing their ego with the woman's emotional sensitivities. The lesson both need to learn, is that people are not either their ego or their emotions, but that these are manifestations of deeper subtle energies within the self. Many couples with problems expend much time, money and energy frantically pruning the dying leaves of their relationship with the aid of marriage counselors and psychiatrists. This is working from the outside in. On one level this is very helpful, as talking about something can open the door to self-improvement.

But the Taoist approach is to nourish the roots of the tree, so that the sap can run strong and feed the entire trunk, branches, and wilting leaves from within. This works from the inside out. The process is more invisible, but it is more lasting. The sap in a human tree is chi energy, and if you want to nourish your woman you must not let your ego block the process of sharing energy. The woman is a mirror to a man. The subtle law of universal energy is that you get back what you project out. If you send her an abundance of love and energy, she will respond and return it to you. The proof of whether a couple practicing dual cultivation has transformed their ego and emotional imbalances will be known internally to each, but also reflected in the tenderness and harmony that develops in their daily living.

A good rule to follow in Taoist dual cultivation, is to make love with your chi energy, not your ego. Sexual energy will begin to cause a degeneration in couples when it is used to feed male egotism or female emotional domination. This is the danger of using sex for spiritual growth when you don't really have your personal life together. The only protection is to give as much love and respect to your lover as you humanly can. A woman needs a certain emotional stability before she can balance higher subtle energies. Likewise, a man's ego will block him from receiving higher energies or experiencing the valley orgasm. If you can self-lessly send your supportive masculine love to a woman, the energy will empower her to return it to you ten times over. This is the yin/yang dynamic. It's a single energy that constantly flows wherever your intention sends it. It then returns to its source, just as you spiritually are returning to your source.

I have begun to notice the subtle domino effect between sexual love and my destiny in the world. When I reach the point of Wu Wei, of spontaneous non-action during sex, it creates a serenity in me that softens the demands of my ego in the outside world. Somehow, the struggle of life gets easier, I find myself resolving problems with less effort.

Life is like one of those puzzle-box eggs: when you open it there is another egg, and inside that another, and so on. Sexual love is one of the eggs halfway to the empty egg at the center of the puzzle. When you make love and transform your selfish ego, raw vital chi energies and raw sex drive into something more refined and radiant, this middle egg shines through to the other eggs in the puzzle, lighting up both the innermost spiritual egg as well as the worldly outer shell.

The idea of Wu Wei and committment to a lover is very confusing. The practice of spontaneous neutrality would seem to encourage the very opposite of long term commitment to another person. Indeed, there are Taoist sex manuals on the market which encourage readers to love as many people as possible to satisfy our spontaneous impulses. I feel this is an irresponsible and misleading oversimplification of the esoteric Taoist teachings on sex. Dual cultivation is directed at experiencing and balancing our inner subtle energy fields, not at acting out with our bodies the same basic sexual impulse again and again. Promiscuity is not the effortless grace of the Tao, but a superficial use of spiritual philosophy to justify dilettantish tendencies and erotic fantasies. The excuse of needing many partners often masks a fear of deeper intimacy with oneself and one's lover. Spiritually, it can block the alchemical union of ching, chi, and shien. The process of transformation requires a certain stability of the lower physical forces that are upset by wild, erratic, or excessive sexual behavior.

While the Taoist philosophy on sex requires a totally non-possessive attitude toward the energies being exchanged, it does not imply acting irresponsibly towards other people. The neutral mind of Wu Wei implies a balanced wisdom in spontaneously choosing the middle course at every moment. This would apply to questions of committment in a relationship as well. The perfect middle choice would naturally balance the virtue of stability in a relationship with the need for freedom to nourish one's subtle energy. These are difficult questions, but there is no ancient Taoist sage who can answer them for you. You and your lover must cultivate your own energy and become subtle beings wise enough to know the truth of your own modern situation. In short, you must become the sage, moment by moment, over the course of your lifetime.

CHAPTER 12

COMMONLY ASKED QUESTIONS ABOUT SEMEN RETENTION

1. I've had a vasectomy. Will that affect my ability to do the Big Draw?

Chia: The effects of vasectomy upon one's sexual life and general health warrant consideration. It is well-recognized that there prevails among vasectomized men a normal level of physical and mental health. Most individuals surveyed after vasectomy have considered their health good to excellent. Many wives thought their husbands' distinctly more virile.

Improved sexual performance may be readily accounted for: sperm is no longer discharged and its energies are no longer wasted. The body reabsorbs active principles of the sperm cells via the blood stream. However, those secretions not formed in the testes are ejaculated.

These benefits and far greater ones are enjoyed by Taoist lovers. They retain not only the sperm but the entire volume of seminal fluid, each part of which bursts with enzymes, vitamins, proteins, trace elements, and electrical energies. Yet this is not the most important advantage.

Secretion of the vasectomized male's testes lessens over a period of time. The volume of hormones available for reabsorption gradually declines. While the vasectomized man never more loses sperm, he ordinarily does not stimulate hormonal production.

The Big Draw Method increases hormonal secretion. First, one focuses energy on the genitals to directly stimulate them. Second, the transformation of sex energy to a higher level produces higher quality hormones.

Fortunately, a vasectomized man may use the Big Draw to "steam" the seminal energies up to the head and vital organs. Moreover, with this method every man, vasectomized or not, may exchange fortifying energies with his love partner.

2. I thought yin energy is supposed to be cool, and yang warm. Why does a woman feel so warm when you have sex with her?

Chia: Relative to the male, however, the woman remains more yin in her basic polarity. Some men may have very yin, female-like qualities that they have cultivated and some women may be very aggressive and yang in their personality. Such a couple would exchange their excess energy to achieve balance. But this doesn't change the polarity at its most primordial, pure level.

In this practice you will eventually get to the point where you experience the woman's energy as cool. This happens normally in the resting stage, during the yin/yang exchange. You will feel a cool fluid running up the spine to the top of your head. It will move up the spine in stages, as if climbing a ladder. When you learn to surrender your fiery hot yang male energy you will feel this cool, soothing yin female within you. At the higher level of practice you can get this effect by simple meditating alone on the yin pole of your yang energy.

3. How long do the Taoists take to make love? It sounds like a very long affair.

Chia: Intercourse lasts as long as both lovers desire and should depend on the quality of the energy being exchanged. Don't force extra orgasms, or if you haven't mastered the method, extra ejaculations. Once you begin feeling deep satisfaction, you won't feel the need to have sex as frequently so when you do have it don't rush. Sometimes perfect polarity can be achieved quickly, but usually when you make love the Taoist way, it is no casual affair. From the beginning foreplay to the final quiet embrace may involve two hours or all day. The Taoist classics suggest one thousand loving strokes to satisfy a woman. You may rest several times and renew more active loving. Allow an appropriate length of time without distraction. Take the phone off the hook, and get rid of the kids!

4. I believe that if you ejaculate, the woman can gain a lot of yang energy directly from the sperm. What's the difference between giving it to her this way versus giving her yang energy and yin/yang exchange?

Chia: So long as you keep the male fluid, you may give her energy and quickly recharge yourself. If you give her the fluid, you lose the means of re-charging for a long time. Give her much energy, but don't give away the whole battery. Unless she is an advanced yogini who has developed the meditative ability to really draw the full power of sperm into herself, she can't use it and you will lose the power to give more. Even an advanced yogini will be limited in the amount she can absorb from physical sperm. Ultimately, she is much better off if her yogi conserves and transmutes his seed. Give her baskets of peaches: don't uproot the tree and send her shaggy roots.

5. When I do the yin/yang exchange, I sometimes feel a mini-orgasm in my genitals. How do I know if I am losing fluid?

Chia: During exhalation and relaxation, the penis will often "jump" as though you were ejaculating. In fact, no seminal fluid pours from the body. The prostate gland and seminal vesicles can also "pop" periodically, yielding great pleasure. The Taoist Method provides this orgasmic pleasure yet keeps the fluid inside the body.

Make sure at first there is no loss of fluid in the popping. When you keep every drop, the method is properly performed. If there should occasionally be some loss, immediately use the Hard Contractions and the Three Finger External Locking together to prevent further waste of seed. You must also distinguish between losing "milk" and "water". Milk is thick and whitish sperm fluid and is the secret elixir Taoists seek to conserve. Water is clear and thin runny seminal fluid that the prostate produces to help deliver the sperm. It is possible to leak some water without ejaculating any milk. If you are at this level you shouldn't rely solely on the method as a means of birth-control, as it only takes one sperm cell in the watery semen fluid to impregnate a woman.

6. I'm just beginning to learn the Big Draw. Will it harm my effort if I fail and ejaculate?

Chia: Don't make it an issue of your failing or not. Nobody expects you to hit a home run the first time you swing a bat. You hit some singles, then a double, eventually you run to third base.

When you've got full control you can hit a home run almost at will. The main thing in learning something new is to keep a positive attitude.

When you begin to practice seminal conservation, try to ejaculate no more than once per week. As you improve keep the loss down to once or twice per month. Continuing to progress, you will lose less and less fluid. Don't worry about losing the seed, simply learn to harbor it for increasing periods of time. Taoists accept what is natural, they never force any sudden change on their body. If you lose your seed, enjoy it and send it lovingly to your partner who will absorb at least a part of its yang essence into her body. Likewise, never force yourself to ejaculate to please yourself or your lover. This is a gradual process: you will spend the rest of your life increasing in knowledge and perfecting the Tao of love.

7. What is the relationship between the strength of the buttock and pelvic muscles and sex? I thought having sex strengthened them, since you get a lot of exercise in your lower body.

Chia: A moderate amount of sex is healthy for your body in many ways; your glands are exercised, especially the prostate, and more chi runs through your meridians. But a lot of these benefits leak out the anus and buttocks because so many men with office jobs develop a fat ass. You wouldn't believe how much chi just trickles out of the body through the buttocks. Ejaculation is opening the flood gates to energy loss, and it has an after effect on your buttocks.

Frequent sex with ejaculation disrupts your health by spasmodically coughing forth vitality. After a period of long abuse, it weakens the tissues so that they are unable to inhale life properly. Frequent ejaculation breaks down the tone of the lower body, inducing chronic flaccidity and steady trickling out of power. I teach pelvic strengthening exercises to improve lower body tone. By maintaining this tone, you constantly save energy that frequent ejaculators lose.

8. I feel less sexual desire after doing the Big Draw every day for several weeks. What's happening to my sexual energy?

Chia: For the first several weeks of Big Draw practice, you may experience slight lessening of sexual appetite. This is more likely to occur if you are in a weakened condition. This indicates that you are successfully transferring power upward from the genital area to the higher centers. Don't be alarmed! This is a sign that you are progressing well. You are conserving energy as never before and beginning to change it to a higher form.

After no more than several weeks the power will complete the microcosmic circuit and return much increased to the sexual centers. The power will recirculate to the genital region, which will then be permanently fortified. Once you have completed the circuit, the power will flow throughout your entire body every time you make love and revitalize you further. Then your appetite for sex may well increase. Its different for each man and his lover.

9. Aren't you being a bit fanatic in trying to save every drop of sperm? There's so much of it. I thought Taoism was a "middle" path that advocated no extremes.

Chia: Semen retention is simple and natural once you've unlearned your old habit. Taoists claim that it was once the middle way, a natural function that all humans could do naturally, and that our current sex habits are a product of degeneration. That's why we've got 4 billion people on earth and all the problems of over population and pollution of a once pure earth. If people felt more fullfillment within, they would create fewer demands without. Not to worry. Nature—the Tao—always finds the proper way to balance itself.

The conventional idea of male orgasm as a few instants of (literally) blinding pleasure is an extreme one. After ejaculation the man is finished unless he digs deep into himself for more energy only to rush forth again before falling off into a pleasant emptiness. To spend the vital seed wastefully is to excrete life. Frequent ejaculation is an infantile attempt to solve our lonely separation from bliss. It is a rejection of the inborn joy that we may all know.

Of course, people can and do love deeply without retaining their seed during sex. But these people are unconsciously transmuting their seed power into love the rest of the time—this is where love obtains its power of spontaneity. But they may miss a deeper joy. Until you learn this deeper joy I must strongly recommend you not be fanatic about losing a few drops of sperm—nature is abundant and forgiving and its best to change gradually. Then the change will be more permanent.

But at the same time you won't be motivated to change your sex habits unless you remember that ejaculation isolates. It cuts you off and enslaves you in small steps to a lower state of energy. Ejaculation is one of many subtle forms of suicide, including drugs, over-eating, over-everything. Your real task is not to prevent ejaculation: it is to establish direct contact between your physical nervous system and the subtle sources of life. To do so you must conserve the vehicle through which your chi life energy flows.

10. Most modern sex manuals claim it's healthy to fantasize about your erotic desires. What do the Taoists say?

Chia: Many sexologists are not aware of the higher possibilities of their mind and don't understand the process of transforming energy into spirit, ching into shien. Above all, Taoists are training the mind. It is very important to keep the mind free of distracting images. Fantasizing about sex ultimately strangles the mind. It breaks the flow of life and provokes orgasm.

Open your mind to the power of life: this will dissolve fantasies. When you empty the mind of thoughts, cosmic energies stream into the void. This is the first principle of meditation. The act of love becomes a meditation on the great life force. Of course, it takes time to cultivate this level of crystal clarity in your mind, so don't worry about your habit of fantasizing. Simply begin by not encouraging it, by catching yourself when you drift off, and return to the present.

The presence of your lover should arouse you. If her company doesn't stimulate you, if you have to turn to erotic fantasizing, wait for another occasion or partner. Obsessive erotic thinking inevitably leads to loss of the life force. Fantasizing causes energy to seep out even where there is no ejaculation, as well as preventing life from flowing in spontaneously. The same is true of electric vibrators or other stimulators. They feel good, but they mechanize your sexual response. You can grow dependant on your machine. If you want to be more human and ultimately find deeper pleasure, follow your natural impulses only, not the ones contrived by your culturally conditioned mind.

11. Will this practice of holding my sperm inside eventually lead to my losing my appetite for the physical passion of sex?

Chia: As you advance in the practice you lessen your need for physical movement. Physical movement is but the shadow of movement of the energy body. Contact with your lover's subtle chi is incomparably more thrilling than the hooked-fish leaps that are often mistaken for the heights of love. Your definition of sex will be radically changed by mastery of these practices that will find you concerned with the quality of your subtle energy relationship with your lover.

12. What's the difference between the physical pleasure of sex and the pleasure of feeling love?

Chia: Your pleasure is limited only by your level of consciousness. The difference between whole body orgasm and ejaculatory orgasm is the difference between human and animal love. The animal frantically ejects his energies. The higher man responsibly conserves vital energy and changes it to love. The truly free and wise man ever restores himself and his partner. This supreme art is his duty, privilege and joy. The purest pleasure is far beyond any sensory feeling perceived through our emotions or intellect. When you cultivate your original spirit, your delicate sense of subtle energy flows as well as your physical sensations are a quantum leap beyond what most people accept as pleasure.

The quality of your feeling determines the quality of energy you generate and absorb. If your desires are selfishly erotic, the energy may temporarily heighten your animal vitality but will not rise and open the higher genius of your heart, mind, and spirit.

These principles apply universally, but the act of love is particularly momentous for a human being. It involves one's entire destiny. The energy of every act and thought is preserved: one who thinks egotistically will find nothing but egotism from others. Another finds love everywhere because he unfailingly brings it within. When you raise your sexual seed-essence to a high level of spiritual intention, it becomes a light-essence, or light seed that illuminates your path through life and beyond. This is the Taoist enlightenment taught in the higher levels of meditation.

13. If the goal is to build up one's sexual energy, what's the harm of sleeping with a lot of different women (or men) to increase your ching chi?

Chia: The goal is not to build up one's sexual energy—it is to transform raw sexual energy into a refined subtle energy. Sex is only one means of doing that. Promiscuity can easily lower your energy if you choose partners with moral or physical weakness.

If you lie with degenerates, it may hurt you, in that you can temporarily acquire your partner's vileness. By exchanging subtle energy, you actually absorb the other's substance. You become the other person and assume new karmic burdens. This is why old couples resemble each other so closely: they have exchanged so much energy that they are made of the same life-stuff. This practice accelerates this union, but elevates it to a higher level of spiritual experience.

So the best advice I can give is to never compromise your integrity of body, mind and spirit. In choosing a lover you are choosing your destiny, so make sure you love the woman with whom you have sex. Then you will be in harmony with what flows from the exchange and your actions will be proper.

If you think you can love two women at once, be ready to spend double the chi to transform and balance their energy. I doubt if many men can really do that and feel deep serenity. For the sake of simplicity, limit yourself to one woman at a time. It takes a lot of time and energy to cultivate the subtle energies to a deep level.

It is impossible to define love precisely. You have to consult your inner voice. But cultivating your chi energy sensitizes you to your conscience. What was a distant whisper before may become a very loud voice. For your own sake, do not abandon your integrity for the sake of physical pleasure or the pretense that you are doing deep spiritual exercises. If you sleep with one whom you don't love, your subtle energies will not be in balance and psychic warfare can begin. This will take its toll no matter how far apart you are physically until you sever or heal the psychic connection. It's better to be honest in the beginning.

For the same reason make love only when you feel true tenderness within yourself. Your power to love will thus grow stronger. Selfish or manipulative use of sex even with someone with whom you are in love can cause great disharmony. If you feel unable to use your sexual power lovingly, then do not use it at all! Sex is a gleaming, sharp, two-edged sword, a healing tool that can quickly become a weapon. If used for base purposes, it cuts you mercilessly. If you haven't found a partner with whom you can be truly gentle, then simply touch no one. Go back to building your internal energy and when it gets high you will either attract a quality lover or learn a deeper level within yourself.

14. Isn't the Big Draw a form of sexual vampirism, teaching men how to suck women's juices, etc?

Chia: This view is incorrect for several reasons. First of all there is necessarily an exchange of energy between partners, all lovers exchange energy; the Big Draw just dramatically adds to its magnitude. You cannot inhale the yin from your partner without surrendering to her an equal measure of yang. This is simply a law of etheric energy.

Generosity is its own reward: the more you give, the more

you will receive. If you selfishly refuse to surrender the yang to your partner, you can absorb little energy from her. Thus, attempts at selfish use of the Big Draw will lead to failure. Their only effect of trying would be to deeply imbalance oneself mentally and spiritually. Likewise, generous and compassionate use of the method guarantees the fullest flow of invigorating energy from your partner.

This "Fail-Safe" aspect of the method not only prevents serious abuse of one's partner, but the natural law of the Tao will ultimately mete out an equal punishment to one who tries to take advantage of his lover. Taoists agree with the Bible here: "As ye give, so shall ye receive."

Secondly, when you draw up power you inhale mainly the energy of your own sexual centers. During the act of love the hundreds of millions of sperm cells swim about frantically in their desire to get out of you and into the egg. Their motion creates a high electromagnetic charge in the semen. In this way your lover stimulates you to produce and concentrate your own energy, which you move to higher centers with the big Draw.

Finally, a major part of the energy you draw from the lover would leave her body at any event as a result of sexual stimulation. If you did not absorb it, the power would dissipate into the atmosphere. By suppressing your ejaculation and your partner's orgasm, both lovers lose much less energy than they would in conventional sex. By following the Big Draw Method both effectively absorb some of the energy the other releases instead of letting it blow away.

15. After practicing dual cultivation for a while, how do you feel when you ejaculate again?

Chia: When you begin to meditate and cultivate your sexual energy and engage in various Taoist exercises, you notice immediately what happens when you ejaculate. There's an immediate feedback in what happens to your energy level. You feel emptied, weakened, sometimes enough to temporarily depress you. The same feeling prior to doing Taoist practices you might have called "pleasant fatigue"; now the loss begins to feel painful on a psychic level, as you are accustomed to living at a higher standard of chi energy. In actual sex, in ejaculation the energy loss is very apparent and very obvious.

16. How are the eyes used in Sexual Kung Fu practice?

Chia: The eyes are very important. Later on, if you just use the eyes and a little breathing you can do the whole Big Draw. You should keep your eyes closed during sex to maximize your internal energy; if you are looking around, the mind will be distracted and chi will escape as the eyes are the most yang organ in the body. Learn to see inside your body and that of your lovers. The eyes reflect your intention psychologically so you can literally direct everything with your eyes. Correct practice of Taoist cultivation will help you develop powerful eyes. The opposite is true as well; improper sex can destroy the sparkle in your eyes. If you're observant, without knowing anything about oriental medicine, you can actually "see" people who have depleted themselves sexually. You see it in the face, the sallowness of the eyes and skin, and lackluster quality in the hair.

17. How will ill health, tension, stress and other adverse psychological states affect Taoist sex?

Chia: A good sex life is closely related to your physical health and mental condition. If you are tense it is difficult to use mind control and the big draw methods. Your ability to use these methods in actual sex is more limited when you are tense, and it's not much fun having uptight sex anyway. Microcosmic meditation and Tai Chi Chi Kung will greatly help you to calm down. If you're not feeling well or if your general level of chi is low, your sex should be passive with your partner moving on top, giving you the healing energy. What happens in your sexual encounters is like a microcosm of daily life that is magnified tremendously.

Your psychological state is very important. Feeling loving, feeling relaxed, feeling calm and not having a lot of negative emotions is essential. If you're very angry or sad or fearful it's very difficult to engage joyfully in sex and to use this kind of practice. It may throw you or your partner off emotionally, as your aura is very open during sex and you absorb negativity easily. Better to sit down together and use the Fusion of Five Elements meditation to calm the mind. Even after years of having practiced the Big Draw, if you are not in a good psychological state you might have to exert considerable effort to hold your seed. On the other hand, when you feel calm and good psychologically you can carry the whole thing off with no effort.

18. What is the difference between mechanically blocking ejaculation through celibacy and the Taoist cultivation method?

Chia: You can mechanically block ejaculation using your mind only by refusing to have sex or masturbate. But this is using willpower against the body impulse; Taoists cultivate the bodily impulses, they put the chi energy to work elsewhere. If you are celibate and can naturally transform your sex energy and you can keep your body fully integrated with your mind, you should be shiny and radiant. But not many men are so naturally enlightened.

There's some negative evidence on health and celibacy based on data that has been collected about priests, using sheer willpower to mechanically prevent sex. This can create long term problems of the prostate, causing failure and inflammation of that organ and very often considerable pain and debility. One study did medical autopsies on over a thousand Catholic priests and found one third died of prostate complications or prostate cancer. The suggestion is that their celibacy was bad for their health. In their case apparently it was true, I've heard of celibate yogis who have similar problems with their prostate.

The problem arises, I believe, because they did not know how to cultivate their sex energy properly. Their energy channels aren't open between their lower and upper body and so their sex energy is blocked and congests the blood and hormones in the genitals and the prostate. To prevent prostate problems, a celibate should squeeze his perineum tightly and relax it several dozen times a day. This will exercise the prostate somewhat, although not as well as the Big Draw, which also circulates chi energy through it. If you try to cure a weak prostate by having more sex it can work, as orgasm exercises your prostate, but you risk losing a lot of sperm energy unless you know the Taoist method. Other men weaken their prostate from excess ejaculation and depletion of their sexual energy. For them celibacy is a cure.

Stopping ejaculation with an internal (big draw) practice may look similar to mechanically stopping sex through celibacy, but the difference is great. The Big Draw consciously transforms your energy up using internal skill, celibacy leaves it to chance or willpower. I've done this practice many years and never had any problems at all. Sometimes, when there's some congestion, just a little massage clears it up. That's why in terms of hygiene, you cannot separate this practice from the larger context of meditation and the energy work in the Taoist system not to speak of other considerations that have to do with ethical, psychological and spiritual aspects.

19. Could you summarize the advantage of the Taoist total body orgasm over a loving normal sex orgasm with ejaculation?

Chia: A total orgasm of the body and mind might be described as a showering of nectar from the head, running down your insides like a springtime shower. It is unmistakable. It is a wave of subtle chi energy that breaks up muscle armoring, releases nerve and lymphatic tension, and opens up hidden powers of feeling. You feel like a new born baby, only instead of experiencing your rebirth as a baby does—as unconscious bliss—you are very adult and conscious. The weight of the world is there, but suddenly it becomes lighter than a feather.

This feeling of lightness happens because the heavy fluid of your sperm-seed has successfully been transmuted into a light-seed which nourishes your higher consciousness. You feel happy deep inside because you know you have found the path home. You are not weighted by yourself or your lover. This is different from a genital orgasm, which is usually followed by either a heavy sleep as the body attempts to recover energy lost or by a still anxious mind that asks: "What next?" With genital orgasm the body is relaxed, but the mind and spirit are not; they are still hungry for nourishment of subtle energy because the polarity between lovers is not complete.

20. Could you explain in detail what happens when you reach the point of no return during an orgasm?

Chia: The curve of sexual arousal in both men and women but especially for men (because women have a greater capacity to maintain a plateau) is to have a gradual (or rapid) arousal, a short plateau and then a rapid and sudden fall off and that's it . . . The Big Bang Theory. Taoist cultivation teaches you to use the Steady State theory, which is continuous expansion and contraction of yin and yang during a series of "valley" orgasms. The Big Bang theory, currently in vogue as the cosmological theory of the Universe, has as its roots the sexual desires of the western male scientist.

Now, the plateau can be likened to a "primal zone", that is an experience of primal time and space. Minutes may seem like hours; however you choose to define it. It is what psychologists call an altered state of consciousness. Women seem more capable than men of extending this plateau. Beyond that there is a critical point of no return and then the "fall off." The plateau can last anywhere from a few seconds to several minutes to a half hour or longer and is characterized by quieting, relaxation and a diminishing erection in the male. In practice, after this period of quiet the couple resumes mutual stimulation, building up the energy, building the chi through thrusting and various other means of arousal. And again a plateau may be reached and maintained a while.

It takes practice to keep from "stepping off the edge" but the rewards are great. It's like climbing a pyramid—the top of each step is safe and flat, but going up over the edge to the next step is a little dizzying. In this step procedure you build a potential to respond to your lover that's enormous and so the probability of losing control increases as you progress to higher steps. It's as though you were building more and more pressure, but it's a pleasurable pressure, because the energy of each plateau is greater than the last. In fact, the plateaus get longer as the energy builds. When sufficient energy has developed and you are at a plateau, the chi energy begins to run through the chi channels in the body and so what had begun as a genital response now becomes a bodily one. If the whole body energy of the male is balanced with that of the female, the energy penetrates the subtle bodies on mental and spiritual levels as well, aligning your total polarity and opening your awareness of both knowledge and bliss. The nature of the Tao reveals itself to be both awesome and ordinary.

The "primal zone" on the plateau is a very precarious place and it is here that the skill of Taoist dual cultivation can really be said to be exercised. The sensitivity and ability to keep from going on to the "point of no return" is a function of your experience, your intention and your overall state of relaxation and health and your relationship to your partner. Now a woman can trigger a man's ejaculation quite easily thru her own orgasm or by stimulating him by contracting vaginal muscles. So this technique does not require a mutual orgasm and especially in the learning phase, the man must be permitted time to gain some stability at the plateau. It's interesting that many women feel that unless a man has an ejaculation he's not satisfied. This is where sexual politics comes in with all the attitudes and expectations which color responses tremendously. Both men and women have to gradually de-condition themselves of their old concepts. This will happen naturally as a couple cultivates their energy together.

21. Does homosexuality or group sex block spiritual development?

Chia: The Taoists are too wise to condemn anything outright, as everything leads back to the Tao. So the question really is how can it be against nature, or the Tao, if the Tao created it? Homosexuality is not against the Tao, but it is also not the highest experience of the Tao possible. It's impossible to experience the full balance of male-female polarity with homosexual love. The subtle energies are lacking and you can't create something if the raw materials are absent. The highest harmony of yin and yang cannot be achieved. It depends on how far on the spiritual path you wish to proceed. If you go deep enough into meditation you may cultivate your opposite polar energy within. But then your homosexual love life might disrupt that balance, so you would constantly be correcting it.

The problem is greater for two men than for two women, because their double yang energy is too expansive and more easily leads to conflict. A double yin energy can be harmonious, as yin is yielding, but neither woman will experience deepest fulfillment. Both cases can lead to subtle organ imbalances that require attention if best health is to be maintained.

The situation for male homosexuals can be somewhat ameliorated if the men seek alternate sources of yin energy. They could eat more yin food, spend more time with female friends and work in the garden cultivating earth chi. You can also absorb energy directly from the earth by lying face down on the ground and meditating, drawing it into your penis and hands. This might help if it were done before or after sex. If you wish to practice semen retention and find yourself in rapidly changing male homosexual relationships, I advise you to become celibate for a period and attempt to gain stability through intensive single cultivation using the Big Draw and Meditation.

In group sex it is even more difficult to harmonize the subtle energies. I recommend you avoid it as it is rarely motivated by love. The only exception might be two women with one man, as the double yin can harmonize his yang if they are also in harmony. For most people this is unlikely to be stable, which is necessary for real cultivation to occur. If you feel attracted to several people the best thing you can do for them is to inspire them to cultivate themselves using Tai Chi, meditation, yoga, or the methods described in this book. Teach by example; you don't have to physically love everyone you feel attracted to. You will never go deep in yourself if you scatter your energy widely.

22. What causes the penis to go flaccid, if you began with a stiff erection but didn't ejaculate?

Chia: It may be that your mind has left the act of love, and is distracted elsewhere. The chi moves with the mind, it is guided by it. If your mind is concentrating on a higher exchange of energy with your lover and you've lost your erection, it may be a sign that physical love is no longer needed and you should relax and enjoy the communion. You should keep your flaccid penis within her or touching her if possible, as the chi can still flow through it. But please, for your own sanity, don't try to force a new erection.

23. If I master the Big Draw and am celibate, but still have wet dreams, what should I do?

Chia: If you really master the Big Draw this should not happen at all, but this might happen to someone who retains the sex energy but hasn't transformed all of it up to a higher center. The sex energy remaining in the lower part might be causing trouble. The Taoist method of Microcosmic Orbit Meditation, Fusion of Five Elements, and Kan and Li contain the formulas for transforming the energy up. If that doesn't work and the wet dreams persist, listen to your body's message and find a lover.

24. Is it o.k. to make specific wishes or project a thought at the moment of orgasm?

Chia: I strongly recommend you avoid projecting your ego at the moment of orgasm or at any time during love-making. This is a magical practice that can have very unexpected effects, sometimes dangerous to your spiritual growth. Evil astral entities can attach themselves if you are not well balanced. Some men have sex with "phantom" lovers in their dream state that are real entities. You might also get what you asked for—and much more that you failed to specify and that you find extremely undesirable. You will also lose energy by sending it all outside. I know one woman who did this "magical child" projection for ten years. It made her pale and sickly. It is best to give the energy back to your lover, as that is where it came from. In this way you pay the universe immediately for its blessing. If you increase your lover's energy instead of some ego desire, she will be transformed to a higher level and be in a position to return even higher blessings to you or others in the universe. Spiritual progress comes from achieving balance of yin/ yang, from being both spontaneously present and neutral, not from fulfilling some mental projection. Taoists refine their chi in their body. We don't send out our dirty laundry and hope it comes back washed—we clean it ourselves. So keep your attention on balancing your chi where you are; that is your entire obligation to the universe.

CHAPTER 13

STUDENT EXPERIENCES OF TAOIST SEXUAL CULTIVATION

This interview was conducted by Michael Winn with a 46 year old psychologist and student of Master Chia who has raised several children.

M.W.: Was it easy to learn the Sexual Kung Fu?

Student: I've been practicing Seminal Kung Fu for a year and a half now. I found it easy to learn when I practiced alone but difficult to implement during sex because of an unconscious resistance from making love for so many years in a different way.

It got easier as I grew more aware that normal sex fatigued me. But it is not possible to divorce this practice from the other practices that I've studied, such as the Microcosmic and fusion meditation formulas, Iron Shirt Chi Kung, and Tai Chi. They increased my sensitivity to energy, particularly the Iron Shirt Chi Kung.

M.W.: How has it affected your daily relationship?

Student: It has produced a very strong bonding. Many times the expression takes the form of energy that flows between us. Sometimes it's translated into telepathic or clairvoyant experiences. That happens in many relationships when partners are together over a long period of time. What's unusual in my relationship is that it's happened very, very quickly. My Taoist practice accelerated the process.

M.W.: Has it been so satisfying to you that you've wanted to have sex less often?

Student: No. The reverse. I want sex more frequently, three or four times a week, depending on the occasion or the situation. Sometimes a number of times during the day. And quite frequently during the week.

When sex does become tiring is when I fail to do the practice and I lose my energy by ejaculation. And I still find that after a year and a half, almost 2 years, of doing this practice that it happens periodically that I lose the will to implement it, I find it quite interesting as a psychologist to see the old conditioning which still remains in myself is not yet totally overcome. That I just want to go for the orgasm. That's something I'm still struggling with. I have control of it now but I have to be pretty watchful.

M.W.: It's like looking at an aspect of your former self.

Student: I owe it much to social and cultural conditioning. This type of sexual activity is absolutely counter to the drive of western sexuality as we understand it.

M.W.: Can you describe any extraordinary experiences?

Student: A number of them. They were characterized by intense energy flow between us after a period of intercourse and repeated control of ejaculation. There were many occasions where the energy would build up and there was an arching between our mouth and genital, like electricity leaping across a gap. Or it would zoom through our Microcosmic Orbits, back and forth between us. At other times it was like a cocoon of energy that just wraps us both, radiating inside and outside our bodies.

M.W.: Is the cocooning valuable to the relationship or is it just for its pleasure?

Student: It is pleasurable but it also has a tremendous compelling emotional quality. It's an extraordinary communication between partners that generates beyond the sex experience to the relationship itself. We feel the energy flow, frequently outside of sex itself. When we meditate together, there is an arching through the head, especially when we do the Fusion formula. Another experience I've had during sex is I felt the thrusting routes connecting. It felt like there was a ladder between the bodies. It formed a fountain at the top and ran down into the bodies and around the bodies so that the thrusting routes were merged at the center point and developed a magnetic field. It was very powerful.

M.W.: Did you ever feel any distinct hot and cold energies?

Student: Yes, that's quite common, just at the point of

ejaculation control. At that point there is a lot of my heat energy
going through the penis. Just then I've often felt a chill go right up
my back. At one point I looked at the window, I thought there was
a draft at my back, it was so distinct. I've often experienced my
partners body feeling cool and moist, while my energy is very hot
and dry.

M.W.: Is this a practice that you would, as a psychologist,
recommend to someone who is emotionally disturbed or is trying to
work out their relationship?

Student: No, not at all. The energy swings would be very
destabilizing.

M.W.: So it's really only for people who already have a fairly
solid relationship?

Student: I think so. It's also very important that people practice this meditation together, the Microcosmic Orbit. It should not
be divorced from the system.

M.W.: You said it brought so much more to your relationship
and so many relationships flounder on sexual compatibility.
Wouldn't this help cure that or have a therapeutic value?

Student: It could in certain ways, in that it cures premature
ejaculation. I think the real benefit is to see the spiritual context but
teaching it as a therapeutic method should be an interesting experiment.

M.W.: Do you think Western sexologists, like Kinsey and
Masters whould be interested in this?

Student: They might if it were in a context where they could
understand it. Masters and Johnson and other sexologists work
with ejaculatory control, so in that sense this method is not dis-
similar. Putting pressure on the seminal duct, manually, is very
similar to Masters and Johnson method. But beyond that they are
still in kindergarden when it comes to understanding the role of sex
in the human energy system, or how to use your mind to control
energy balance and sex drive.

M.W.: A lot of men your age go through a mid-life crisis
which is partly seen in sexual terms. How does the practice relate
to that?

Student: I had my mid-life crisis these last few years. A lot had
to do with a career change and decisions about what kind of work I
wanted to do. So this Taoist work has helped me decide on what I
want, how I use my energy and how I use my energy in sex and

what my purpose is. So, yes, the Taoist practices and Seminal &
Ovarian Kung Fu have helped to clarify the picture, because a lot
of the mid-life crisis is about your spiritual direction in life.

The following excerpts were tape recorded following a Sexual
Kung Fu workshop in Denver, a discussion between Master Chia
and his students.

Student: I've been around the esoteric world for about twelve
years now and I've heard about chakras and energy flows and what
the properties are and how to understand it. Sexual energy, I think
is a very potent force in life and controls many people's minds. So
to put this in order, to put it in a proper perspective is very important and I'm happy to have found someone to teach me to do it.

Chia: There's an order in going to school. You wouldn't attempt to take a Master's when you haven't finished grade school.
In the same way you shouldn't attempt Tai Chi Chuan, which is
comparable to taking a Master's until you've developed a good
foundation in your esoteric practice, at the very least, the Microcosmic Orbit. The style of Tai Chi Chuan is not so important as
developing an internal flow of energy.

Student #2: I found that doing the testicle breathing really
gives you a lift, it keeps you awake and refreshes you. I used to use
No Doze to stay awake when driving long distances. Now I use
testicle breathing instead, and it really works.

Student #3: I really appreciate the details that you offer in the
Taoist Sexual Kung Fu. I'd practiced a Buddhist Tantric method
that made use of the Microcosmic Orbit, the tongue and the anal
sphincter muscle, actually the perineal area. My experience with
the Taoist method was different. Immediately upon drawing in my
penis and testicles as you suggested, I pulled up through the perineum and the energy shot to the top of my head.

Chia: Can you describe this Buddhist Tantric Method?

Student: Yes, I'd hold my breath, push my tongue up and look
into my head. So you bring the tongue up, the breath up, the eyes
up and then squeeze the perineum, but the details were lacking, as
I said, as soon as I pulled in my penis and testicles, it made a
tremendous difference. I thought the power that I derived here was
at least twenty times what I'd experienced in that Tibetan approach. During the last workshop with you I actually felt the tendons around my penis and the testicle cords pull up. When the
perineum was closed, the rush of energy was overwhelming.

Occasionally, in the Kundalini approach, a practitioner will spontaneously draw in air thru his urethura into his bladder. That can be painful, and even troublesome later when a pressure bubble forms in the bladder, in the practice of drawing water up into the bladder, where the same sphincter is used, that air bubble can interfere and again cause pain.

Chia: I must point out an important difference between the methods that you've described and the one you've just learned here. In that approach the perineum is left open during the big draw. When you close it off first and then pull up (or draw), air doesn't get into the bladder. In the practice of drawing water into the bladder you must be sure to have expelled everything out of it first. Otherwise you can have pain. That is why I do not teach it. Besides, it's not really necessary. Here you close off before the "draw" to prevent air or water from getting in. When you get to Lesser Enlightenment, Greater Enlightenment and Greatest Enlightenment, you'll also find that when you mix the higher cosmic energy you have to close off so that no air gets in when you "draw". In fact, a spontaneous "draw" occurs by then, which means that you should have mastered closing off first to avoid the trouble of pulling in air.

Student: In that Tibetan Tantric teaching we were told that the Buddha could pull his penis in, but it was never presented as a technique. Here, it's as though the whole thing is brought together, on both physical and spiritual levels. By the way, the packing of chi in the body, done in Iron Shirt, reminds me very much of Tumo Yoga or the Inner fire, because a very important part of that is "packing". There again I appreciate the way you've described exactly what to do inside your body. The Tibetan teacher would demonstrate and the way that many of us imitated him we might have been doing a comical dance.

Student #4: In the male, in the normal course of ejaculation, there is a strong charge in the perineum that switches the parasympathetic stimulation to a sympathetic one, which quickly leads to exhaustion. By contrast, the female remains in a parasympathetic state of arousal throughout. After the ejaculation reflex takes place there is a sympathetic nervous system stimulation in the male. This is evident in the flush and the dryness in the mouth that is experienced. Each time ejaculation takes place it leads to an outright catabolic state. Instead of building there is a tearing down.

Chia: And that leads to anger or in extreme cases even crime.

Student #5: This Taoist method is very, very, good. It's my second time taking this class. The first time I didn't practice on any regular basis. About three weeks ago, I found the Big Draw without even looking for it. I found energy coming from the perineum. I then concentrated on bringing it into the coccyx while making love and my whole body filled with an enormous bubble of energy. The next day I repeated the "Big Draw" with great success. One thing I would caution everybody—I forgot to bring my energy down. About a week or so later, I became very, very angry and flew off the hook very fast, and I realized in today's session that you really have to concentrate on bringing it down. I was just letting the energy shoot up. I forgot to go through the practice and bring it on down. So I caution you. It's very important to bring it down. It's a terrific practice and it really gives you enormous energy, and a great vitality. It's fabulous.

The following statements were taken from interviews with students of Taoist Esoteric Yoga who studied the methods taught in this book.

EXPERIENCE OF A LAWYER, AGE 29

I'm a lawyer, age 29, from New York. Taoist cultivation of sexual energy has brought a revolutionary change in my life. This is not because I was a failure as a lover. As an adolescent, of course, I had periods of insecurity about my virility and occasional impotence due to fear of particularly powerful women. But after leaving adolescence my self-confidence gradually improved and I learned each year how to please women more and more.

As I learned something of the arts of love, I realized that there could never be lasting satisfaction unless I learned to retain the seminal fluid and avoid the breakdown at the end of normal love. This point was the flaw in an otherwise marvelous experience. I could often have sex for a long time without ejaculating, but it was a hit or miss affair. I didn't know how to transfer the energy away from the genital region at will, nor to swiftly calm myself if I was in an overexcited state.

I sensed that sex-love relationships were so perishable because men and women didn't know how to nourish the life flame between them. I realize that even when I had been a superb lover, at the end of the act I always felt insufficient. Ejaculation forced me to stop making love whether or not desire continued.

When I first began to practice with Master Chia, I immediately recognized the immense value of his teaching. This was surely to be the most important thing I had learned to this point in my life. At first, it was not very pleasant to do the muscular contractions and I was a little embarrassed. But since I made love to one partner who cared very much for me, my embarrassment quickly faded. She really wanted to help me accomplish my goal. This is so important.

I cannot urge too strongly other students of Taoist cultivation to stick to one loving partner. There is so much more to know in one good soul than in 50 good bodies. The adventure and variety of experience that comes from diving into the soul of another person is incomparably superior. After all, the body, like all material things, exists on one plane. The depths of the human soul, however offer multiple worlds to explore, the one more fascinating than the next. The analogy in the physical world is that playboy never really moves from that hick town called the body; whereas, the faithful lover may travel vast continents of hidden worlds within.

When I began to practice Sexual Kung Fu it was somewhat awkward at first. I had to concentrate on these seemingly unnatural movements and this deprived me of the small degree of freedom I had already attained in my ordinary, good old, down home loving. But I persisted and everything quickly became much easier. I found I could soon abandon the Hard Contractions, which most seemed to disrupt the smooth harmony of the act. I did this when I had learned to calm down to a certain degree. After that I had to use the Big Draw for several months to keep calm enough to hold the seed. However the Big Draw didn't disturb me or my partner's delight. Over the course of months, I have attained to virtually effortless control of the seminal fluid.

Just after entering I still must sometimes consciously cool off due to the initial stimulation. After that I have no difficulty holding the seed with the sheer strength of my thought. I rythmically inhale the power and exhale it to my partner. I am always sure to give her more than I take. There are certain times when it is more desirable to maximize the exchange, others when I prefer to lessen it. These things must be learned for oneself and are intensely personal.

The zone between high excitement and ejaculation has grown continually greater. When I got very excited before it was very unpredictable when I would come. Sometimes I could go on for a long time, sometimes I would lose control just as I reached a state of high excitement. Now there is a much larger space between excitement and ejaculation. The plateau has grown wider and I can stroll around there joyfully without danger of falling into the pit.

After about 1½ years, I can see that there are no limits to this practice. It has grown more and more pleasurable, and has deeply changed my relations with women.

I attribute much of the historic repression of woman to man's fear of woman's sexual potency. There is no way he can match her unless he learns to control his seed. My sex drive has always been tremendous and women have come back to me for more, but ejaculation always flawed love fatally in the end. Even if the woman didn't realize it and thought she was getting the greatest possible time, I knew that something crucial was lacking. A valid method of seminal retention is the only way to overcome that hidden fear of women. And as long as man continues to fear his mate, nothing of lasting beauty may be accomplished. The loss of fear of woman is a magnificent new freedom. Even when I don't make love, the power of the fluid pervades and fills my life.

EXPERIENCE OF A BUSINESSMAN, AGE 45 YEARS OLD

I'm a 45 year old businessman from Connecticut. About one year ago I had a chance to study Seminal Kung Fu with Master Chia. Originally, I took the class out of curiosity. Seminal Kung Fu, to my surprise, has turned out to be the most valuable technique I ever learned. The method is simple yet so powerful.

During my ten years of marriage I always failed to reach orgasm at the right time. I usually came too early and too fast for my wife to have full pleasure. This problem didn't destroy my marriage, however it troubled both me and my wife.

Seminal Kung Fu changed the whole experience of love-making. With the controllable orgasm, sex has become much more enjoyable for us. The method began to be effective from the first lesson. A year of practice has made me more skillful. Now I am enjoying a much happier life with a sweet wife, two lovely children, and good health.

We are living in a highly tense society. We are heavily loaded with work, worries, endless desire, and abuses like smoking, drinking and promiscuity. It is difficult for an average middle-aged man to survive in his sex life without trouble. That is why impotence is a common word today.

I sincerely wish that every man on this earth has the opportunity to experience sex as it's really meant to be.

EXPERIENCE OF A TEACHER, AGE 37

I'm a 37 year old teacher from San Francisco. I'm Chinese but have been in America for 10 years. At the age of 15 I had my first ejaculation. I was intensely curious about it and began to read much on the subject including esoteric books that a friend of mine had. I later talked to yogis and monks from a temple near my house who might know what it meant apart from its reproductive function. I began to appreciate the value of the semen and the importance of its retention. But I couldn't help ejaculating often and masturbated once or twice a week.

When I was 18 I went to a Chinese medical doctor who told me I had kidney trouble. He said this caused my frequent ejaculation. He prescribed a very expensive course of medication and said that if I didn't follow his prescription I would be impotent by middle-age. Being unable to pay even one-quarter of his fee, I began to despair.

I experimented with many methods over a long period of time. None of these methods were really effective. Some times I abandoned even attempting to control the outflow of my semen.

Then I was taught the External Locking Method. The first time I used it I had a little pain in the perineum. My teacher said that this was from never using these muscles and organs in this way before. He assured me that there was no danger to my body. After this first time I used External Locking 300 to 400 times without any discomfort or problem.

When I learned the Taoist internal method, I realized they had a very deep understanding of human sexual power. The importance of opening the energy route in the back to bring power up to the head cannot be overemphasized. When I opened this route, I could store much more power, for the head can hold more than the lower back. I gradually produced more and more power for the well-being of myself and my wife.

During my first three years of marriage I have used Sexual Kung Fu as an effective means of birth control. When I wanted to have a child, I needed to ejaculate only three times before my wife conceived our beautiful son.

I know that I could have never achieved my present happiness and success without Sexual Kung Fu. My health is wonderful, and I am told that I look much younger than my age. In fact, I've noticed that after a good night of love-making, my partner and I actually look several years younger the next morning. My wife says the power I give her when we make love is the world's best beauty aid.

EXPERIENCE OF AN ELECTRICIAN, AGE 27

I am 27 years old and work as an electrician in an electronics firm in Long Island.

When I was 20 years of age I had to work to help support my family and put myself through school. It wasn't long before I became physically run down and it was during that time that I experienced wet dreams, sometimes as often as three or four times a week. These made me feel weak and ashamed and somehow guilty. As time went on things seemed to get worse.

If I looked at pictures of naked women or went to porno shows I would get so sexually aroused that If I just touched my penis I would ejaculate. If I went on a date and if the girl and I petted a little and she rubbed against me I would ejaculate. It made me so embarrassed that after a while I dreaded going on dates.

By the time I met Master Chia, about two years ago, my emotional and physical health were pretty far gone. When I described the situation to him, he advised me to open the Governor route so that I could practice Seminal Kung Fu which directly related to my problem. He advised me to do the exercise thirty-six times in the morning and the same number of times at night. Instead, I did it 100 times in the morning and 100 times at night. In one week, the wet dreams stopped and after two weeks had passed I still didn't have any.

I practiced every opportunity I had. Some days I did the exercise as much as 400 times. I found it invigorating. If I grew tired or sleepy while driving, I would pull over to the side of the road and practice a while and in no time I was wide awake and full of energy. In fact, whenever I found myself with nothing to do I would practice. Waiting in line in a supermarket or when alone and not having anything to do, I might practice the "Big Draw" and "Scrotal Compression".

When I get up in the morning I rub my penis and then again when I go for a b.m. When I have an erection I draw the energy up using the "Big Draw" exercise. As soon as the power rises up to my head the erection subsides. Six months after I began this practice, I ceased being troubled by wet dreams. When I do dream of a girl, which has happened many times, I have an erection, but instead of ejaculating, the energy is drawn up to my head, at which time I wake up with a sense of a cool, fragrant nectar, beyond description. This nectar of heaven, as I've heard it called, tastes like nothing I've ever tasted before.

After practicing the "Big Drawing" for a year, my memory has improved, the wet dreams have stopped, my health has improved and I'm not afraid to date anymore. It wasn't easy. There were many setbacks along the way but practice makes perfect. After doing the "Big Draw" exercise many thousands of times, a feeling now develops which is so pleasurable that I am sure that nothing can be compared to it. The sexual pleasure that I had experienced earlier, prior to and during the ejaculation were nothing by comparison. What I experience now can only be called spiritual. I feel as though it penetrates my very soul. The Seminal Kung Fu pleasure transcends all that we know of in our everyday world.

EXPERIENCE OF DRY CLEANER, AGE 67

I am 67. I am still working at a dry cleaner upstate. I first noticed my sex life falling off when I was 39. I was no longer easily aroused and when I finally was, I had trouble maintaining a firm erection. I began to read anything I could lay my hands on relating to the subject. Nothing seemed to really work, so I devised my own way. Upon reaching the point of ejaculation I just held it back. That didn't work too well either because after a time I simply had a wet dream. Yet, I continued the practice thinking it could help. By the time I was 50 my sexual activity had diminished considerably. At 60, it had dropped off to just 4 or 5 times a year.

I met Master Chia when I was 64. I listened to him give a talk on "Seminal Kung Fu" but really couldn't believe him. After all, by that time, I'd been practicing it, I thought for almost 30 years. But he said something that caught my attention. He said that one had to complete the Microcosmic route after which the Ching power would more effectively be utilized. I recall that he compared the Microcosmic Orbit to a highway and explained that unless you had such a highway, it would be very difficult to transport goods from one place to another. It took me four months to open the route after which Master Chia taught me "Seminal Kung Fu" and the "Big Draw."

In the beginning, I practiced 36 times a day whenever I could, or just a few times if I was too tired. He taught me a number of techniques during that time. I was told to rub my penis until it became erect, expose myself to the sun and absorb power from the earth. After six months I found myself frequently awakening in the morning with a very firm erection—a most impressive sign of improvement.

However, when I had a wet dream for the first time in ten years I quickly called Master Chia to thank him. Six more months more went by with no success. I told him the way I felt—that I had no faith in the method. He introduced me to other students who were practicing Sexual King Fu.

Talking to them and hearing of their success first hand I grew very confident that I could succeed too. Though I practiced for two years I had difficulty succeeding in deriving much pleasure because of my age. In fact I succeeded only three times, however I did develop much control. Master Chia said that I am only 40% effective because I am now 67. He promised me, though, that if I continued to practice, I would still be able to have intercourse in my eighties and will be able to produce sperm to maintain my health and vigor.

After three years of practice I suddenly realized that I am fortunate in not having any prostate gland trouble—an affliction that troubles men between the ages of 60 and 70. I think that Master Chia's suggestion that I rub the area around my prostate, the Hui yin and the area around that, has been of most help in the matter. Before I started this practice I had to urinate three or four times a night, the frequency of which is just half that now.

EXPERIENCE OF A COOK, AGE 30

I am 30 years old and work as a cook. My main problems are that I ejaculate too quickly and have occasional wet dreams. I read extensively on the subject and talked and meditated to no avail. Then a friend introduced me to Master Chia saying that he had found him to be very good. Even after I'd practiced Seminal Kung Fu for six months, however, I still had trouble with control, because as Master Chia said, I am not married. Going to prostitutes as I do I cannot practice the method. They want to have me ejaculate as quickly as possible so that they can go on to their other clients. Master Chia advised me that I find just one girl, who will work with me and he assured me that with practice I would succeed. He urged me to practice the "Big Draw" and to rub my penis more, thinking that that could also help. I really have a problem, though, because I don't think I can stick with one girl, let alone get married. I have improved, though. I'm nowhere near as bad as I used to be. At one time I'd ejaculate within a couple of seconds after entering a girl's vagina. Now I can go as long as a minute and a half.

EXPERIENCE OF GARMENT FACTORY OWNER, AGE 38

I am 38 years old and own a garment factory. I'm young, I'm prosperous and I am proud of my sexual prowess. I've never had any problems getting girls nor have I had any trouble after we get together.

For years I studied and practiced all kinds of variations of sex a man and a woman can enjoy together. Then I heard that a Master Chia was teaching Seminal Kung Fu and Taoist Yoga and I was so intrigued that I went to see him.

I've been going to see him for around three and a half years. At this point, I am convinced that Seminal Kung Fu is the heart of Taoist Yoga. Now that I have practiced these methods I can satisfy my wife much more fully than I had when I was younger. Besides, my own pleasure has been greatly heightened.

There is no comparison between what I call worldly pleasure and my new found beyond-worldly-pleasure. In the normal, everyday sort of ejaculation my pleasure is quickly over with. Not so in Seminal Kung Fu. The pleasure generated here stays with me throughout the day. There seems to be no final peak to this pleasure, either. Each time I seem to go to newer, more delightful levels of loving my wife, which cannot be described. This practice offers the added bonus of affording extra energy, so I am just never tired. Now I can have as much sex as I want and I can control it rather than have it control me. What more can a man ask for?

EXPERIENCE OF AN EXECUTIVE, AGE 38

I am a 38 year old executive for a well known company in New Jersey. When I was 25 years old I was taught a method of sexual control by a Master who forbade me to teach it to anyone else. After about a year I could indulge in sexual intercourse for more than an hour without ejaculating. I've been in this country for about 10 years and I am still not married. I was thankful for having learned such self control because it has enabled me to have continuing relationships with women who enjoy my company.

I heard about Master Chia three years ago and went to see what he could teach me. In three months I opened my Microcosmic Orbit. Then, he taught me Seminal Kung Fu. I was just curious to know whether there was any difference in approach in his method and was willing to pay to find out. I discovered that Master Chia taught a much more detailed and higher level of practice and presented a much more complete program for overall development.

My previous Master had never taught me anything about opening the Microcosmic Orbit nor had he told me what to do with excess power. Master Chia has even taught me how to transmute Ching Ch'i, during sexual intercourse, into power that can be sent up to the head. I feel confident now that I am learning a more complete system. Furthermore, I feel better and stronger and enjoy more feelings of pleasure than ever before. It is most important to transmute the sperm energy into a type that can be used throughout the system. Simply retaining it is no use and doesn't even really manage to keep you from losing fluids.

It is like building a dam. After a while the water just runs over the top. But when I transmute power and send it to my head, I feel my energy routes getting joined and cleared. Otherwise energy builds in areas like the head. Having nowhere else to go, it might cause damage. Right now I'm working on opening the 32 routes that must be opened. This should allow me to accommodate much more power, as there is much more room for it to occupy. So what's the end? Immortality seems like a long way off, but it beats the hell out of my job. I think I'm going to go for it.

CHAPTER 14

PRACTICAL GUIDELINES TO KEEPING SEX RADIANT AND HEALTHY

"The Way of the Tao is to unify the spirit. Do this by gathering your vital energy, calming your mind, and harmonizing your will. The body should be regulated neither too hot nor too cold, neither hungry nor overfed. In this way sex is always leisurely and relaxed."
—*Plain Woman's advice to the Yellow Emperor*

Over the centuries the Taoists observed there were many different ways to maximize the power of love-making and minimize the harmful loss of the sexual energies being exchanged and transformed. For example, assume you had mastered the "Big Draw" so you had perfect control over your orgasm. Suppose you then ate a big meal before making passionate love with your partner for several hours. Afterwards, you took a shower right away and then lay about naked under a cool summer breeze coming through the window.

You very likely neutralized the energizing effects of the sex, or worse, harmed your health by ignoring that the flow of energy before and after love-making is as important as the flow of chi felt during sex.

Mastering semen retention is an essential step in transforming your sexual energy, but it is worthless if that energy generated is not harmonized with the rest of your life. The big dinner ties up your digestive energy and the shower and breeze disperse the chi so carefully conserved during sex. Taoists are concerned with keeping the overall flow of life energy in balance and this demands growing awareness of the subtle events that control your life. Here are some observations culled from Taoist teachings on keeping sex radiant and healthy.

1. GET TUNED WITH YOUR PARTNER'S ENERGY 48 HOURS IN ADVANCE

Sex really begins 48 hours in advance of the act, as the energies you accumulate then will express themselves when you go deep into sex. So the day before, during and even after sex you should try to calm down any feeling of agitation or anger, as this, more than almost anything else, will block the balanced flow of energy with your partner and within yourself. A woman's yin nature gives her sensitive antennae to hidden under-currents. So if you are clear, it will help her be clear and relaxed when you begin to make love. If you start on the plane of serenity, sex will more easily take you to a higher level of ecstasy. Be sensitive, stay with your partner; the effort is to move to a deeper state of being together, not just share a momentary climax. Let the sex become part of the larger meditation that is your life.

2. FOREPLAY BEGINS WITH A RELAXED ATMOSPHERE

Remember a woman's erogenous zones are different and often broader, than a man's. Caress her by creating an intimate "home" or bedroom conducive to love-making. Foreplay begins before you even touch a woman's body; dim lighting or candles, soft pillows and loose, natural clothes, sweet smells, music and gentle talk will appeal to her sexual energy and expand her openness to your own.

3. DON'T MAKE LOVE AFTER A BIG MEAL

This common mistake can ruin either your digestion or your love-making. Sex and eating are two separate functions that work best when there is no competition for body energy. Sex on a full belly reduces semen production, causes indigestion and harms the spleen. Wait until your food is fully digested, and the quality of your love making will be much higher. After sex is over, it may be nourishing to eat some warm sweet foods. Herbal tea can be especially tonifying and help a man regain his energy. Avoid cold drinks, ice cream, or ice cubes afterwards—your body has to heat them up which burns off your subtle sexual energy.

4. AVOID INTERCOURSE IN ANY EXTREME STATE

If you are too tired, angry, hungry, afraid, sad, weak, or angry don't have sex. The energy required to make love may throw your health further off balance, and accelerate the development of a minor illness into a major one. A cold acquired from a partner can develop into a flu. If you feel sexual frustration and are literally "bursting" with extreme yang sex energy, engage in sex but with restraint. Don't exhaust the yang energy so that you flip into the opposite "yin" state of exhaustion. This is like a thirsty man dying from gorging on water suddenly found.

You may feel passion and should fully enjoy the body sensations and feelings stimulated by sex, but try not to get lost in their extremes, or the pleasure may turn to pain. When the atmosphere is one of relaxed enjoyment both lovers will find it easier to open to the higher energies within themselves. If one lover moves to an extreme state of arousal, the other may feel left out or unbalanced.

5. DON'T MAKE LOVE WHEN DRUNK ON ALCOHOL

It's hard to control your semen flow much less your chi flow when you're drunk. The feeling of warmth you feel on alcohol is temporary, caused by your blood capillaries opening and releasing your inner energy. Strong physical exertion while drunk may damage your lungs through loss of breath control. One or two drinks may help some people relax without causing loss of control; if you must drink alcohol learn your own limits and stay within them. When your own energy becomes more intensely satisfying than that offered by alcohol, your need for it will drop away naturally, without struggle.

6. URINATE 20 MINUTES BEFORE YOU HAVE INTERCOURSE

Making love on a full bladder puts stress on your kidneys and thus makes it difficult to feel relaxed during sex. The only time it's advisable to urinate after intercourse is if the woman has her period. The urine will prevent her blood from drying inside the urethra of your penis and blocking it which can be very painful.

You should wait a short while after urinating before having intercourse to give your bladder (or intestines if you defecated) and other vital organs time to return to balance. A short rest lying down should quickly restore them. Otherwise your love making may suffer from irregular rhythm and contribute to the development of ulcer tensions.

7. SEX DURING EXTREME WEATHER CONDITIONS CAN BE UNHEALTHY

Severe cold or heat, rain and dampness, fog and great winds, thunder and lightning all have an input on the function of your vital organs and electro-magnetic field balance. These can lead to imbalances between love partners and even illness if one is already in a weakened state. Weather is a very powerful force and should be respected. This is especially true if you are attempting to conceive a child, where it is important to create a balanced "home" (parents energy field) for his/her spirit.

8. AVOID HARD PHYSICAL WORK BEFORE AND AFTER SEX

If you engage in vigorous activity for the couple of hours before and after intercourse it may temporarily deplete the organs and muscles being exercised. This may interfere with the transformation of sexual energy into your higher centers, since the energy will be needed for physical recovery. When you are sweating or feel physically exhausted your life-force can easily leak out of the body. Sex is a proper cure to this condition only if the love making is totally passive and restful.

9. DON'T RELY ON ARTIFICIAL SEXUAL AIDS

Vibrators and dildoes can be of a great help to someone who suffering from a sexual dysfunction (can't erect or have orgasm). But for most men it is better to "sharpen your own weapon" and strengthen your sex organs through exercise, diet, and sexual kung-fu than to rely on artificial aids. The goal is to have love making become an internal process between the energy poles of man and woman, so the sooner you can leave behind external aids the better.

10. DON'T BATHE/SHOWER IMMEDIATELY AFTER SEX

Water is a strong conductor of electricity and that includes human electricity as well. If you bathe immediately after love making it will draw off some of the charge built up. Wait until your body/mind has had time to relax and absorb the sexual energy of your lover before showering. Yoga tradition extols the virtue of water in cleansing negative particles and energy from the body, but this should be done daily or in any case before sex. The skin will smell and feel fresher if it is not washed excessively with soaps that remove natural oils. Experiment by washing only the armpits and groin with soap and scrubbing the rest of the skin with a sponge only. This will make it soft and natural.

11. DON'T THRUST TOO POWERFULLY INTO THE WOMAN

The woman's vagina may grow numb if you pound her continuously with your pelvic bone and penis and lead to exhaustion or negative association of pain with sex. Firm but gentle thrusts will provide the most lasting enjoyment. In the beginning it will also make it easier to hold your seed; as you master the process of sexual transformation, you can play with more passionate variations.

12. YOUR SEXUAL POWER IS GREATEST IN THE SPRINGTIME

Your body has four seasons, just like nature. Don't force yourself to relate with the same intensity. It's not natural and will ultimately wear you down. April and May are the best months for sex, as the sperm is in an expanding state. The same amount of sperm is far more dormant in winter, when your energy naturally contracts to survive the cold. If you must ejaculate spring is the best time, with summer and fall next as your surplus declines toward winter.

13. IF YOU ARE ILL MAKE LOVE PASSIVELY

Sex can be very healing for a man in a weakened state, but only if the man assumes a passive role with the woman moving on top. This will allow you to absorb her healing yin energy without losing more of your already depleted yang energy. If you are strong and lover is weak, you can help heal her by assuming the active role. If you feel ill from too much sex, passive love-making without movement can work as a cure. Symptoms will include pain in penis, damp scrotum and low energy.

14. STOP MAKING LOVE IF IT HAS BECOME A ROUTINE CHORE

Sex becomes mechanical for men when they forget or ignore the proper preparation of women for love-making. Warm the woman with proper foreplay and with warmth of feeling. If you take her body or the sex act for granted the woman will not be properly readied to exchange her love energy through her breasts and lips. If the only contact is genital penis and vagina the energy will not flow to her higher heart and centers into the man. So a man defeats the very goal of what he is seeking if he uses her for a kind of masturbation. He cuts off the return flow of his own sexual energy by engaging in mechanical sex. Better to stop sleeping with your lover than to have "dead" sex—at least then the polarity between you may build up and reawaken you to the attraction that still exists.

If you feel sex is becoming boring, cut back on the frequency of your intercourse. Treat love-making like it was a feast and do it only when you are both feeling extremely healthy and passionate. Stop using sex as an escape from boredom or anger or as a means of masking your hidden fear that the love between you is dead. Quality of love-not quantity of sex is the important thing.

15. DON'T RELY ON SEXUAL FANTASY TO GET AROUSED

The danger of reliance on sexual fantasy is that sex will become limited to a mind trip. The yin and yang energies moving through man and woman are real, not a fantasy. If you limit sex to an idealized image taken from Playboy or invented by your imagination you will find it difficult to experience in your body the profound flow of your deeper energies. If sex becomes a mental play, it can block the deepest play of your being because it is not centered in the body in the present moment but in projecting ahead into the future. How can you love a woman in your arms if you are busy holding another one in your dreams? Both lovers are cheated by this.

The common tendency of the male is to project ahead in time a plan of action. This imagination is a strength when it leads to positive accomplishment. A joint projection of spiritual will shared by lovers can certainly lead to deeper fulfillment.

But sexual fantasy becomes a negative projection, an escape from the present, this is impossible for any real woman to fulfill. Worse, it reduces real women to the level of fantasy objects. It can be an excuse to leave the real woman in your life to go off and pursue an imaginary one. The classical Taoist texts speak of "ghosts" that visit men in their dreams and make intensely passionate love to them. These men are never happy, with their life, constantly seeking their intensity in dreaming, and never awaken to the possibility they could have a more satisfying love with a real woman, with a flesh and blood body and soul if only they spent their energy cultivating that possibility.

But how does one escape the powerful lure of sexual fantasy? By cultivating the flow of one's own energy through healthy physical exercises such as sports, yoga, martial arts, and the Microcosmic Orbit meditation. The Big Draw is also effective if done whenever you catch yourself falling into fantasy. If you transform your energy up to the crown of your head each time you get an erection or feel a sexual fantasy coming on, you will eventually master that tendency in yourself.

Another way of mastering sexual fantasy is to live it out if the opportunity presents itself-engage in your idea of wildly erotic behavior or pursue women you know at heart are not for you—but observe yourself carefully and ask what the real satisfaction gained is. This is often enough to diffuse the charge built up around the fantasy as the real life experience of your fantasy can rarely match the perfect fantasy of your dreams. The Taoists would say that you cannot make "this world" more perfect. Only that simple awareness of the forces in your life will lead to a profound experience that the world is perfectly made.

16. KEEP SEVERAL PILLOWS HANDY

Because the Taoist love methods can be lengthy, it's important to use pillows to avoid crushing your partner during the long periods of resting and exchanging energy. A man's leg can be heavy over a woman, and will cut off blood circulation. At least two pillows are needed if you are lying side by side.

CHAPTER 15

EXERCISES TO INCREASE MALE POTENCY

In this chapter for increasing male capability potency, there are many exercises. Each one works on a particular aspect of the male sexual organs and energy. Choose one you like or one that is suited to your particular specific health needs. Once sexual vitality is restored the main exercises to use are taught in chapter six, the Testicle Breathing and PowerLock, combined with solar energy absorbtion and massage of the penis, prostate, and anus.

HOW TO CURE IMPOTENCY

For those who are impotent, the most important means of curing impotency is stopping sex for a while. It's like a man who has no money saved and starts saving; when he has saved a few dollars he spends it all again. Likewise when you want to regain potency, most important is to stop having sex until the body is repaired. No hormones or medicines or drug stimulation will help. It's like bankruptcy, you borrow and borrow until you cannot borrow anymore. No one will lend you any money. You keep on drawing from your life reserve energy.

Save your seed, do exercises, and try to eat right by stopping all bad habits like smoking, alcohol and sex movies—which will stimulate you to lose much power just by thinking of it. For those times you engage in sex prepare yourself with the technique known as "Sharpening the Weapon". This will help you to retain your potency as well as develop your ability to prevent premature ejaculation.

This first method is practiced while the man is immersed in a hot bath. While in the tub, and the water is still hot, rub the penis as if to masturbate. When it is fully erect, at optimal size, and maximally stimulated, grab the testicles with your hands and forcefully grab, squeeze, pull, and hold the testicles. Perform this an uncountable number of times (at least 100–200 times). At first rub the penis slowly, but persistently. This method gradually builds up a man's sex power.

The idea here is that by practicing this exercise under water in a tub, the water pressure is increased by grabbing, pulling, and squeezing the testicles. This stimulates hormone secretions and sperm production. Over a period of time, sexual potency is increased dramatically. During the exercise, the man should refrain from ejaculation at all costs because he will be defeating his purpose.

HOW TO AVOID WET DREAMS

Wet dreams have different causes: one is from daily stimulation along sexual avenues and the other is because of the over richness of food and eating too late at night. Another cause may be that the blanket is too warm or the underwear is too tight. Another cause is drinking too much water, causing the bladder to press into the prostate gland and thus producing wet dreams.

In the normal adult having a wet dream once a month is considered normal. But some lose the seed 4 or 8 times per month because they are too weak or have too much sex or you masturbate too much. So when sperm is too full and stimulated, you will have ejaculation. Sickness such as infection of the uterus or prostate or venereal disease damages the genital parts and may cause you to ejaculate very easily.

Even worse is to have wet dreams with still greater frequency, as much as every night. Some even have them during day time naps. Their face is very pale, their eyes are dull, their body is clumsy, they have a loss of memory and they are always in a physical low. After practicing this method for a few weeks their power begins to return.

First try to stop the leak. Because the weaker the body is the more the sperm will leak. The main thing is to close or seal the leaking penis. This practice is called "Seal the Leaking Door". If you diligently practice this method you can stop the leak in one week. The method we teach here has been used by people who have had serious problems with wet dreams with good results.

There are two positions. One is lying flat on your back, thinking and concentrating on bringing warmth to the hiu-yin and testes. Do this for about ten minutes. After doing that for ten minutes, do the Big Drawing, clenching the teeth and fists, putting your tongue up to your palate and drawing in by tightening the feet and buttocks. Start to pull in from the Hui-Yin, testes and penis, holding your breath while doing this. Hold this for one to two minutes and gradually increase to five minutes.

Do thirty-six repetitions five times a day: 180 times altogether. Or use a sitting position with back erect and meditate to the Hui-Yin region for ten to fifteen minutes and gradually tighten the teeth, hands, feet and buttocks. Do the big Draw also for 36 repetitions, 5 times per day for at least 2 weeks to one month.

The second position is to lie flat on the bed and rub your hands until they are hot. Use the right hand under the head and the left hand under the testes. . . . . pulling the penis up, use the palm to press the whole testes and start to draw in thinking the power transferred from the back to the head and from the left hand to the right hand. Tighten your feet, clench your teeth and do the big drawing 24 repetitions for 5 times a day.

A third method is to sit down on the floor, back straight, and put the left foot over the right foot. Rub the whole foot, especially on the yung ch'uen for 36 times. Change legs and repeat, bringing the power down to the feet and later back up to the head.

The most effective method is the first, especially for those people who have been meditating and can gradually transfer the power to the head. This technique is also the most powerful one for those with no training in meditation. It will take a bit more practice but will produce good results. The second is only for those with no training in meditation and can't control the mind very well. The third method is good for any condition or time, as rubbing the feet is very good for the entire health.

I mention again that these methods have been kept extremely secret. Many books talk about this but never reveal the secret.

Though the method is simple, the effectiveness is real because it has already helped so many people.

WARMING THE STOVE

The next method of increasing male sexual potency is a variation of the Male Deer Exercise, called Stoking the Golden Stove. To perform this exercise stand in a slight horse posture, or sit on the edge of a chair so the scrotum overhangs the edge of the chair. Optionally it may be performed lying down on the right side with the right leg extended straight and left beg bent at the knee leaving the testicles hanging freely. The left arm may be resting on a cushion, and the right hand supports the head with the thumb and fingers surrounding the ear.

DIAGRAM 35

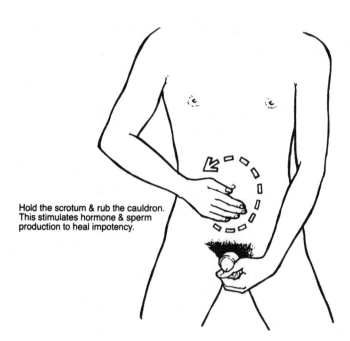

Hold the scrotum & rub the cauldron. This stimulates hormone & sperm production to heal impotency.

To perform the exercise, rub the palms of the hands together until they are hot. With one hand, cup the scrotum, with the other hand, rub the lower abdomen (Tan Tien) back and forth for at least 100–300 times. As you rubbing the lower fanteu inhale and contract the anus, perineum, and buttock muscles. Hold the breath and contractions for as long as you can. Try to conduct the energy generated up the spine to the brain, then down the front of the body to tte navel again. After a time you can switch hands and use the other hand to perform the rubbing. If you have been lying down doing the exercise switch to the other side.

MASSAGE THE FIELD OF PILLS (LOWER TAN TIEN)

This exercise is a variation of Warming the Stove and is simply called massaging the Field of Pills. To perform it the man briskly rubs his palms together until hot, with one hand pressing firmly against the base of the thigh at groin level and with the other hand pressing hard against the Tan Tien. The man begins to rub with the hand pressing the root of the thigh from the right thigh to the root of the left thigh, then massage the Tan Tien area. The hands should not touch or press against the genitals. Rub each area a total of 36 times in the above sequence. When you rub the Tan Tien area, the force of the massage stould make the penis lift up and move. This shows that energy is reaching the penis and scrotal area. This technique will cure impotence and increase the man's energy. Also, this will indirectly stimulate the prostate gland and increase semen production.

HARMONIZING THE TENDONS, MARROW, AND BONES

To perform this exercise, sit with your feet outstretched in front of you on a mat or bed, etc., with your hands relaxed on your knees. While inhaling, bring your arms up to your sides and with your hands, make fists with your palm facing up, elbows bent at your sides. Suck up your genital organs, anus and squeeze buttocks tight. Press your legs straight out with toes bending back toward you. At the same time, press your arms up. Rotating the wrists so the palms remain facing up and turn your eyes to glare at the backs of your hands. Inhale air into your Tan Tien. Hold this posture for as long as comfortable, focusing the energy 1–2″ below the navel.

Exhale and as you exhale, bend from your hips, foward to touch your toes (or knees if you can't touch your toes). Inhale, and come back to a sitting posture, and relax. Take a breath and repeat. Start with ten repetitions and increase to 36 times or 100 times. You may perform this exercise in the morning upon rising and in the evening before retiring.

SECRET TAOIST METHOD OF URINATING

Another technique that strengthens the kidneys is to pass urine while standing on the tip of the toes. In order to increase one's sexual potential, it is very important to strengthen one's kidneys. The practice of this exercise helps cure impotence and helps prevent premature ejaculation because it strengthens the kidneys when practiced over a period of time. It is very simple and consists of passing urine while standing on the tips of the toes and at the same time keeping the back and waist straight. Clench the teeth, lock the buttock, and keep pressure in the abdominal and forcibly discharge urine while exhaling slowly. This process increases and tones kidney energy.

Impotence and weak sexual capability is usually associated with other symptoms of weak kidney energy including fatigue, laziness, and a lack of will-power to carry out ones aims. You can easily test your sexual strength by observing the strength of the discharge of your urine. How forceful is it? If it is forceful, then the sexual power is good. If it is weak with no force and dribbling at the end, then the sexual strength is weak.

Another simple method for strengthening the kidneys and thus increasing sexual potential is to sit on a backless chair or stool or on the floor. Sit with your knees bent and your hands placed on your knees. Rock backward to a 45 degree angle, then back to beginning position. Do this as many times as you can and repeat this exercise at least ten times a day. This exercise places a great deal of stress on your abdominal musculature, thus increasing abdominal strength. A strong abdomen is another indication of strong sexual potential.

SIX EXERCISES FOR THE KIDNEYS AND BACK

The following is a listing of a set of exercises that work both the abdominal muscles, the waist musculature and the lower back. A strong lower back and abdomen are indicative of a strong sexual potential, thus helping to prevent premature ejaculation, lumbago, lower back pain and urogenital problems of all kinds. These exercises and the movements work to strengthen the kidney energy as well.

Exercise One:

Lie with back on the floor or mat with both legs held up, outstretched at a 80–90 degree angle. Begin to slowly lower legs to the left until they reach an angle of 45 degrees. Then bring them back to the beginning position. Then slowly lower them to the right side until they reach a 45 degree angle and bring the legs back to the beginning position. You may perform this exercise at least 10–12 times at each sitting.

Exercise Two:

Lie with your back to the floor on a mat. Raise both legs so they form a 45 degree angle with the ground. Then cross each leg over the other three to four times. Repeat this exercise ten to twelve times.

Exercise Three:

Lie with your back on the floor or on a mat. Hold your hands on your waist and lift up the upper half of your body until it forms a forty-five degree angle with the floor. Hold as long as you can, then lower your body to the floor. Repeat the exercise 10–12 times or more, if desired.

Exercise Four:

Lying on your stomach on a mat, with both arms bent at the elbows and hands held out next to your ears, lift the upper half of your body off the floor. Hold this position for as long as you can, then lower your body slowly to the floor. Repeat the exercise 10 times.

Exercise Five:

Lying on your stomach on the floor on a mat, grasp both hands behind your back at the level of the small of the back. Lift the upper half, and the lower half of your body simultaneously off the ground so that just your abdomen touches the ground. Hold for as long as possible. Lower both halves of your body to the floor and repeat ten times eac.

Exercise Six:

Lying on the back, alternately lift the legs one at a time and hold it in the lifted position for as long as you can. Do ten sets of the exercise.

The above set of exercises should be performed on a daily basis and in the early A.M. is best.

The following is an exercise taken from the Pa Tuan Chin (Chinese Health Exercises), and is very good for the kidneys. Stand with feet shoulder width apart, hands at your sides, with tongue touching the palate. Inhale, bend from the waist, and exhale as you go down, touching the floor with your palms if you can. Inhale while straightening up. At the same time as you straighten up bring your hands out-stretched over your head and stand up on your toes as you reach maximum outstretched reach. Exhale, as you come down off your toes and at the same time place your fists on your kidneys, on the back under the rib cage, relax on both sides,and then inhale as you press your fists into your kidneys while leaning as far back as you can. Exhale as you come back to the starting position and repeat 10 times.

HOW TO ENLARGE AND ELONGATE YOUR PENIS

Inhale the air through the nose into the throat from there swallow and press it down to the stomach. Do not keep it in the chest. Then the air, which you may experience as energy, is imagined as a ball, and is rolled down the front of the body beneath the abdominal muscles. When the air reaches the lower-most part of the abdomen, press it into the penis itself. This exercise for enlarging the penis differs from scrotal compression, because in the latter the air is pressed into the scrotum.

As you direct the air to the penis take the 3 middle fingers of the left hand and press them to the Hui-Yin midpoint between the anus and the scrotum. This pressure prevents the air power from flowing back into the body. The power lodges in the penis itself.

Resume normal breathing while keeping the left fingers on the Hui Yin midpoint. At the same time begin to directly exercise the penis. Pull it forward and backward, stretching it out in a smooth rhythmical movement for 36 times. Next use your thumb to rub the glans of the penis. This should erect the penis. If there is no erection, continue pull and rub the glans until the penis stands.

The right hand then circles the penis firmly at its base and, while holding firmly, slides forward about an inch. In this way the air energy is locked into the body of the penis itself and driven toward the tip of the head. Feel the pressure pushing forward toward the head and maintain it but don't force it too hard.

Then the penis is pulled out to the right and rotated with a stirring action thirty six times clockwise and counterclockwise. Then it is pulled out to the left and rotated another thirty six times clockwise and counterclockwise. Simultaneously maintain the outward pressure locks in the air.

This exercise massages the entire urogenital system including the penis, the prostate gland, and the veins, arteries, and surrounding nerves; the bladder and even the kidney are beneficially stimulated. The energy of many bodily organs flows into the penis, and the tone and function of all are enhanced.

In the final penile manipulation, gently beat the inner right thigh with the erect penis 36 times, while simultaneously you are maintaining the air-lock pull. Then beat the inner left thigh 36 times.

Upon completion of these calisthenics soak the penis in warm water for one minute. This will help it absorb the warm yang energy and to expand. This completes massage of the organ and should produce growth of a healthy inch during the first month or two of practice. Depending on individual bodily structure, further gains may be realized.

HOW TO DECREASE PENIS SENSITIVITY

Techniques for reducing penis sensitivity have been sought for millenia as a way of preventing premature ejaculation. I prefer Seminal Kung Fu methods to those surveyed here, yet I do not discourage anyone from trying others, so long as proper precautions are observed. (Also see chapters on sharpening Your Weapon and Salvation for Impotence.)

Some have worn coarse material inside their underpants. The cloth rubs the penis and nervous sensitivity may gradually subside. Many have counseled thrusting every day into sand or bags of rice. However, sand may get inside of you and cause irritation and infection. Rice may actually cut and abraid the member.

These methods may provide a little extra stimulation, but they are primitive, painful and dangerous. They miss the point: the naked penis is perfect when used with understanding of its laws, rigorous training and the invincible force of Love.

STRENGTHEN YOUR ERECTION

This method helps a man to obtain a stronger, healthier, more energetic erection. Place the thumb on the top of the penis at the root, and the index finger at the bottom of the penis at the root. Inhale, hold your breath, then squeeze and grip the shaft in a wave toward the penis tip. The thumb, index finger, pinky finger push so that the blood is forced to the penis head. Hold this grip for as long as you can hold your breath. Do nine repetitions. This forces the blood into the penis and it can't get back out again. As you hold your breath, count to nine and with each count, squeeze more toward the head of the penis. This technique strengthens the penis and reflexively strengthens the entire body.

REFLEXOLOGY MASSAGE OF THE PENIS

A healthful reflexology massage can be performed on the penis, just as a similar massage can be performed on the hands, feet, and ears. This results from the fact that on some areas of the body there are reflexive zones that refer to other areas of the body and the internal organs. Just as the entire pattern of internal organs is found on the soles of the feet, so is the pattern for the internal organs found on the shaft and head of the penis.

This massage is both pleasurable and very beneficial to health. This can be clearly seen when the penis is rubbed and feeling how quickly pleasurable sensations emanate to other areas of the body. There are two parts to this massage. (a) First spot massage with the thumb and fingers starting at the base, and massaging along the entire shaft of the penis in both directions with a circular motion on the top sides, under side, to the tip of penis, and back toward the base.

(b) "Rubbing the Turtle Head"—To massage the head of the penis, grip the head of penis with index and third fingers. Massage the tip with the thumb in a circular motion while gently pressing in on the head. This reflects to the prostate gland and massages this gland which is very beneficial. Repeat this massage 100–300 times in both directions. This builds up and energizes the prostate gland.

Exercise Note: Don't ejaculate. If you feel yourself getting too excited, perform the Big Draw technique or slow down for a few moments.

This massage builds sexual potential by building up the prostate gland. This is a prostate gland cancer preventative exercise, which may be performed 100's of times daily.

DIAGRAM 36

PENIS REFLEXOLOGY

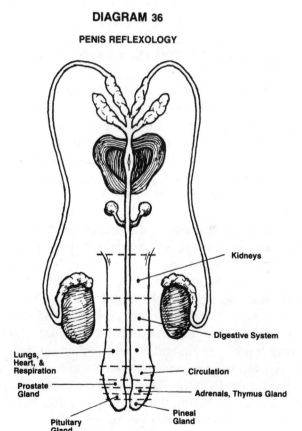

Different zones of the penis
connect with the vital organs.

THE INDIAN ROPE BURN MASSAGE

In this massage, rub the palms of the hands together until they are hot. Hold up the penis with one hand and with the other hand grip the penile base firmly with thumb and index finger. Perform the Indian Rope burn technique back and forth 9 to 36 times. This stimulates the kidneys. Performing this same technique on the middle of the shaft stimulates the digestive system. Massaging under the penile head stimulates the heart, lungs, and respiratory system.

With one hand hold the penis up, while with the other hand perform the Rope Burn technique.

FOUR WAYS TO INCREASE SPERM COUNT

1. Testicles Grip and Squeeze Massage: This exercise stimulates sperm and hormone production and builds up sexual potential in the man. To perform, rub hands until hot. With one hand hold penis up and with the other hand grip the testicles and gently squeeze them. Gradually squeeze them harder with definite short and pronounced grips while gently tugging on testicles. Perform a minimum of 100 grips before switching hands and repeating from the other side.

2. The Testicle Rattle: Like the above exercise, this stimulates sperm and hormone production for the man. Rub the hands together till they are hot and with one hand, hold penis up. With your other hand cup testicles starting the testicles shaking gently and gradually increasing the intensity of shaking. Shake testicles for at least three to five minutes. Switch hands and repeat.

3. Testicle Tapping: Again rub hands until they are hot. With one hand hold penis up and with the other hand, gently tap and pat testicles, gradually increasing intensity and strength of pats. (Don't do it too hard). Perform for at least 3–5 minutes and then switch hands and perform from the other side. Also, pat at the root of the testicles at the base, on the perineum.

4. Testicle Spot Press Massage: Rub hands until hot. With one hand hold penis and with the other hand massage testicles with the thumb, in a circular manner in both directions for at least 3–5 minutes, (at least 100–300 times). Switch hands and repeat in both directions 100–300 times. Or, you can support the testicles with the fingers and thumb and massage in a circular manner with the heel of the hand.

All of these exercises increase sexual potential and hormone production, stimulate the ching energy and prostate gland, and build power to the penis and lower energy centers. After you perform these exercises you must perform Seminal Kung Fu to transmit this sex energy to the higher centers. If you should happen to waste the energy by ejaculation, you are definitely defeating your purpose.

MASSAGING THE PROSTATE GLAND

Besides massaging the "Turtle Head," you can also massage the prostate directly. This is done by placing a finger in the anus. This is done using your index finger, a glove, and a little saliva, vaseline, or massage oil for lubrication. Gently thrust and massage on the prostate gland. You can also thrust in and out, varying the rate to get maximum stimulation, at the anal sphincter. Or, vibrate the sphincter, this will also stimulate the large number of local nerves and the prostate gland. You can also press the Hui-Yin point in the perineum. Rubbing this point back and forth hundreds of times will also stimulate the prostate gland.

Spot pressing points around the anus will also stimulate the prostate gland. First wash the anus very clean with mild soap and water when you shower or bathe. Press and rub around the sphincter. This will stimulate the prostate gland and all of the higher endocrine glands, including the pituitary and pineal glands. This is the best way to preserve, harmonize, and increase blood circulation.

ANAL PUMP SQUEEZE EXERCISE

Inhale through the nose and hold your breath while you pump and pull up the anal sphincter, the muscle around the anus. That is, you squeeze the anus like you're holding in a bowel movement. This stimulates the prostate gland. The method is easy and effective and can be done anytime, anywhere. It is important to contract the anal sphincter with maximum grip to get the most out of this exercise. Exhale slowly and relax. This is a simple way to relieve stress and tension at the same time build up sex potential and energize the body.

Eventually you will feel a warm sensation in your lower groin and anal area. This feeling may spread to the back and up over the head, eventually returning to the solar plexus and navel area. By constantly gripping your anal muscles, you can energize the prostate gland and cowper gland and circulate the blood, strengthen your penis, and gain control over ejaculation. After a period of practice, you can test your rectum strength by trying to suck up water while squatting in a tub of luke warm water via the anus grip exercise. (Make sure the water is clean).

They say the last act before a man dies is to take a bowel movement, and that a flaccid rectal sphincter is indicative of poor health. By doing this technique, the sphincter will never become flaccid. Maintaining a strong healthy prostate gland is one of the secrets for leading a long healthful life.

So squeeze and rub yourself for good health and happiness!

TONGUE KUNG FU

The first major strategic tool in love-making is the tongue. Learn to maneuver this erotic arm par excellence. It has miraculous powers of sensual stimulation and can, by itself, wage brilliant love campaigns. Use of this arm may be mastered through practice of Tongue Kung Fu.

The tongue combines more virtues for the bedroom than any other organ. It is warm and moist. Its file-like roughness wears down resistance. Besides these perfect attributes for erotic arousal, it changes size and shape. It flicks about with quickness, strength and infinite variety of movement.

The "Illusion of Descartes" proves the tongue's magnificent sensitivity. This philosopher observed that a pinhead-sized cavity seems as large as a matchhead to the tongue: such is the organ's unique capacity to magnify tactile impressions. More importantly, the tongue is the major means of directing your chi into your lover prior to intercourse. This is because the tongue is the main switch for the chi flowing in your microcosmic orbit. Whenever you kiss deeply or lick her, your life energy flows into her, and hers into you. A power tongue is like a magic wand, sprinkling bliss wherever it touches, making the spark that connects two life forces.

The essential Tongue Kung Fu exercises follow:

A. Serpent Tongue: Thread an orange with string and secure one end of the string with a 1″ section of toothpick. Hang the orange at mouth level. Then lash out at the orange precisely in the manner of a viper. Shoot the tongue straight out of the mouth, making it very firm and sharp-pointed. Fire it directly forward and with practice increase speed. This serpent-movement is useful in stimulating breasts, genitals, and ears. Ears are especially sensitive, as each ear has dozens of acupuncture points that connect to the whole body when activated by chi flowing through the tongue.

B. Hook Tongue: Using the hanging orange, stick out the tongue as far downwards toward your chin as possible. Stick the tip forward. Then try to hook the orange as you lick up its side. This action is especially exciting to the genitals; if you touch her g-spot, it may cause her to release her "elixir of moon," the female ejaculate considered by Taoists to contain a super powerful yin essence.

C. Slap Tongue: With the hanging orange stick the tongue quite far out while drawing it to the extreme left. Then quickly swing it to the right, forcefully slapping the orange with the rigid tongue side. Then start with the tongue at the extreme right and slap at the orange with a quick movement to the left. Slap the orange around with increasing power and speed. Teach this to your lover, she can use it to arouse your "Jade Stalk" (ancient Chinese term for "penis"). It will increase your own oral dexterity and nimbleness much to her delight.

After some practice you should be able to dribble the orange. Catch it on tongue tip, side and surface, balance it with flashing movements. Use the orange for the first month; then move up to grapefruit for the second. In the third month graduate to a hanging glass jar filled with little steel balls or with nails, beginning with ballast of ½ lb. and progressing to 1 lb. As you improve larger jars may be used.

Wash citrus fruits before and after each workout. Keep them in a plastic bag in the refrigerator. In this way the fruits may be used for a few weeks of practice, and you will avoid infection. It is of the highest importance to keep your mouth clean and free of offensive odor. Casanova himself commented on the discouraging effect of bad breath. In fact tongue Kung Fu will stimulate the production of fresh, clean saliva, which you should swallow in a single gulp to your navel. Taoists consider saliva to be a very potent elixir that can be used to intensify and center one's chi. If you have an ongoing problem with plaque coating your tongue, eat less meat and more vegetables and use a tongue scraper to clean it daily.

The graduate school of tongue exercises involves the use of a plastic ruler, which you alternately lift up and depress with the broad base of the tongue. These Power Lifts strengthen the tongue muscles and complement the darting practice. You may use any flexible material such as wood, metal or bamboo for the ruler. Use only smooth rulers, since any wound in the tongue is slow to heal. It sits in a medium full of microbes. If your tongue should happen to suffer a cut for any reason, you may find it helpful to rinse the mouth with boiled salt water thrice daily.

Once you have practiced the secret tongue gymnastics, you are ready to approach the fortunate partner of your choice. Find the spots of her greatest sensitivity and lavish your skill upon them. Often you may find those points by watching where the woman directs her hand or eye.

When you've found the places where she wants you, enjoy playing with your full complement of tongue techniques. What pleases best in one place may not be what she craves in another. Watch for her responses; she will tell you with unmistakeable eloquence when you hit the mark.

D. For tumescent nipples you may unfold the Drill Tongue. In this esoteric practice the tip of the tongue drives the projecting nipple back into the breast where it is whirled around in a little circle, creating a thrilling spiral of energy.

If you perform Tongue Kung Fu in the vagina, moisten the right thumb and index finger. Put the thumb inside the vagina and the wet index finger over the anus opening. Seal the anus to prevent loss of your partner's energy. When your partner kisses your genitals, have her seal your anus with a moistened middle finger while she stimulates your scrotal region with the other fingers.

I must emphasize the importance of being with partner who observes reasonable standards of hygiene. The genitals and anus are warm and moist, ideal conditions for bacterial growth. Wash and keep them clean especially when you have sex. Odor can spoil or lessen the enjoyment of sex.

Like the tongue, the index finger is also a very powerful stimulator. You may have it lightly explore the vagina and gently massage the clitoris. Keep your finger nails clean, especially the index finger. Trim the nail quite short and file it to a smooth surface which will not scratch sensitive tissues. The utmost gentleness must be used in these attentions. Pain may upset your mate and bring her pleasure to a screaming halt.

The gentle of the index finger can easily stimulate the gland (critoris) and the G spot which lie behind the pelvic bone, one inch behind the gland (cretoris).

DIAGRAM 37

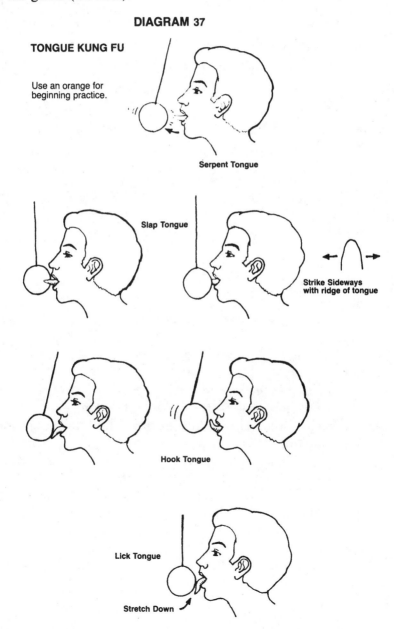

TONGUE KUNG FU

Use an orange for beginning practice.

Serpent Tongue

Slap Tongue

Strike Sideways with ridge of tongue

Hook Tongue

Lick Tongue

Stretch Down

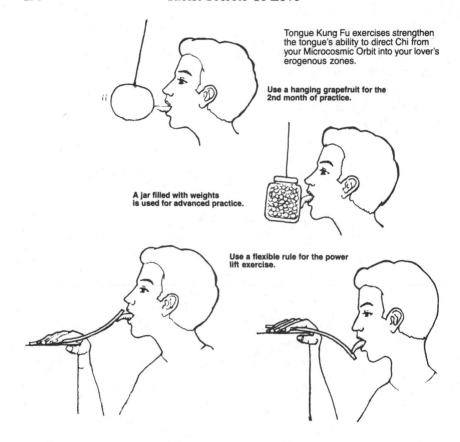

Tongue Kung Fu exercises strengthen the tongue's ability to direct Chi from your Microcosmic Orbit into your lover's erogenous zones.

Use a hanging grapefruit for the 2nd month of practice.

A jar filled with weights is used for advanced practice.

Use a flexible rule for the power lift exercise.

HOT AND COLD BATHS FOR SEXUAL HEALTH

These ancient time tested methods that have come down to us help build the body's resistance to disease.

(a) Cold Water Sitz Baths

This technique is extremely good to alkalize the blood of the genital groin area. This increases blood flow to the genital area, stimulating the prostate and production of sperm for the man (and stimulating the hormones in a woman), thus increasing sexual potential. The procedure is quite simple. Just squat or sit in a tub of cold water so that your genitals, anus, and coccyx are submerged in the water. Minimum time for this is ten to twenty minutes. Start with cool water and gradually accustom yourself to colder temperatures.

(b) Alternating Hot and Cold Water Baths, Showers or Sitz Baths

This also is an ancient technique in which one alternately plunges into first hot, then cold water. This method increases blood circulation, tonefies the body, increases resistance to disease, and stimulates hormone production, thus increasing sexual potential. One must stay for a minimum of three minutes in either hot or cold baths before one alternates to the other temperature extreme. And, one must alternate at least six times to be effective. Try for 12 times is best, with at least three minutes in each one. If you don't have time, during your morning shower begin it hot—while soaping—and finish with a cold rinse.

One may also instead of plunging into the bath, gradually enter first with your toes, then legs, body, back, shoulders, abdomen, and lastly the head. This way the body gradually acclimates itself to the temperature change. Those suffering from high blood pressure, heart disease, kidney disease, etc., can also enjoy alternating hot and cold baths, but be careful and go slowly.

(c) Exposing the Skin to the Air (Air Bath)

This is very healthy for the body, aerating the skin. It gets rid of musty odors, builds the body's resistance to disease, and helps blood circulation. It keeps the male genitals cooler than the rest of his body temperature thus increasing his sexual potential. The thought of running naked on a beach or in a mountain field has much appeal. One gets exposed and absorbs much needed negative ions. The weather should be moderate to warm, the temperature typical of late spring through early fall. This can also be done sitting inside your house naked with the windows open. Do not use this practice as a way to exciting your sexual fantasies as it will waste the chi. Think about how healthy you feel.

HARMONIOUS ENERGY FOR THE HOMOSEXUAL

In Chinese practice Heaven is Yang or male and Earth is Yin or female. When both lovers are of the same sex, there are two poles of Yang (homosexuals) or Yin (lesbians). There is an inherent imbalance in this type of relationship which favors instability and violence, and blocks progress to higher levels of balancing sexual energy.

To attain a more harmonious balance it is essential for those that love their own sex to find a source of the opposite type of energy; otherwise, they will receive too much imbalanced force.

Fortunately, there are sources of female energy which the male may absorb to his great benefit. Likewise there are available means whereby the lesbian may obtain additional yang energy. This is because man and woman are not the only sources of yin and yang but small reservoirs of these energies which stream through creation.

The key is in the very first line of this chapter: heaven is male and earth is female. Thus the man who needs yin energy but prefers not to receive it from its human container will absorb it from the earth; and woman will draw in the male potency from its source, the heavens.

For the man to draw in the yin energy, he lies belly down, embracing the earth. One leg is straight and one bent at the knee. He will pull in the energy from the earth. He must try to have no sexual thoughts. The genitals should not touch the ground, but hang a little above it. Relax and gather your concentration by breathing deeply in and out through the nose. Think the power

DIAGRAM 38

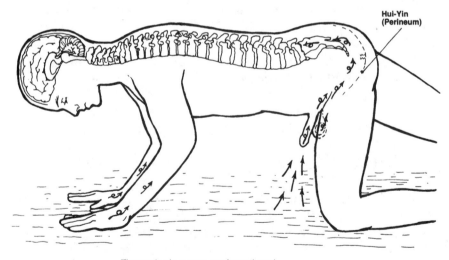

The earth, yin energy can be gathered
using this palms down position. Think the earth energy
up into the penis, up past Hui-Yin into the spine
up the back to the head.

from the earth slowly into the penis. This basic practice applies to man: think the power up through your breathing.

As you inhale, draw the power up as if you were absorbing up fluid in a straw: the fluid is the power and the straw is the penis. From the penis draw it past the hui yin, chang-chiang, and up the back to the head. Store the yin power in the head. In due course it will overflow the crown and move down the front of the body and return to the hui yin. When this point is reached, you may bring it up the front of the body to the navel and work the centers navel, solar plexus and heart, respectively, in the manner described in the Yin-Yang Exchange. Put away all obsessive erotic thoughts or it will cause the power to drain out.

HOW TO ABSORB SEXUAL ENERGY FROM THE SUN

Throughout the civilized world there is an increasing enthusiasm for nudism and nude sunbathing. Our body can in fact absorb energy from nature. Some parts are more absorptive of the life energy than other parts. The lower part of the body, penis and testes especially, can absorb more power than other lower parts (perineum and Hui Yin).

During the course of civilization, man has hidden the reproductive organs as secret things. So we have what is commonly called "underpants" and "panties" to protect from the outer world. That is the part that can absorb much natural energy to strengthen the body or greatly increase force and endurance in sex life. The more we keep it hidden from nature the weaker the parts will be. It will effect your entire body deleteriously.

This method of absorbing the solar power into the penis is regarded as top secret and rarely revealed.

Practice: Morning sun from 7 to 11 is much preferred or 3 to 6 in the afternoon. If the sun is not too strong we can gradually absorb its power into the glans (head) of the penis much easier.

To expose to the sun, hold stem of the penis with one hand and use it to rub the glans until penis is erect. Put it down facing towards the sun and imagine the power coming into the glans, absorbing it, so that it fills the organ with warm power. It will fill the entire organ with energy if your thought is properly concentrated. When your penis softens, do the whole procedure again. Do this exercise three to four times.

Pull the testes up and expose them to the sun. Use your right hand to rub the Hui-Yin and imagine the power being absorbed through the Hui-Yin to the whole genital region, and especially the testes. Rub the testes with both hands gently for a few minutes. Rub the stem of the penis (which is beneath all the glands) and the prostate gland by using one hand to hold the testes up and the other to rub gently. Start with 5 to 10 minutes and increase gradually up to, at most, one hour. This may require months to attain.

The lower part of the body is rarely exposed to sun. Moderate exposure to the sun, in this way, is a preventative measure against skin disease in this part of the body as well as a strengthening measure. This sensitive part will feel much stronger and less sensitive, thus reducing the difficulty of withholding or retaining the seminal fluid.

DIAGRAM 39

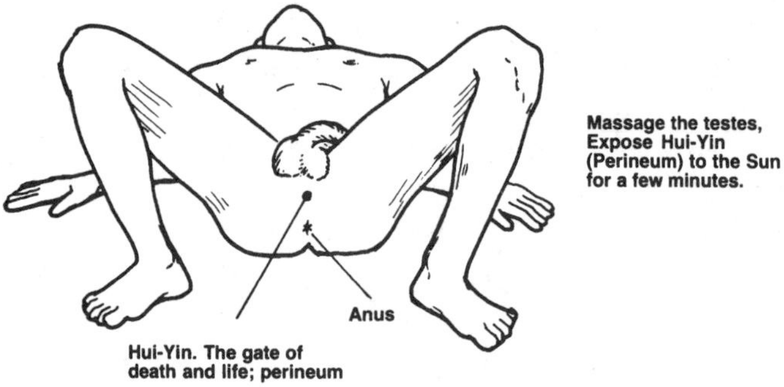

Massage the testes, Expose Hui-Yin (Perineum) to the Sun for a few minutes.

Anus

Hui-Yin. The gate of death and life; perineum

When rubbing the glans, start with light rubbing and don't heat too much. When rubbing the Hui-Yin begin gently and gradually; take care not to injure yourself. Injuries to the reproductive organs are the hardest to cure.

Be sure to be in a covered place and don't show other people, so that you don't get in trouble. Some people might find these meditations and hygienic practices provocative. These exercises will greatly help reduce premature ejaculation, impotence, and nocturnal emissions.

The second position I recommend is the "head stand", "shoulder stand", or lying on the back with hands under back of

DIAGRAM 40

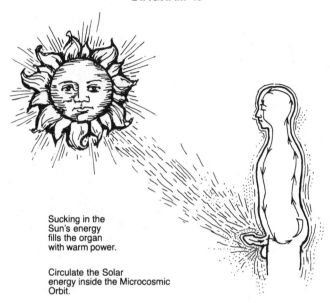

Sucking in the
Sun's energy
fills the organ
with warm power.

Circulate the Solar
energy inside the Microcosmic
Orbit.

lower thighs to hold the anus, Hui-Yin, scrotum, and penis up to the sun. People never expose these parts to the sun though they are highly permeable to energy and readily draw it into the body.

Male and female reproductive organs are never exposed to solar energy. Yet the organs are very powerful. They can expel energy or absorb it in from the universe, but because man ignores this method by wearing clothing that close this way of absorbing power from the universe. The best position is the head stand, with the two legs facing down. Absorb with your mind the solar power through the anus and penis in from both directions to the prostate and then forward into the scrotum. Keep the scrotum warm and try not to expose too much at first; start with 1 or 2 minutes. Do not absorb excess heat, because the scrotum can't be too hot or the sperm cells will die, and that defeats our purpose.

CHAPTER 16

ACUPUNCTURE, MOXIBUSTION AND HERBS CAN HEAL WEAKENED SEXUAL ENERGY

ACUPUNCTURE–MOXIBUSTION METHOD TO HEAL IMPOTENCE

Moxibustion is a very old Chinese tradition more than 5,000 years old. It is a way of increasing the chi energy to stimulate the glands, organs, nerves, and circulation of blood using heat applied to acupuncture points. Moxa or moxa-rolls can be bought from a Chinese store selling acupuncture equipment. You can also use a cigar or a cigarette, but the moxi-roll is better, although both will give you a lot of smoke in the house. You can also use a fish tank heater attached to a long glass tube.

The best way to overcome impotence is to generally keep oneself healthy and to protect oneself from excessive sexual stimulation, which will only fan the flames of your feeling of impotence. You should abstain from sex for a period, make sure you sleep and eat well until your health and sexual potency recovers. If you modify your life-style to allow a renewal of your life energy, moxibustion and acupuncture can be used to quicken the recovery of your potency by aiding the flow of chi energy to your hormonal system and reproductive organs.

You can treat yourself at most points, but should probably obtain a good book on acupuncture or moxibustion to aid you with the location of the points described here. DO NOT moxa any points on the body at random, as some are forbidden to moxa heat as dangerous. Without further instruction, you should moxa only the points I describe here.

It is best to use garlic and onion with mox. Garlic is the best, which you should slice or chop and put in a piece of cheese cloth. You then put it on the acupuncture point to be treated and apply the heat of mox or the roll or the cigar or heater to the garlic. Don't overwarm it, as you can hurt yourself. Garlic is a very strong stimulus. If kept on the place too long it will "burn" the skin, and you may suffer from superficial heat burns as well. So, be careful. If allergic to garlic you can use the onion. If allergic also to onion, you may use heat alone, which is still effective.

DIAGRAM 41

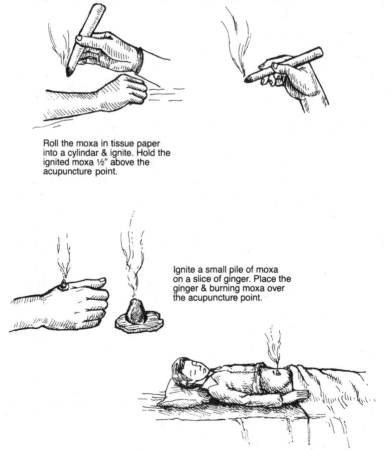

Roll the moxa in tissue paper into a cylindar & ignite. Hold the ignited moxa ½" above the acupuncture point.

Ignite a small pile of moxa on a slice of ginger. Place the ginger & burning moxa over the acupuncture point.

Moxa each point for 3 to 4 minutes, but hold the heat roll at the point for a few seconds only, moving it up and down all the time, pressing deeply unless discomfort sets in. Do not exceed this time of 3 to 4 minutes. When doing moxa try to keep the room warm. Be careful of a cold room, especially when you are nude, as you will lose a lot of chi. If you are using the cigar, moxi rolls, or cigarette, afterwards the room will be smoky for awhile. So you must have very good ventilation to exhaust the smoke out.

Do this moxa treatment every day for ten days and then stop for 3 days. Then start another 10 day period of application. Don't drink wine or take a bath for two hours after mox treatment. During mox treatment stop having sex until you recover. If the condition is serious, stop sex for 1 to 3 months. After a thorough rest you will recover your strength and potency. If you discipline yourself to follow the cycle of 10 day treatments and 3 to 4 day rest, most men will recover their potency unless suffering an anatomical defect (which is extremely rare).

1. URINARY BLADDER MERIDIAN-KAN-SHU BL-18 THE MAIN LIVER POINT

Start at back, the urinary bladder meridian, called the Foot Tai-Yang. The first point is the Kan Shu BL-18. Kan-Shu is one and one-half tsun beside the lower end of the spinous process of T9. One and one-half tsun (1 tsun is a thumb-width) is the width of your index and middle finger. This is considered the main liver point. The liver stores the body's energy. With too much intercourse or stress, the body must draw its supplies from the liver and deplete it. For this reason this treatment is helpful in hepatitis. The spinous process is the outer tip of the vertebra as you move outward from the center line of the spinal cord.

2. PI-SHU BL-20 MAIN POINT OF SPLEEN

Second point is the Pi-Shu BL-20, which is one and one-half tsun beside the lower end of the spinous process of T11. This is the main point for the spleen. It also helps backaches and indigestion.

3. SHEN-SHU BL-23 PALACE OF SPERM/TZU-LIAO BL 32

Third point is the Shen-Shu BL-23. (Palace of Sperm). One and one-half tsun beside the lower end of the spinous process of L2. Used for kidney, this helps fight infections, lower back pain and sexual problems. Shen-shu means "palace of sperm". Do on both sides of the spine for all points.

Finally come down to Tzu-Liao, BL-32 on the 2nd posterior sacral foramen and midway between the lower part of the posterior superior iliac spine and the median line. It's easy to find; start with the sacrum, the large piece of bone above the coccyx. Put your thumb on the point BL-27, which is the last point between the spinal vertebrae on the sacrum. Put your little finger on your coccyx, and spread the fingers out, and your index finger falls on the Tzu-Liao. Your thumb should be just at the upper rim of the sacrum and the fingers evenly spread out.

Another way is to find the point where the sacrum meets the spinal column. Place the thumb at this junction and then spread the fingers. This may be easier. Surrounding the outline of the hand are eight holes of the sacrum. Shang Liao upper hole is on BL-31. The most important point is the Tzu-Liao BL-32 on the second hole, then Chung-Liao BL-33 on the middle hole and Hsia-Liao BL-34 on the lower hole.

There are more points than those mentioned here. Not all of the points need moxa every day. Do your back if you have someone to help you. You can do it once every two or three days on the back, combining and alternating with points on your back and front.

4. GOVERNOR MERIDIAN-CHANG-CHIANG GO-1
FUNCTIONAL MERIDIAN CHI HAI CO-6
THE OCEAN OF ENERGY

Another point is on the governor meridian, the chang-chiang, GO-1 at the lower end of the coccyx between the tip of the coccyx and the anus. It's also good for lower backache. Another point is on the Functional Meridian. The point is Chi-Hai CO-6, one and one-half tsun below the umbilicus, known as the ocean of the chi energy. This also helps disorders of the bowel. Next go to Kuan Yuan

CO-4, three tsun below the umbilicus. All points on the functional (conception) meridian on your back help increase energy in the abdominal organs, including the small intestine, large intestine, bladder, and prostate gland. By stimulating all these organs you greatly help to reduce your impotency.

DIAGRAM 42

THE MAIN MOXIBUSTION POINTS TO
RESTORE MALE POTENCY.

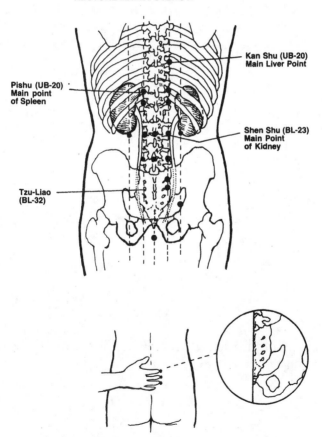

Kan Shu (UB-20)
Main Liver Point

Pishu (UB-20)
Main point
of Spleen

Shen Shu (BL-23)
Main Point
of Kidney

Tzu-Liao
(BL-32)

With the thumb on the sacro-iliac to the left side,
spread out the three fingers evenly on the right side.
They will touch S1, S2 & S3.

THE SPECIAL POINTS FOR IMPOTENCE:
1. HEAD OF THE PENIS, GLANS PENIS, ROOT OF PENIS, HUI-YIN

All back and front points on the governor and functional meridians stimulate the organs. The points listed here are the special points for impotence. First point is the head of the penis, or the glans penis. Best way to use is slice the garlic (don't chop it and don't use garlic if you are allergic to it) and punch a hole in it with a needle. For the first few times put on a silk cloth to prevent burning the penis glans and then use the heater. Second point is the 2 points at the under root of penis. Third point is hui-yin, the perineum located between the anus and the penis, which is included in the special points.

DIAGRAM 43

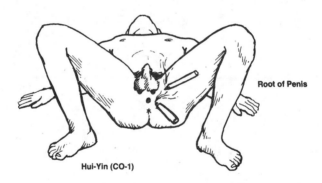

Root of Penis

Hui-Yin (CO-1)

2. FU-LIU KI-1 (MASSAGE ONLY)

On the leg, point Fu-Liu KI-7 is two tsun above the posterior media malleolus on the inner ankle bone.

DIAGRAM 44

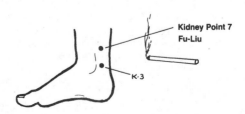

Kidney Point 7
Fu-Liu

K-3

3. LAO-KUNG (MASSAGE ONLY)

The point mentioned here cannot use moxa, but responds to massage and rubbing. On the hand, the Lao-Kung is between the middle and fourth fingers when the hand is closed so that all fingers run along the line in the hand. Rub this point every day.

DIAGRAM 45

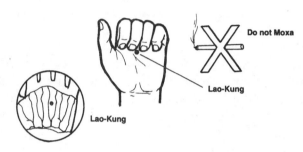

4. YUNG-CHUAN KIDNEY POINT (MASSAGE ONLY)

Another point is on the Kidney meridian, called the Foot Shao-Yin. The point is the Yung-Chuan. KI-1 point is on the inside of the ball of the foot (where your weight falls directly) on a line below the second toe, counting your big toe as the first. Never moxi this point. Only rub with a finger or rub the bottom of your feet together every day. This will help to stimulate the kidney energy, the most important in regulating sexual activity.

DIAGRAM 46

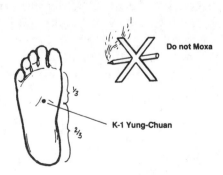

I have used moxa treatment for many years and helped many patients and students with the problem of impotence, and most recover in a very short time. Some have very serious nocturnal emissions (wet dreams). Some have emissions every two or three nights or sometimes in the daytime. They lose too much seed essence, or ching, and so lose the ability to have sex. They usually feel weak, and their face is pale. Using the moxa method combined with the power lock exercise (described in chapter 6) is the most effective, and the students who do both recover the most quickly, you should clench 108 times each morning and evening until your erection returns.

Many people get desperate and try to cure impotence with other methods. They try to stimulate themselves with even more sex, with hormones, spanish fly, etc., but these only drain off their energy more quickly. The best way I can advise to cure impotence is to use Taoist methods of cultivation. I'm not telling you to have sex as much as you want but to have sex as a meaningful and delightful act in your life.

Any compulsive sex is meaningless and dangerous to your health. It's better to complete one very successful sexual act than 10 or 100 of unprepared, unpracticed sex. If you regard every act of sexual intercourse as a special or sacred occasion, take a bath, put perfume on, brush teeth, wash penis and anus, wash hair, ears, change bed cover, clean up the room, have some flowers, etc., it will help you reduce your compulsiveness.

If you have a gun you can't go out and begin shooting any person you see on the street. You'll get yourself in big trouble. Sex is the same; it's a powerful tool that becomes a dangerous weapon when fired indiscriminately. If you practice the Taoist method, your sexual organ will become strong but you need not give it to every woman you see. Use it meaningfully. A tool like a gun can help protect life or it can kill you and others. Using these things one must be very careful. If you know that excess ejaculatory sex can harm you and that cultivation of harmonious sexual energy with love makes life meaningful, you can cure yourself of impotence and return to full sexual fulfillment.

RESTORE SEXUAL VITALITY THROUGH DIET

Food is alive, and each kind of food contains its own energy vibrations that when eaten forms part of the overall vibration of your body. The process of food selection, therefore, becomes a process of selecting vibrations for ourselves that not only are in harmony with the universe but that will bring us into harmony with a love partner.

Factors involved in food classification include size, shape, color, taste, nutritional level, and animal or vegetable origin. Everybody's balance of chi energy and bodily health is different, so everyone needs to choose the foods most balancing for their specific state of health. Thus the Taoists avoid prescribing any one dietary regimen such as macrobiotics, vegetarianism, fruitarianism, etc. although these diets may well be suited to particular individuals or good at certain times of the year. The topic of diet is a large one that I intend to cover in another book. Here is a superficial outline that will give you a sense of the possibilities of balancing yin and yang energies in your body using food.

Very Yin: (Drugs) Sugar, Alcohol, Fruit. Yin: Beans, Veggies, grains, fish. Yang: Poultry, Meat, Eggs, salt. Very Yang: garlic, ginger, red pepper.

EATING FOODS IN EXCESS

If men eat very yin foods in excess after a while sexual activity will diminish. When their yang energy is exhausted it will peeter out all together. Yin foods include foods that grow below ground level: roots, fibers, and bulbs.

Men eating very yang foods to excess may cultivate a strong, even violent sexual appetite characterized by egotism, insensitivity, and its short duration. Eat from both extremes and your sexual activity and desire will fluctuate, sometimes on and sometimes off.

SEX AND SEASONS OF THE DIET

According to the Taoist Lui Ching "In Spring a man can allow himself to emit semen once every three days, in Summer and Autumn twice a month and during the Wintertime he should save his semen and not ejaculate at all. The loss of yang energy caused by one emission in Winter is considered a hundred times worse than one emission in Spring.

In accordance with nature Winter was believed to be the season of storage and accumulation of energy. For a man this means he should conserve his semen and increase his "hot" energy by eating hot and warming and fortifying foods during winter, and cooler foods in the summer.

SEPARATE STEPS TO TAKE FOR MEN AND WOMEN TO ACHIEVE
YIN/YANG BALANCE

Women:	Men:
Less salt	Slightly more salt
More vegetables	More grains
Shorter cooking time	Longer cooking time
More green, leafy veggies	More Root veggies
Little or no fish	Very moderate to low fish
Little or no animal food	Very moderate to low animal food

Too much yang food makes a woman hard and insensitive (foods such as meats, eggs, and dairy foods).

Too much yin food can make a man soft and incapable of having an erection.

FOOD FOR SEXUAL ORGANS

During sexual intercourse a great deal of "hot chi" is released, and anything that supplements this hot chi is considered a great help. This means that foods that are extremely cold should be avoided because they bring down the chi quotient of the body. On the other hand, foods that are cold but stimulate the Kidneys can be eaten since the Kidney is in charge of the sexual apparatus and is thus stimulated. Examples of extremely cold foods to be avoided are: coconut milk, mentholated wines, chrysanthemum tea, and ice water.

Foods that provide nourishment to the entire organism are adviseable after sexual activity, for example, muscle and organ meats, ginger, red dates, sharks fin, swallow nest, and sea cucumber. These are examples of tonic foods, in that they build the energy of the body.

CHAPTER 17

BIOLOGICAL FACTS EVERY MAN SHOULD
KNOW ABOUT FEMALE SEXUALITY

Few things confuse men more than women's bodies and their monthly cycles. Women's bodies are different from men and this alters their psychological and spiritual path of development. Many spiritual groups don't discuss the female body because it carries such a loaded charge of sexual energy they don't like dealing with it. But men need to understand woman and her biology if he is to move beyond the level of emotional struggle and come into complete harmony with her yin essence. As Taoist sex brings a man into the most intimate contact he'll ever have with a woman's body, I am including some brief but important pieces of information about their sexual organs and reproductive cycle. This will be vastly expanded in volume two of this series, "Taoist Secrets Of Love: Cultivating Female Sexual Energy," also known as Ovarian Kung Fu.

The best education you can get is from loving a woman and observing how her particular subtle energies change with the moon and seasons of nature. If a man cultivates his yang energy he can have a powerful effect in strengthening his lover's body and stabilizing her energy cycles. When the subtle energies of yin and yang have proper intercourse, the hormones and vital organs function at a more refined level and produce radiant good health.

THE UTERUS

The uterus, a muscular organ smaller than a woman's fist, is suspended in the pelvis by large ligaments which attach to the pelvic bones. It is like an upside-down pear. The lower part, the cervix, (like the stem end) is the only part that is visible in the vagina, and is at the end of the vaginal canal. It is pink, round, and has an opening in the middle (called the cervical os) which leads through the cervix (about 1½″ long) and into the uterus. The fallopian tubes extend out at the right and left side of the uterus and form an umbrella over the ovaries. The ovaries are white, about the size and shape of an unshelled almond.

OVULATION

Around the middle of a woman's cycle (the timing can be extremely variable) an egg breaks out of one of the ovaries. Some women experience a brief twinge at ovulation, some women have severe pain that can last up to a day or two. Most women are not aware of any changes at all during this process.

Although the egg only lives for 12 to 24 hours, a woman's fertile period can be as long as five days. How is this possible?

DIAGRAM 47

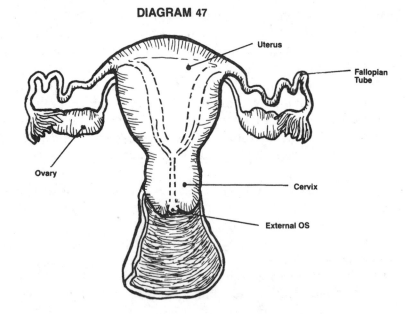

FERTILE MUCUS

Before ovulation, the glands lining the cervical canal start producing a slippery, stretchy clear or translucent mucus which flows down the cervical canal and into the vagina. There may be enough for a woman to be well aware of it, or she may just notice a slickness around the opening to her vagina. The molecular structure of this mucus is like tunnels and ladders, giving sperm direction and support in their journey toward the cervical canal.

Ten minutes after ejaculation into the vagina, some sperm can be found in the fallopian tubes. Sperm also find their way into the crypts lining the cervical canal where they are nourished by the mucus and time-released out over a period of three to five days. So, if a woman and a man have intercourse on Saturday night and she has fertile mucus but doesn't ovulate till Tuesday, she could get pregnant some time on Wednesday.

NONFERTILE MUCUS

During the rest of her cycle, a woman may notice periods of relative wetness and dryness. The cervical mucus produced during the nonfertile times varies in quantity and is usually white and sticky. The molecular structure of this mucus is like a mesh or grid, preventing most sperm from entering the cervix. Observation of the mucus cycle aids many women in determining their fertile times.

MENSTRUATION

About two weeks after ovulation, if a woman has not gotten pregnant, the lining of the uterus, which has been building up to make a nest for a developing embryo, sloughs off and another period begins.

The menstrual cycle is measured as the time between one period and the next, counting the first day of bleeding as Day 1. Most women menstruate about once a month, although few women have periods exactly every 28 days, which is denoted as the "norm" or "ideal." Regular cycles can vary as much as from three to seven weeks. Some women who have only two to three periods a year are often unaware of any cycle.

PERIODS

For many women, their periods are a sign of the health functioning of their body, occurring more or less "on time," lasting three to five days, and requiring a certain amount of paraphernalia and attention to hygiene. For sexually active heterosexual women their period is the sign that they are not pregnant. From the Taoist viewpoint, the loss of blood is a loss of valuable energy that can be minimized or altogether stopped if the woman has finished bearing children. The Taoist method is reversible should the woman change her mind.

The typical period often starts out "light," that is with a small amount of pink-tinged mucus or a few drops of blood, increasing to a bright red full flow on the second day and perhaps going on for a couple of days, then diminishing to brownish "spotting" as it tapers off. Some women bleed a lot; for some, their periods start and end dramatically, like turning on and off of a faucet; some have very little bleeding. Some women's blood is dark and can have clots varying from specks to the size of a dime; some women's periods have a lot of mucus. The blood as it comes out of the cervical canal has virtually no odor or taste. These characteristics change with exposure to air and the passage of time as cells break down.

Many women commonly experience some discomfort during their periods: swollen, sore breasts, fluid retention, pimples, headaches, low back pain, diarrhea or constipation. Some women with chronic herpes are likely to have an outbreak around the time of their period, indicating some of the "stress" imposed on the body by her period. The uterus, which is a muscular organ, can contract, which sometimes feels like a cramp does in any muscle of the body, or may be described as pressure, ache, or a bearing down feeling. A few women are absolutely incapacitated by their periods, e.g., with severe pain or vomiting. Virtually no research has been done to understand such recurrent misery and Western allopathic doctors only offer these women strong and possibly dangerous medications to relieve the symptoms.

Women are intimately familiar with their own cycles but rarely exchange these details with friends or relatives. Most American women are deeply ashamed of their menstrual blood, feel humiliated and embarassed if they stain their clothes, and are very self-conscious about bulges of sanitary pads, odors, and the discreet disposal of bloody pads or tampons.

EMOTIONAL CHANGES

Some women experience mood changes around the time of their periods, but studies have not been able to document any patterns in large numbers of women.

Most women can identify a part of their cycle when they feel "horny" and indeed every portion of the menstrual cycle, including the period itself, has been claimed by some women as being the time when she feels her sexual desire most strongly.

WOMEN'S SEXUAL ANATOMY

So, let's take a look at women's genitals. Starting at the front and top is the Mount of Venus (mon veneris, or mons, for short). The amount, texture and distribution of pubic hair can vary from a few straight hairs to a bushy growth going up the abdomen or down the thighs. The mons is a cushion of fat protecting the pubic bone underneath (which is joined together by cartilage that softens during pregnancy so that the bones can separate if necessary during childbirth). The mons divides and separates into the large outer lips (labia majora).

INNER LIPS

Inside the outer lips are the inner lips (labia minora)—very different in color and texture, they are related to the mucous surfaces, like the lips of the mouth. In the unaroused state they vary in color from pink to dusky to dark maroon/purple. Sometimes the inner lips are long and can be seen protruding from the outer lips. During sexual arousal the small lips, which are well-supplied with blood vessels, get engorged and swell to two or three times their resting size! As the point of no return approaches orgasm they can go through a color change sometimes turning to crimson or dark wine. (Masters & Johnson)

Follow the small lips to the top where they join together to form the hood that protects the glans of the clitoris. Usually the glans, in the unerect state, is nestled under the hood. You can see it by pulling back on the hood. The glans of the clitoris is loaded with nerves, and for most women the glans is the most acutely sensitive spot in their sexual anatomy. Some women find it is so sensitive that direct stimulation can be irritating.

THE SHAFT OF THE CLITORIS

The shaft of the clitoris can be felt like a strong rubber band under the surface between the glans and mons. As sexual excitement mounts, the shaft thickens and shortens and the glans, shaft and supporting structures erect. As with men, there is often a dramatic change in size and shape.

THE GLANS

Travelling down from the glans is the opening to the urethra. Below this is the opening to the vagina. A woman's urethra is about 1½" long from the outside to where it opens into the bladder. Surrounding the urethra is a plexus of blood vessels. Since these blood vessels had no name in medical books, a group of women named it the urethral sponge (A New View of a Woman's Body). During sexual excitement the blood vessels engorge and a bulge can be felt through the vaginal wall. This bulge has been named the G spot (after Grafenberg, one of the first sexologists). It can be explored by feeling around the front and upper part of the vagina. (It has also been said that the G spot is located ½ inch deeper than a woman's longest finger).

THE POSITION OF THE G SPOT

Making love in a face-to-face position, the G spot can be difficult to reach directly (with the exception of those men whose penises, when erect, press right up against their bellies). Shallow thrusting gets closest to the G spot and can cause that stimulation of the suggestive and tantalizing kind.

However, a change in position may be necessary if a woman wants her G spot stimulated more directly. Fingers are often most effective and direct. A woman stimulating herself might choose to squat or lie with her legs up in order to reach it better. Her partner might find it easier to reach if she is lying on her stomach; during coitus, if the woman is on top she can position herself more precisely.

Some women, when holding their man tight, enjoy the sensation of an erect penis rubbing on their lower abdomen, right above the pubic bone, stimulating the G spot from the other side.

When the G spot is massaged, often a woman's first impression is that she has to urinate. However, sexologists assure women that if the pressure is continued there will be a transition to sexual arousal. The sexual response to G spot stimulation may also have to be learned by some women and it can take several sessions for it to feel good. (Perry and Whipple)

Some women find that stimulation of the G spot can trigger their orgasm, while many women enjoy G spot stimulation as part of the whole panoply of sexual stimulation.

With or without G spot stimulation, there are women who ejaculate when they orgasm. This ejaculate, which can be quite copious, is much like seminal fluid. It is not urine. However, many women who experienced ejaculation report they were dismayed, felt sure they had urinated, and they learned to withhold this reaction. Now that the word is out about women's ejaculations there will probably be much relief and relaxation and increased enjoyment by the women who have this particular capacity. No research has yet uncovered where this fluid is made or stored.

THE WALLS OF THE VAGINA

Inside the vagina, the walls rest against each other, creating a potential space. The walls of the vagina are pink and have many folds, accounting for its tremendous elasticity. During sexual arousal lubricative fluid oozes out of the walls in a kind of sweating action.

Across from the urethral sponge there is an area of blood vessels protecting the anus called perineal sponge. This can be felt through the lower back part of the vagina. During the plateau phase the perineal sponge thickens, further narrowing the entrance to the vagina.

THE CERVIX

At the end of the vaginal canal is the cervix, the neck of the uterus. Most sexologists agree that women have little sensation beyond the first (outer) third of the vagina. However, many women strongly disagree saying that they experience terrific pleasure with deep thrusts at the back of the vagina in the area of the cervix and many women feel pleasurable contractions of the uterus during orgasm.

The perineum is the skin from the vaginal opening to the anus. The anus is a sexual orifice for some women, and quite taboo sexually for others. Those women who enjoy anal sex usually prefer lots of lubrication such as, K-Y or spermicidal jelly, to reduce irritation and discomfort to these delicate mucous surfaces. Also, for hygiene, men are discouraged from putting their finger or penis in the vagina directly from the anus.

LOVE MUSCLE

Below the surface level of the visible genitalia is the figure-eight pubococcygeal (P-C) or "love" muscle. The P-C muscle encircles the urethra, vagina and anus. A well-exercised P-C muscle is considered by some sexologists to be the key to healthy sexual functioning for both men and women. Poor muscle tone leads to sexual difficulties as well as other physiological problems, such as difficulty in childbirth and urinary incontinence. In fact, the first person to understand the importance of good P-C tone taught exercises to women in preparation for childbirth. His name, Kegel, is still associated with these exercises.

Men and women can test their P-C muscle by starting and stopping a stream of urine and then starting it again. This ability is due solely to P-C muscle tone. Many women have found on their own the pleasure they can get for themselves and give to their men by squeezing this muscle. It is in the vagina, and many women have become quite dextrous at this.

SEXUAL RESPONSE CYCLE

Women's sexual response was described by Masters and Johnson as being in four phases: excitement, plateau, orgasm, and resolution. These phases are marked by physiological changes in the sexual organs: beginning engorgement in the excitement phase with sweating of lubricant in the vagina; pulling up of the broad ligament which supports the uterus, which in turn enlarges the back of the vagina in the plateau phase: a myriad of changes during orgasm, including for some women changes in skin color on the back and chest, tingling, or contractions in the hands and feet; and gradual return to resting state in resolution. What is truly notable is that women are described as having a long arousal period. Yet, in Shere Hite's research, most women describe themselves as reaching orgasm very quickly once they start masturbating. Whether it is women's capability to extend sexual pleasure or the ineptitude of their lovers coupled with her reticence to instruct her lover (Shere Hite's Report on Male Sexuality) is not clear, but is an important question.

DIAGRAM 48

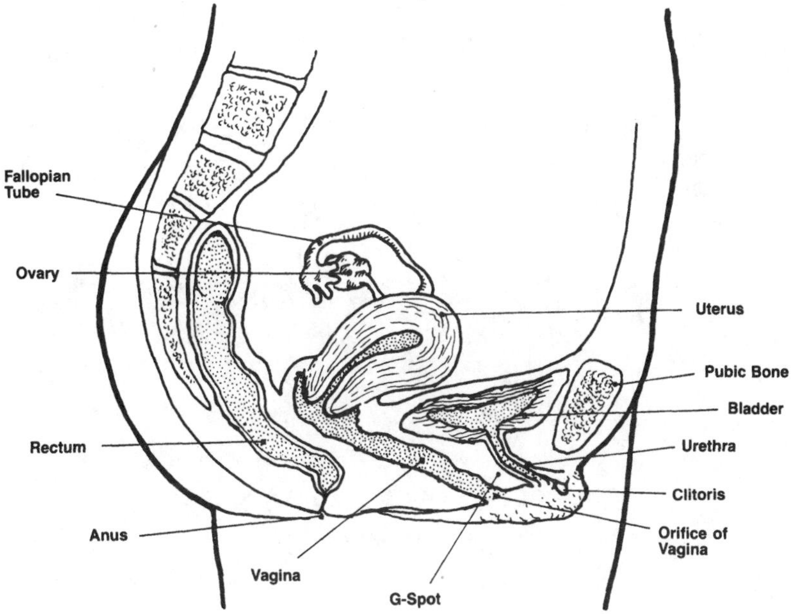

The most sensitive part of the
vagina is the outermost 2 inches.

CHAPTER 18

SUMMARY OF THE SEVEN STAGES OF TAOIST ESOTERIC YOGA

SMALL HEAVENLY CYCLE (MICROCOSMIC ORBIT)

The introduction to the seven higher formulas of Taoist practice is the Opening of the Microcosmic Orbit, or the rebirth process of return to the mother's womb. This route is composed of the Functional and Governor Channels, which must be purified and linked to form a free-flowing circuit.

The life of a human being begins with the piercing of an egg by a sperm cell. From this original act of Kung Fu, an enormously complex human being develops, which is capable of real genius. The fetus develops around that point, which is called the navel. It is from this point that nutrients are absorbed and wastes expelled from the developing creature. Therefore, in the Warm Current Practice the navel is a point of overriding importance. While in the womb the human being doesn't breathe air (the lungs do not function at all). Energy and oxygen are passed to the fetus through the umbilical cord. When the energy flows into the fetus' body, it enters at that point at which the navel will later be after the umbilical cord is severed. Then it proceeds downwards to the bottom of the trunk, flows all the way up the spine to the crown of the head and from there, flows down the middle of the face continuing on to the navel, again to complete the circuit.

The fetus, it is said, automatically touches its tongue to its palate. This serves to link the two energy channels and allows the power to flow. The crown of the baby's head is open and moves up and down. This is due to the waxing and waning of the flow of power through this particular part of the body.

Thus, the tongue is the terminus of the Functional Channel. This energy pathway begins at the bottom of the trunk at the point midway between the anus and the testes, called, the "Hui-Yin". From there it flows up the front of the body through the Kuan-Yuan and the Chi-Hai and then through the Chi-Chung (the navel). Then it passes through the Chung-wan (solar plexus) and proceeds to the Shan-chung (the heart center). Thereafter, it passes through the Hsuan-chi (throat) center and up to the tongue terminus. When connected with the Governor Channel the energy path reverses direction and flows down from the tongue, navel, to the Hui-Yin.

The Governor (or control) Channel also starts at the Hui-Yin. From this point it moves up the posterior of the body. In doing so it passes through the Chang-chiang (the base of the spine) and goes up to the Ming-men (L2 and L3) or Door of Life where it continues up to the Chi-chung (T11) between the adrenal glands and then proceeds upwards to the Yu-chen or the Emerald Pillow of the medulla. From there it rises to the crown of the head or Pai-hui (the crown) and then goes to the Shen-ting and down to the Yin-T'ang between the eyebrows. Here it passes to the San Ken (the tip of the nose) and finally travels down to the palate, which is the terminus of the Governor Channel.

DIAGRAM 49

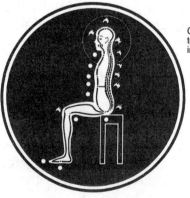

Open the Microcosmic Orbit to aid your practice of interal locking.

THE TONGUE IS A SWITCH OF THE CIRCUIT

The circuit may be closed when the tongue end of the Functional Channel is raised to contact the palate terminus of the Governor. Thus, during practice, we must keep the tongue in contact with the palate. Placing the tongue against the palate has a calming effect for those who practice the Warm Current Method. It also generates saliva, which is regarded as the water of life in Taoist practice. Saliva is said to be the chief lubricant of all bodily functioning. In the Taoist view the soft palate is regarded as a direct link to the pituitary gland.

As a man grows older he suffers increasingly from an imbalance of Yin (female) and Yang (male) energies in the body. As these disharmonies multiply, the bodily organs begin to suffer from the receipt of too much or too little energy. How different is the vital power of the infant! He grows nearly an ounce a day. This represents an astounding accomplishment in the assimilation of energy by the material body. The baby's body can do this heroic job of cell building because its routes of energy are thoroughly open and the flow of power is, consequently, very strong.

The Governor Channel controls the Yang organs of the body. These are the lungs, spleen, heart, kidneys, circulation-sex, and liver. The Functional Channel controls the Yin organs, which are the colon, stomach, small intestine, bladder, triple warmer, and gall bladder. The tissues are Yang in tendency and the blood is Yin.

THE SEVEN FORMULAS OF THE SEVEN BOOKS OF THE TAO*
THE FIRST FORMULA: FUSION OF THE FIVE ELEMENTS

This formula literally combines the separate energies of the five principal elements into one harmonious whole. The meditation has a particularly powerful filtering and purifying effect upon the human nervous system.

The Earth is the Mother of all the elements. All life springs from her generative womb. This reunites the other four elements of Chinese cosmogeny with the mothering Earth. Thus, metal, wood,

---

*The Taoist Masters traditionally referred to each level of esoteric practice as a "book" with a formula even though, until now, they have never been written but passed down only by word of mouth)

water and fire are drawn back into the earth and are simmered gently at this point. Each element is purified but is not so hotly fused that it loses its integrity and dissolves into ashes.

This formula is regarded as a highly secret method of Taoist meditation. In Chinese Philosophy each element corresponds to a particular organ. The Earth corresponds to the spleen, metal to the lungs, water to the kidneys, wood to the liver, and fire to the heart. The five elements interact with each other in three distinct ways: producing, overcoming, and threatening. The producing or creating cycle runs thusly: wood burns to make fire, the ashes decompose and seep into the earth, where are born and mined metals, which when melted become water (liquid), which nourishes trees and plants. The overcoming or destruction cycle runs thusly: wood is cut down by metal, fire is extinguished by water, earth is penetrated by wood, metal is melted by fire, and water is interrupted and cut off by earth.

The life cycle also has its relative elements thus: birth corresponds to wood, growth to fire, maturity to earth, harvest to metal and storage to water. In climatic types, wind corresponds to wood, heat to fire, dampness to earth, dryness to metal, and cold to water. Their corresponding emotions (sympathy, sadness, joy, anger, fear) blend one harmonious whole, raising the morale and encouraging kindness, gentleness, rightousness, respectfulness and humor. The formula of the five elements combined into one involves the mixing of the Yin and Yang to attain a higher state of bodily harmony and beauty. The ancient alchemical formula SOLVE ET COAGULA corresponds to the second stage in the meditational forms.

SECOND FORMULA: LESSER ENLIGHTENMENT OF KAN
AND LI
(YIN AND YANG MIXED)

This formula is called Siaow K'an Li in Chinese and involves a literal steaming of the sperm (Ching) into life force energy (Chi). One might otherwise say that this begins the transfer of the power of the sexual hormones into the whole body and brain. The crucial secret of this formula is to reverse the usual sites of Yin and Yang power, thereby provoking liberation of the sperm's energy.

The first and second books are the preparation of the paths for the greater energy flow of the sperm so that the body will be able to handle the great influx of energy (power which might correspond to the awakening of the Kundalini). This formula includes the cultivation of the root (the Hui-Yin) and the heart chakras and the transformation of the sperm energy to sperm power at the navel. This inversion places the heat of the bodily fire beneath the coolness of the bodily water. Unless this inversion takes place, the fire simply moves up and burns the body out. The water (the sperm and seminal fluid) has the tendency to flow downward and out. When it dries out that is the end. This formula reverses the normal, energy-wasting relations by the highly advanced method of placing the water in a closed vessel (cauldron) in the body and then cooking the sperm with the fire beneath. If the water (sperm power) is not sealed, it will flow directly into the fire and extinguish it or itself be consumed. This formula preserves the integrity of both elements, thus allowing the steaming to go on for great periods of time. The essential formula is to never let the fire rise without having water to heat above it and to never allow the water to spill into the fire. Thus is produced a warm, moist steam containing tremendous energy and health benefits.

The Second formula consists of:

(a) Mixing of the water (Yin) and fire (Yang) (or male and female) to give birth

(b) Transforming the sperm power (generative force) into vital energy (Chi), gathering and purifying the Microcosmic outer alchemical agent

(c) Opening the twelve major channels

(d) Beginning of the half immortal (joining and sublimation of the body & soul)

(e) Circulate the power in the solar orbit (cosmic orbit)

(f) Turn back the flow of generative force to fortify the body and the brain and restore it to its original condition before puberty

(g) Gradually reduce food intake and depend on inner self, sun, moon and water, a beginning of the cosmic energy. (beginning of the Half Immortal)

THE THIRD FORMULA: GREATER ENLIGHTENMENT
OF THE KAN AND LI
(GREATER YIN AND YANG MIXED I)

This formula comprises the Taoist Dah Kan Li (Ta K'an Li) practice. It uses the same energy relations of Yin and Yang inversion but increases to an extraordinary degree the amount of energy that may be drawn up into the body. At this stage, the mixing, transforming and harmonizing of the energy in the Solar Plexus (it might correspond to the Manipura Chakra) takes place. The increasing amplitude of power is due to the fact that the third formula draws Yin and Yang energy from within the body, whereas, the third formula draws the power directly from Heaven (above) and Earth (ground wire-Yang and Yin, respectively) and adds the elemental powers to those of one's own body. In fact, power can be drawn from any energy source, such as the moon, wood, earth, light, etc.

The Third Formula consists of:

a. Moving the stove and changing the Cauldron.

b. Greater Water and Fire mixed (male & female intercourse).

c. Greater transformation of sperm power into the higher level.

d. Gathering the outer and inner alchemical agents to restore the generative force and invigorate the brain.

e. Cultivating the body and soul.

f. Beginning the refining of the sperm power (generative force, vital force, Ching Chi).

g. Absorbing Mother Earth (Yin) power and Father Heaven (Yang) power. Mixing with sperm power (body) and soul.

h. Raising the soul.

i. Retaining the positive generative force (seminal) force and keeping it from draining away.

j. Gradually do away with food and depend on self sufficiency and Universal energy. (Breatharian)

THE FOURTH FORMULA: GREATEST ENLIGHTENMENT
OF THE KAN AND LI
(T'AI K'AN LI)
GREATEST YIN AND YANG MIXED II

This formula is Yin and Yang power mixed at a higher bodily center. This is to reverse the aging process, to re-establish the thymus glands to increase natural immunity. This means that the radiation of healing energy stems from a more powerful point in the body and provides vast benefits to the physical and etheric organism.

The Fourth Formula consists of:

a. Moving the stove and changing the Cauldron to the higher center.
b. Absorbing the Solar and Lunar power.
c. Greatest mixing, transforming, steaming and purification of sperm power (Generative Force), soul, Mother Earth, Father Heaven, Solar and Lunar Power for gathering the Microcosmic inner alchemical agent.
d. Mixing the Visual power with the Vital power.
e. Mixing (sublimating) the body, soul and spirit.

This might correspond to the heart Chakra (Anahata).

THE FIFTH FORMULA: SEALING OF THE FIVE SENSE
ORGANS

This very high formula effects a literal transmutation of the warm current or Chi into mental energy or energy of the soul. To do this we must seal the five senses, for each one is an open gate of energy loss. In other words, power flows out from each of the sense organs unless there is an esoteric sealing of these doors of energy movement. They must release energy only when specifically called upon to convey information. This might correspond to the Brow (Ajna) and Throat Chakra (Vissuddha).

Abuse of the senses leads to far more energy loss and degradation than people ordinarily realize. Examples of misuse of the senses are as follows: if you look too much, the seminal fluid is harmed; listen too much and the mind is harmed; speak too much and the salivary glands are harmed; cry too much and the blood is harmed; have sexual intercourse too often and the marrow is harmed, etc.

Each of the elements has its corresponding sense through which its elemental force may be gathered or spent. The eye corresponds to fire; the tongue to water; the left ear to metal; the right ear to wood; the nose to earth.

The Fifth formula consists of:

(a) Sealing the five thieves: ears, eyes, nose, tongue and body

(b) Controlling the heart, and seven emotions (pleasure, anger, sorrow, joy, love, hate, and desire)

(c) Unite, transmutes the inner alchemical agent into life preserving true vitality

(d) Purifying the spirit

(e) Raising and educating the spirit, stopping the spirit from wandering outside in quest of sense data

(f) Do away with decayed food, depending on the un-decayed food, the universal energy is the True Breatharian.

THE SIXTH FORMULA: CONGRESS OF HEAVEN AND EARTH IMMORTALITY

The sixth formula is difficult to describe in words. It involves the incarnation of a male and a female entity within the body of the adept (this might correspond to the Crown Chakra, Sahasrara). These two entities have sexual intercourse within the body. It involves the mixing of the Yin and Yang powers on and about the crown of the head and being totally open to receive energy from above and regrowth of the pineal gland to its fullest use. When the pineal gland is at its fullest, it will serve as a compass to tell us in which direction our aspirations can be found. Taoist Esotericism is a method of mastering the spirit, as described in Taoist Yoga. Without the body, the Tao cannot be attained, but with the body, truth can never be realized. The practitioner of Taoism should preserve his physical body with the same care as he would a precious diamond because it can be used as a medium to achieve immortality. If, however, you do not abandon it when you reach your destination you will not realize the truth.

The Sixth formula consists of:

(a) Mingling (uniting) the body, soul, spirit and the universe (Cosmic Orbit)

(b) Full development of the positive to eradicate the negative completely

(c) Spirit returned to nothingness

THE SEVENTH FORMULA: REUNION OF MAN AND HEAVEN
TRUE IMMORTAL MAN

We compare the body to a ship and the soul to the engine and propeller of a ship. This ship carries a very precious and very large diamond, which it is assigned to transport to a very distant shore. If your ship is damaged (a sick and ill body), no matter how good the engine is, you are not going to get very far and may even sink. Thus we advise against spiritual training unless all of the channels in the body have been properly opened and have been made ready to receive the 10,000 or 100,000 volts of super power, which will pour down into them. The Taoist approach, which has been passed down to us for over 5,000 years, consists of many thousands of methods. The formulae and practices we describe in these books is based on such secret knowledge and the author's own experience in over twenty years of study and of successfully teaching thousands of students.

The main goal of Taoists:

1. This level—overcoming reincarnation, or enlightment.
2. Higher level—the Immortal spirit.
3. Highest level—the Immortal spirit in an immortal body. This body functions like a mobile home to the spirit and soul as it moves through the subtle planes, and allows greater power of manifestation.

TAOIST ESOTERIC YOGA COURSE OFFERINGS

There are now Taoist Esoteric Yoga Centers throughout the U.S. offering personal instruction in the complete Taoist Body/Mind/Spirit system. Opening the **Microcosmic Orbit** is the prerequisite for all other courses. If you are having difficulty mastering the methods taught in this book, it will help to study the Microcosmic with a teacher and follow that with a class (usually a weekend) in the **Taoist Secrets of Love/Cultivating Male** and **Female Sexual Energy**. This will answer personal questions and allow discussion of many related topics that could not be included in this book. The Microcosmic course includes the Inner Smile meditation, the Six Healing Sounds, and the Taoist Rejuvenation exercises.

Complementary to the cultivation of sexual energy are the course offerings in **Iron Shirt Chi Kung**. This teaches how to pack energy in various organs and cavities of the body and strengthen the connective tissue which gives our body its integrity. These powerful exercises can be performed in a few minutes and will greatly increase your "rooting" power in the earth. It is an invaluable aid to anyone who meditates and tends to get "spacey," for martial artists, or anyone seeking to increase their immunity against disease. The higher level Iron Shirt classes strengthen the tendons and bone marrow, increase sperm count, allow your internal organs to gain super strength leading to the development of what Taoists call the "steel body" impervious to attack or illness.

A short five minute **Tai Chi Chi Kung** form is taught in addition to a longer Yang style **Tai Chi Chuan** form. **Five Finger Kung-Fu**, **Chi Massage**, herbology and many other related courses in healing are offered in addition to all the meditation levels described in the seven formulas.

AWAKEN HEALING ENERGY

THE HEALING TAO

Bibliography

Bach, E. Heal Thyself: An Explanation of the Real Cause and Cure of Disease. London: C. W. Daniel, 1978.

Chang, Jolan. The Tao of Love and Sex. Dutton, N.Y.

Douglas, Nik, and Slinger, Penny. *Sexual Secrets* New York: Inner Traditions.

Dowman, Kieth. The Secret Life and Times of Lady Teshe Tsogyel. Routledge, Kegan, Paul. London.

Flatto, E. Warning: Sex May Be Hazardous To Your Health. New York, Arco publishing, 1973.

Free John, B. Love of the Two-Armed Form. Middletown: Dawn Horse Press, 1978.

Gourmont, R. de. Physique de l'Amour. Paris: Mercure de France, 1940.

Grant, K. Cults of the Shadow. New York: Samuel Weiser, 1976.

Gurdjieff, G. All and Everything. New York: E. P. Dutton. 1964.

Hartmann, F. Paracelsus: Life and Prophecies. Blauvelt: Rudolf Steiner Publications, 1973.

Hua Ching, Master Ni. Book of Changes and the Unchanging Truth. College of Tao, Los Angeles.

Kinsey, A. C. Sexual Behavior in the Human Male.

Rawson, Philip. Tao: The Chinese philosophy of Time and Change. Thames and Hudson.

Scheimann, E. Sex Can Save Your Heart and Life. New York: Crown Publishers.

Scheingold, L. D. & Wagner, N. Sound Sex and the Aging Heart. New York: Human Services Press.

Schwaller de Lubicz, R. A. Symbol and the Symbolic/The Temple in Man. Brookline: Autumn Press, 1978.

Suares, C. The Cipher of Genesis. Boulder: Shambhala, 1978.

Woodruffe, J. The Serpent Power. New York: Dover Publications, 1974.

AWAKEN HEALING ENERGY THROUGH THE TAO

The Taoist Secret Of Circulating Internal Power

Mantak Chia

Taoist Esoteric Yoga is an ancient, powerful system of physical, psychological and spiritual development encompassing meditative and internal energy practices. This unique and comprehensive book reveals the Taoist secret of circulating Chi, the generative life force, through the acupuncture meridians of the body.

This comprehensive list includes:

- Opening the Energy Channels
- Proper Wiring of the Etheric Body
- Acupuncture and the Microcosmic Orbit
- Taoist Yoga and Kundalini
- How to Prevent Side Effects
- MD's Observations on the Microcosmic Orbit
- Commonly Asked Questions

Written in clear, easy-to-understand language and illustrated with many detailed diagrams that aid the development of a powerful energetic flow, for psychological and spiritual health and balance.

> *"A treasure of ancient profound knowledge of subtle energy patterns in the human body. These simple exercises which balance, harmonize and focus energies, can be of great benefit to anyone seeking a state of physical and emotional well-being. To those who, due to an imbalance of energies, fill the growing ranks of "Kundalini Casualties" of various meditative practices, this approach offers hope for relief."* **MIRTALA BENTOV**

ISBN: 0-943358-07-8   Paperback   6×9   205 Pages

 # INITIATION
ELISABETH HAICH

Written at the request of her advanced students, *Initiation* is an illuminating autobiography that connects the twentieth century European life of internationally beloved teacher Elisabeth Haich and her lucid memories of initiation into the hidden mystical teachings of the priesthood in ancient Egypt. A compelling story within a story emerges detailing the life experiences that catalyzed her spiritual path.

In an earlier life in ancient Egypt, a young woman is prepared for initiation into the esoteric secrets of the priesthood by the High Priest Ptahhotep, who instructs her step-by-step, consistent with her development, in the universal truths of life. Throughout this extraordinary book, Elisabeth Haich reveals her in depth insights into the subtle workings of karma, reincarnation, the interconnectedness of individual daily life choices and spiritual development Elisabeth Haich shares usually hidden truths that only a few rare individuals in any generation, seek, find and communicate to others, enabling the reader to awaken within the essential understanding necessary to enlighten any life no matter what events manifest.

In twentieth century Europe, from childhood to adulthood, through war and remarkable meetings, she demonstrates the power of turning the searchlight of one's consciousness inward and using every life event towards expanding consciousness.

Initiation is a timeless classic communicated in modern terms inspiring generations of spiritual seekers globally. Whether read as an autobiographical novel unveiling mystical truths or as a unique glimpse into Elizabeth Haich's exceptional journey to initiation, the personal impact on the reader is profound.

To read *Initiation* is to be part of the initiation itself.

ISBN:0-943358-50-7 Paperback 5½x 8½ 376 Pages June

THE EAR: GATEWAY TO BALANCING THE BODY
A MODERN GUIDE TO EAR ACUPUNCTURE

Mario Wexu, D.AC

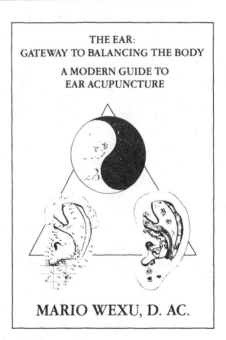

THE EAR:
GATEWAY TO BALANCING THE BODY

A MODERN GUIDE TO
EAR ACUPUNCTURE

MARIO WEXU, D. AC.

T his is the first comprehensive modern textbook of ear acupuncture. The author uniquely combines his extensive personal clinical experience with traditional and modern Chinese and European sources. Anatomical descriptions with detailed charts clearly illustrate how to locate and use over three hundred ear points, both alone and in combination with body points, to treat and prevent illness. Case histories with specific techniques cover problems such as:

- Deafness
- Otitis
- Otalgia
- Drug Addiction
- Tobacco Addiction
- Alcoholism

- Obesity
- Anesthesia
- Oedema
- Insomnia
- Acupuncture Anesthesia
- Electronic Acupuncture Devices

An incredible repertory listing 130 diseases facilitates an understanding of this incredible and valuable healing art.

ISBN: 0-943358-08-6   Paperback   6×9   217 Pages

CRYSTAL ENLIGHTENMENT

The Transforming Properties of Crystals and Healing Stones

Katrina Raphaell

This book is a comprehensive, yet easy to understand guide to the use of crystals and gems for internal growth, healing and balance in your daily life. Discover new resources, learn how to extend your personal awareness and center by attuning to crystal energies. The magnitude and potential of crystals and gems to impact positively our personal lives and the evolving planet we live on is significant.

Some of the topics explored in this book are:

- What are crystals physically and esoterically?
- Working with crystals for self-healing
- The ancient art of laying on stones
- Psychic Protection
- Generator Crystals
- Important healing stones and their uses
- Double terminated stones and their functions
- Crystal Meditations
- Black Holes

Crystal Enlightenment is designed for the lay person, as well as the professional, to give the basic understanding necessary to use the healing properties inherent within the mineral kingdom to improve the quality of our external and internal lives.

ISBN: 0–943358–27–2   Paperback   5¹/₂ × 8¹/₂   175 Pages

CRYSTAL HEALING

The Therapeutic Application Of Crystals and Stones
Katrina Raphaell

Volume **Two** of the Crystal Trilogy further refines the practical applications of crystal therapeutic techniques. Katrina introduces innovative, previously unavailable methods for discovering and removing internal imbalances. This wealth of information derived from the author's first-hand experience is practical, while inviting the reader to explore deeper levels and gain insight into the processes underlying our disease and health patterns.

Unique in its content, **Crystal Healing** reveals for the first time:

- 6 Master Crystals
- Time Bridging
- Maintenance-Personal Responsibility
- Exorcising
- Past/Future Life Recall
- Laser Wands
- Protection & Guidance
- Conscious Reprogramming
- Mind, Body, Heart & Soul Correlations
- Window Crystals
- Dematerialization
- Channeling Crystals

To facilitate a complete understanding of the specific techniques described, **Crystal Healing** is strikingly illustrated with detailed color photographs. Step-by-step instructions encourage an understanding of all you need to know to reap the benefits emanating through crystals and stones. This invaluable guide enables the lay person and professional to use crystals and healing stones for soul activation, complete healing and expansion of consciousness. In addition to the information in **Volume One**, this book will help activate hidden potential and open up a world of light into your life.

ISBN: 0-943358-30-2   Paperback   5¹/₂×8¹/₂   220 Pages

AURORA  PRESS

For our online catalog visit
www.AuroraPress.com

Write, fax, or email:
Aurora Press
PO Box 573
Santa Fe, N.M. 87504

Fax 505 982-8321

www.Aurorapress.com
Email: Aurorep@aol.com